"YOU SAVED MY LIFE . . .

. . . I suffered and ran from doctor to doctor. Nothing wrong. I couldn't go on living this way. Living? I was existing. Then into my life came the answer, *THE BOOK OF HOPE*. I only hope that everyone reads it . . . It gave me back my identity and desire to face reality—to live again."
—Redwood City, California

"It seemed like most of my life I had been wrestling with many of the problems and emotions you explore in your book. I never found reasons for them or answers to them . . . Just reading *THE BOOK OF HOPE* made me feel better. I've already taken steps (pretty crucial ones) to try and deal with my feelings, and my total outlook is more positive and hopeful . . . Thanks for understanding so much so well."
—Kailua, Hawaii

"When I read the first chapter of the book, I broke down terribly. It was as if I were crying with relief . . . That one chapter gave me the words to my life which I have never been able to put into words myself. Even my husband has been able to understand me more now . . . I can actually believe in a future . . . I can actually believe in real happiness."
—Syracuse, New York

"Every woman should read this book."

"Are you a woman, married or single? Are you a mother or are you childless? Have you ever suffered from depression, loneliness, loss of self-esteem, shyness, anxiety, boredom, or inertia? In other words, are you an American woman living in the seventh decade of the 20th century? If you are, this is the book you have been waiting for."

"Women who would not label their malaise 'depression,' but merely feel edgy, bored or angry with their lot, will profit by a reading of this easy-to-follow, encouraging volume . . . It gets down to the symptoms and cures of the real problems —in and outside the home—that are limiting instead of liberating women today."

THE
BOOK OF
HOPE

*How Women Can
Overcome Depression*

by Helen A. De Rosis, M.D.
and Victoria Y. Pellegrino

BANTAM BOOKS
TORONTO · NEW YORK · LONDON

THE BOOK OF HOPE

*A Bantam Book / published by arrangement with
Macmillan Publishing Company, Inc.*

PRINTING HISTORY

*Macmillan edition published September 1976
5 printings through March 1977*

Bantam edition / November 1977
2nd printing .. November 1977   4th printing .... February 1978
3rd printing .. December 1977   5th printing .... March 1979

Grateful acknowledgment is made to reprint lines from:
"Daddy" and "Getting There" from Ariel by Sylvia Plath.
Copyright © 1965 by Ted Hughes. Reprinted by permission of
Harper & Row, Publishers, Inc.
(First two lines) of "In Plaster" from Crossing the Water by
Sylvia Plath. © 1971 by Ted Hughes. Reprinted by permission
of Harper & Row, Publishers, Inc.
"Lorelei" from The Colossus by Sylvia Plath. Copyright ©
1959 by Sylvia Plath. Reprinted by permission of Alfred A.
Knopf, Inc.

ISBN 0-553-12878-7

Published simultaneously in the United States and Canada

*To our husbands,
whose support
and minimal demands
enabled us
to do our work*

Today is my life.
But only when
There will be a tomorrow,
Can I hope.

Contents

Introduction

Do YOU FEEL that something is "missing" in your life? Do you want "something more," but find it difficult to put your finger on what that "something" is? We think we can help you. Countless numbers of women who suffer from some form of depression do not realize they are depressed. Consequently, you accept a restricted life. You feel your vague feelings of restlessness and dissatisfaction are "normal." Yet these feelings are not "normal" and they do not have to be part of your life. These are feelings generated by symptoms of depression, an illness that is so common, especially among women, that it often goes undiagnosed and uncured.

We are going to describe the symptoms of depression so that you can better understand your feelings. We are going to explain what causes depression; and we are going to tell you how you can reclaim your rightful heritage—your right to be yourself, your right to a satisfying life, your right to grow, your right to decide your life goals.

We interviewed several hundred women who suffered from depression, finding them largely through the placement of ads in community newspapers, women's club newsletters, health clubs, women's centers, colleges, and high schools. The response was immensely gratifying. Many of the women with whom we talked had suffered from depression throughout their lives. Some of them were learning to deal with it, to overcome it; others were seeking answers. We believe that these women's stories (the names of these women have been changed, of course) will be helpful to you, perhaps even inspiring, for they demonstrate the importance of strength and courage when one is fighting for health.

Of course, we have no easy answers for you, for anyone. Quick steps for relief can be taken, but only long-term efforts will effect the changes you seek. Much has been written about depression already. You may have heard that depression is anger turned against the self, or that forcing yourself to "do something" is the best antidote to "the blues." These points have validity, but they do not begin to explain the tenaciousness of depression. Therefore, we have attempted to explain in detail why certain feelings and moods arise, why and when depression occurs, and the myriad ways you can help yourself.

There is still great misunderstanding about the way women are raised—the self-expectations women have, the excruciating conflicts they face. For a deeper understanding of women's problems, we are going to explore the ideas of Dr. Karen Horney, who was the first female psychiatrist to disagree with Dr. Sigmund Freud's theories about women and neurosis. She rejected, for example, Freud's theories about penis envy and the idea that anatomy was destiny. Dr. Horney believed that *culture* was certainly as important in molding human destiny. Eventually, Dr. Horney broke with the Freudian New York Psychoanalytic Institute and set up the American Institute for Psychoanalysis, the first independent psychoanalytic school to be founded by a woman.

Women are not destined to suffer from "nerves," "tension," or "just not feeling good." Many of the women we interviewed suffered from these feelings, but were beginning to learn to overcome and cope with them. Yes, we believe that living can be more rewarding than it seems for so many of our sisters, for where there is life, there can be hope.

PART I

1

Garden Variety Symptoms

DEPRESSION HAS BEEN called the social disease of the seventies. It has been estimated that approximately eight million people suffer from depression each year.

Depression often affects people who are reliable, capable, and conscientious—sometimes women and men who were taught to assume responsibility *early* in life. In fact, it is more frequently seen in adults who were expected to be self-disciplined, independent, and emotionally in control even as young children.

Depression seems to be far more common among women than among men. One national study covering hospital admissions for all depressive disorders showed 175 women affected for every 100 men. A similar study of outpatient psychiatric services showed the ratio as 238 to 100. Moreover, while actual suicides are most common among middle-aged men, suicide *attempts* are far more common among relatively young women—and among housewives.

The reasons for this phenomenon, we believe, are cultural rather than genetic. *The cultural roots for depression among women, as we shall see again and again, center around learned helplessness and a position of self-effacement.* It is those cultural roots which create the extraordinary conflicts women now experience in their strivings toward changing their assigned roles and realizing and asserting their own needs.

However, women *can* begin to live with more zest

3

and satisfaction. Take the first step. Ask yourself the following questions.

1. *Are you tired even when you've had enough sleep? Do you have difficulty getting yourself going in the morning? Do you accomplish less than you like?*

"I'm just not a morning person," says Elaine. "I get up at eight, but it takes me until about lunch time to get myself going. But then I go all day."

What do you think about Elaine's statement that she is not a morning person? This may surprise you, but her statement indicates she may be suffering from *low-grade, chronic depression*. Healthy human adults are like children in this respect: they wake up feeling good, ready to meet the day.

The truth is that Elaine doesn't like the way she spends her days and she is angry about her situation. But she feels guilty about her anger. "I should be grateful for what I have," she thinks, so she keeps from awareness her feelings of anger and guilt. She muffles them so she won't have to deal with them. Finally, by lunch time, she is able to get on with her day. But what a strain she is under!

A feeling of constant fatigue, a tiredness that no rest can cure, is a key symptom of low-grade, chronic depression. Moreover, a tragic result of this fatigue can be a generalized inertia. Involvements and activities become curtailed because you feel you have to spare yourself. You may not feel like going to the theater—it's too much trouble. You'll buy those records you want *next* week. You'll think about getting a new job—later. Inertia can rob you of the active exercise of two crucial factors: your creativity and your initiative.

Meanwhile, excessive fantasizing takes over as you weave all kinds of static images. Says Joan, "I spend hours thinking how wonderful life will be once I get myself together." Such nonproductive fantasizing serves to provide a *facsimile* sense of involvement and aliveness.

Inertia may be experienced physically, intellectually, and emotionally. Actually, inertia serves a "useful" function: it can protect you from anxiety. But what a price you pay. Yet somewhere, buried deeply in the center of one's being, remains a longing, a yearning, to be free of this hampering burden of inertia and the feelings of deadness that accompany it.

2. *Are you restless?*

Sally says, "I had a good job and a nice life. But it wasn't enough. I had this terrible restless feeling, and, at the same time, I'd feel bored. Sometimes, I'd get manic and throw myself into ten activities at once."

Sally's restlessness is an outward manifestation of anxiety. Some people become restless and remain restless, even though they are inert. Others get up and move around as do children in school who "can't sit still." When Sally sits down, she often finds she has to move again. Her restlessness is really a need to be active in order to distract herself from feelings of continual anxiety.

Women who are alternately restless and depressed are often very susceptible to any idea, event, or person (especially a new man) that holds out the promise for making them feel better.

3. *Have you lost interest in things? In your family? In your work? In your friends? In your sex life?*

Mary says, "I just don't feel anything toward my kids—or even my friends. I'm *trying* to keep acting normally, but I'm just putting on an act. I feel like I'm just going through the motions of being alive. But I'm not alive. I'm dead inside."

"I just can't be bothered with sex," says Tanya. "I now Ralph is upset with me, and I feel bad about t. I don't want to reject him. I simply don't like sex ore. I've changed."

Mary and Tanya, as we'll explain in later chap- uffering from low-grade, chronic depression.

u unable to make decisions?

ess is another indication that low-grade, ion exists. A woman who is not de- ey her options, make a choice, and hoice. She'll feel strong enough to ices of her actions without feeling anxious. The depressed woman may be unable to decide what to cook for dinner, what dress to purchase, what man to marry.

Martha has problems making decisions because she needs to satisfy other people. She fears criticism because her self-esteem depends solely on other people's estimation of her. She prefers that others make decisions for her. That way, she feels she won't run the risk of being criticized. When she is *forced* to make up her own mind, she feels "incompetent," and becomes even more depressed than ever.

Jenny also can't make decisions, but for a different reason. Jenny cannot stand to be wrong. She unwittingly demands of herself that she always make the *perfect* choice. Otherwise, she becomes filled with self-contempt. The pressure this puts on her is enormous, and it is understandable that she remains crippled with indecision.

Harriet is afraid to commit herself to a definite opinion or course of action. Even if she isn't content with her life, she feels momentarily safe. Any change —which entails risk—endangers her precarious position of safety. So she is stuck and will feel anxious about making even the smallest commitment, which is what any decision entails.

To further see how indecisiveness is tied in with depression, let's look at twenty-seven-year-old Ellen. One afternoon Ellen bought a lovely, expensive dress. Once she was home, she worried whether her mother would like the dress. After several hours of anxiously weighing the pros and cons, she returned the dress. However, she continued to feel miserable. Her action didn't solve anything.

Ellen had placed herself in an impossible, but not uncommon situation. She wanted a dress she and her mother would both like. She wanted a beautiful dress, but she didn't want to spend a large sum of money. Unconsciously, she demanded of herself that she be both thrifty *and* beautifully dressed, and that she always please her mother as well as herself. The impossibility of making the one choice that w

satisfy all these demands depressed Ellen. She became furious with herself for not being able to make
that choice!

5. *Are you continually angry and resentful?*

Studies have shown that depressed women frequently complain of conflicts with their families,
friends, and others. A young mother says, "I hate to
hear myself. I just seem to nag all the time. Nothing
my kid does is right. The other day, he dropped a
glass of milk and I slapped him for it. Then I felt
guilty. I don't know what's wrong with me, but I do
know I don't like myself very much."

This young woman cannot accept herself as an ordinary mother who nags, who gets angry, who has a
child who spills milk. She feels this is not the kind of
mother she *should* be. She becomes angrier and angrier at herself for not being a special, superior, perfect
(yes, perfect) parent. She may not be aware of what
she is doing to herself. All she knows is that she gets
furious with her child—and then feels guilty.

Cynthia finds that she is constantly irritated with
Bill. She feels tense and anxious much of the time.
"We don't seem to communicate," she says. "He's in
his world and I'm in mine. We don't talk, we snap at
each other."

Cynthia has many questions she can ask herself. She
can let the situation continue, although she'll probably
become more and more depressed. She can consider
a break-up. Or, she can work at finding new interests
for herself and re-building the broken-down com-
munication with Bill. Cynthia has, in fact, many options. Her depression, however, stems partially from
the fact that she isn't able to *see* the options she does
have. And because of that, she feels hopeless about
any possible change. This hopelessness, as we shall
see again and again, is one of the largest components
of depression.

6. *Do you have bouts of anxiety? Do you often
have feelings of dread, as if something terrible is going to happen?*

"My heart starts pounding," says Maureen, a buyer

at a department store. "But I don't know why. This has to be the worst feeling in the world. I sit down and tell myself everything will be all right. But the sudden panic is debilitating. I try to call a friend on the phone. It usually helps."

All women who suffer from depression hold within themselves a large element of anxiety. But in some depressions you don't experience the anxiety so keenly; it has gone "underground." In fact, that is one of the purposes of depression: to drive painful anxiety underground.

Anxiety is not experienced for no reason at all, although it *may feel* that way. Anxiety comes from within and can be caused by a variety of factors, just as the feeling of happiness comes from within and may be elicited by a nice day, a smile, a compliment. You might become anxious before a job interview, before a blind date, before making a speech, before moving to a new environment. This anxiety can usually be overcome in a number of ways: by preparing yourself adequately for the challenge that is making you tense ("doing your homework"), by going through the experience with optimism and courage, and perhaps by using a method of your own, such as relaxation techniques or prayer.

However, if your expectations are too high, or if you have too little confidence in your abilities, your anxiety will remain, and will, in fact, act as a block in the path of your effectiveness. In other words, *impossible expectations generally lead to anxiety*. Some women use tranquilizers to calm them when their anxiety becomes too painful.

7. *Are you a chronic complainer?*

It's often impossible to be accurate about the cause of an illness. We do know, however, that chronic, psychosomatic illness, such as migraine headaches and ulcers, point to the presence of inner conflicts. Other complaints like backaches, sore feet, muscle spasms, constipation, palpitations, vague aches and pains are common in chronic, low-grade depression.

Marsha says, "When I think of the last year, I can

hardly believe it. I had pains in my breasts and was sure I had cancer. Yet tests revealed that I was healthy. After that I began to have terrible headaches. Finally, a friend of mine whom I'll always be grateful to, suggested that my unhappiness was causing me to feel ill. At first I protested that I wasn't unhappy—that I just didn't feel well. But she looked me straight in the eye and said, 'I don't believe it.' As the words 'I'm happy' came out of my mouth, I started to cry. I had to face that I really felt I was wasting my life."

8. *Are you self-destructive?*

Self-destructive behavior is common in depression. There is, for example, the destructiveness of being consistently ineffectual. Soon no one will depend upon you or require you to be responsible. Expectations diminish, both externally and internally. You can then say to yourself, "See, I can't be effective under any circumstances. I shouldn't even try because it's no use." Some sort of peace might result from that maneuver. But you might also find yourself becoming more depressed, as you become more and more helpless.

Inertia is another form of self-destructiveness. As you find that you can initiate fewer and fewer projects, that you are interested in less and less, your guilt will reach greater proportions. A circle of destructiveness has set in, which can only end as you begin to tap your many real resources and areas of strength.

Those of you who suffer from inertia often feel you must meet not only the impossible expectations you place on yourself, but the ones you believe others are placing on you. Soon your balance goes awry and you begin to experience *all* demands as external pressures. You garden not because you want to garden, but because you feel you *should* garden. You cook a gourmet meal not because you feel like it, but because you think you *should*. It is expected of you! Your resentment over these feelings of pressure may lead to your not wanting to do anything.

IMPOSSIBLE EXPECTATIONS ⟶ ANXIETY + ANGER
⟶ INERTIA

Other common extremes of self-destructive behavior are alcoholism, drug addiction, and gambling. Harriet's success at poker, for example, allowed her to buy a business. (Contrary to what you may think, there are many female gamblers.) For the first time in her life, she could feel a measure of financial security. But after the first flush of success in her business, she became progressively depressed. She found she could "feel better" only when she was gambling again. The excitement of taking risks and competing with others kept her from experiencing a depression she had had—and masked—for years. Her uncertain financial existence had always created enough tension for her to feel excitingly alive. Now that she was comfortable financially, the dead feelings of her depression surfaced. Harriet needed the tension of uncertainty to maintain her feeling of aliveness.

Not all self-destructive behavior is motivated by a wish to destroy. That the particular behavior is destructive is incidental or accidental. You may have heard that people make themselves unhappy, or that they *want* to be unhappy. This is highly unlikely, however, for people generally want only to do the *best* for themselves. However, that best may often be terrible and self-destructive, even though they do not intend to hurt themselves or make themselves unhappy. *The motive for self-destructive behavior is the same as that for any other form of compulsiveness— that is, to avoid anxiety and depression, and to achieve a sense of safety.* Destructive behavior is often used to *mask* depression. And so the gambler often pursues the excitement of gambling; the alcoholic seeks the euphoria of alcohol. The drug addict as well is out to avoid feelings of depression when she pops a pill or shoots a fix. But any feelings of well-being in these situations are only transient.

Women who *have* to keep busy are often using

their busyness to mask depression. For example, Theresa married, furnished a lovely apartment and "settled down" to a life of raising a family and dabbling in some hobbies. One night, lying in bed next to her husband, she announced, "I feel dead." He was shocked. He knew she had never been a ball of fire, but he couldn't understand her remark about deadness and insisted she see a physician. One of three doctors she saw ventured the diagnosis of depression. But she rejected this diagnosis and "cured" herself by taking on the presidency of the PTA and the leadership of a Brownie troop, and by starting to play tennis vigorously. She left herself so little time that she didn't have the opportunity to confront or experience her "dead" feelings. Yet there was a frantic quality to her activities that kept her from actually enjoying them.

It is not easy to overcome self-destructive behavior, but it can be done. We have all met ex-alcoholics, ex-gamblers, ex-drug addicts, ex-work addicts. Change may come about slowly. But it can come about.

9. *Are you critical of yourself? Do you often feel inferior or inadequate?*

Rebecca says, "Mark constantly had to bolster me. I'd call him up feeling terrible and he'd tell me how silly I was being. Often, after a party, I'd come home really down on myself. The women I'd see always seemed prettier, more competent, more charming."

Nothing Rebecca ever did was good enough. She constantly chastized herself for wearing the wrong clothes and acting inappropriately. When her frustrations reached frightening proportions, she would "cope" by becoming depressed.

One often doesn't think of depression as a way to cope. But one often becomes depressed in order to obscure intolerable feelings of self-hatred. By "playing dead" emotionally, you are coping—even at great cost. In other words,

SELF-CRITICISM + SELF-HATRED ————→ DEPRESSION

Charlotte, for example, was critical of Len. She felt he should do more around the house, that he should express more warmth and affection toward her, and that he should be more ambitious in his work. The more critical of him she felt, the more depressed she became.

In Charlotte's case, her depression was based partially on her failure to marry a man who would meet all of her expectations. This failure to find the man of her dreams, as we'll see later, was in fact, Charlotte's *lost dream*. She experienced that failure as a humiliation. In addition, she felt guilty that she was imposing such demands upon her husband. An attempt to keep all of this from awareness led to her need to depress these feelings.

However, this move was far from a positive one. Charlotte's depression only increased the tension between her and her husband. He felt angry that she was making what he felt were unreasonable demands. Both of them were caught up in a circle of anxiety, rage, and depression. Instead of dealing with her relationship with her husband, instead of working at making her life more satisfactory, Charlotte chose the option of becoming depressed. No, she didn't do this intentionally. But the result was the same. At that time, her self-criticism and depression kept her from making growth-promoting changes in her life.

10. *Do you spend a great deal of time daydreaming?*

For many, daydreaming is a way of avoiding conflicts and the inevitable feelings of anxiety that always accompany conflicts.

Marilyn had been in art school, then married, and had a daughter. At first she was content to stay home and take care of her daughter. After the first year, however, she found she spent a good part of each day thinking about what life would have been like if she'd gone to France. She pictured herself as the mistress of a French painter. She fantasized sitting in cafés, having conversations about art, life, beauty. This was her lost dream—the dream she thought she'd buried years ago.

As time went on, her fantasies became more and more compelling. She found it difficult to concentrate on her "real life," which could never compete with her fantasies. That led to her greater dissatisfaction, for her fantasies inadvertently served as an on-going "put down."

However, fantasies can also provide the base for constructive action. Ada, for example, had gone back to work as a secretary but she didn't like being confined and dreamed of selling real estate. However, she kept putting off her dream; it was always "next year." When she was feeling good, she could say to herself that at least she was "thinking about" what she wanted to do. And this was true up to a point. By giving her imagination free rein, she was beginning to see herself in a new role—as a real estate agent. *This is a positive first step.* However, for Ada to actualize her dream, she had to take the second step: planning how to reach her goal. Only by taking her fantasies one step further, could she ward off disappointment at never having striven for, and reached, what she wanted.

11. *Do you have "up" weeks and "down" weeks?*

"Before I learned what it is like to feel good most of the time, I accepted moodiness as part of my fate. I thought, okay, I'm just a moody person. I just have up weeks and down weeks. But you know, it's hard to live that way," Sheilah says.

Of course it is. Being on a continual emotional seesaw causes problems—with ourselves and with other people. Of course, there are disappointments and tragedies in life which we can't predict. Pain and sorrow and anger are inevitable parts of life we have to accept. But we're not talking about that reality. We are talking about feeling "down" for vague reasons, and about continual depressions which ebb and flow like waves breaking upon the shore.

Instead of continual ups and downs, one can strive for a centeredness—a position in the middle of the seesaw, a sense of self which can't be tossed so far up and down by day-to-day problems. Says Bobbi, "Two years ago, there was a frantic quality to my life. I would make elaborate plans in which everything was going to be different. I would lose weight. I would get a new job. I would learn how to drive. For a week or two, I would keep very busy and do all this—the dieting, the job-hunting, the driving lessons. I would feel great! But then, something would happen and things would slow down—or I wouldn't be able to accomplish what I wanted to accomplish—and I'd become moody and depressed."

This would, in turn, make Bobbi angry at herself. She would eat more and more. She'd stop the lessons and become inert. Then she'd feel guilty and become even more depressed. Bobbi had to learn (and we'll explain this later in more detail) that she was placing too many simultaneous demands on herself at one time. She was not pacing herself realistically—and, by not doing so, she set herself up for the great downers that inevitably followed her "highs."

The eleven points mentioned above are the most common symptoms of low-grade, chronic depression. As you've probably surmised, this illness isn't as easy to diagnose as a broken leg. Mostly, you feel just "blah" or "draggy" or "blue." You're exhausted. Things —even things you used to enjoy or might enjoy— become too much trouble. But often, at the same time, some part of you knows that you want more from life. And from those positive feelings—that "there must be more" or that "there must be a different way to live"—spring hope and health.

Unfortunately, if healthy striving is not actively encouraged, low-grade, chronic depression can sometimes develop into the more severe forms of depression. Physicians refer to these forms as *clinical depressions*. If you are clinically depressed, you may be only too painfully aware that there's something wrong. However, if you're not sure, ask yourself the following questions.

12. *Do you cry often? Do you cry more than you used to?*

"I didn't know what was happening to me," says Daisy. "I just cried more than I ever had before. I cried when I did the dishes. I cried when I took a shower. And I was withdrawn. If anyone said anything, you know what I did? I cried."

Depressed people cry for a variety of reasons. Most common are tears of impotent rage because of the sense of helplessness they experience regarding any possible change. (The feeling is, "Nothing will happen.") Tears also accompany feelings of hopelessness and loss. The loss, as we'll see later, is usually the loss of some dream.

13. *Have your sleeping habits changed? Does it take you longer to fall asleep? Do you wake up several hours earlier than you want to?*

"I would wake up at five o'clock every morning and be unable to go back to sleep," says Lorraine. "My friends whom I'd complain to didn't know what to do with me. I felt I was going crazy." Even though Lorraine is depressed, her inability to have a good night's sleep tells us that she is anxious too. The depression has not been able to keep her anxiety from surfacing.

In Lorraine's case, her anxiety was triggered by the end of a love affair. Although she said she thought it was probably for the best, she felt deeply unlovable. These painful feelings were responsible for her anxiety and concurrent depression.

14. *Do you sleep more than you used to?*

Bonnie says, "I take three naps a day. I don't have the energy I used to have." Excessive sleeping fits in with the constant tiredness we've previously discussed. As your depression worsens, you may find you're sleeping more and more. In Bonnie's case her anxiety is alleviated by sleeping.

15. *Does the thought of food make you almost sick?*
Have you lost weight recently without consciously
dieting?

"Every time I look at food, I feel ill," says Jill, who
also has not been sleeping well. "I used to love food,
but lately I just can't eat."

Jill's depression causes her to lose interest in food
just as it causes loss of interest in other areas of her
life. Her lack of appetite may also be caused by a
sluggish digestive system. (In depression, it's not
uncommon for bodily functions to become sluggish.)

16. *Do you feel full of guilt?*

"I used to wake up and think about what an awful
mother I was," says Mary. "It was like a record. I
couldn't shut it off."

The feeling of guilt is almost always present in depression. It is usually tied in with a feeling that high
demands have been violated. Guilt is not productive.
Of course, there are decent standards of behavior
which we all try to live up to in some way or another.
When we do not, we feel ashamed. But as we'll see,
the standards that produce feelings of guilt are not
realistic.

17. *Do you often have nightmares?*

One night, Marlene dreamed a gang was going to
kill her. Another night, she dreamed this same gang
was stealing the belongings from her house. For Marlene, the gang symbolized the destructive forces within herself which she was gradually becoming aware
of. Dreams, as we'll see, provide wonderful clues to
our true feelings about ourselves.

18. *Do you think about ending your life?*

Suicide is often a desperate attempt to escape the
negative and painful feelings within yourself. "I kept
thinking life would never get any better," says Jane.
"Nobody could understand why I was unhappy. And
I felt guilty because I had people who needed and
depended on me. But I just wanted to die, that's all. I
wanted my misery to end."

Suicidal feelings, we must emphasize, are cause for
great concern. Such thoughts, impulses, and state-

ments are to be taken seriously. In many instances, professional help should be sought.

19. *Do you feel "unreal," as if you're "in a fog?"*

Helene explains, "I feel like I'm in outer space. My body doesn't seem to be part of me. I'm not here." Doris complains that her head "feels heavy" as if something had "snapped." Another woman says her head feels as though it were "filled with cotton."

This "fogginess" serves as an emergency defense mechanism to prevent a massive complex of feelings of deprivation, rage, and anxiety from erupting into consciousness.

Just as novocaine would numb a toothache, this "fogginess" can numb your inner pain. But as you may know, feeling "unreal" or "in a fog" doesn't feel good either. There is a more satisfying way to feel—and live.

20. *Do you find you can't concentrate and that you go over and over certain thoughts?*

Iris complains she couldn't concentrate on her schoolwork. "I just can't think," she says. "I don't have any idea how I'm going to get through each day. I look at one page in my book over and over." Janice says that only a few thoughts go round and round in her head. "And they are only the things I hate myself for. I can't seem to shake them loose. I feel them devouring me."

These are two examples of what is called ruminative thinking. Questioned closely, Iris described the same phenomenon as Janice. It was discovered that she couldn't concentrate on her schoolwork because she was concentrating on these hateful, ruminative thoughts.

The most important thing we can tell you right now is to try to stop feeling guilty about being depressed. It isn't your fault. You are not depressed because you *want* to be, but because it seems the best way to keep yourself together, to keep your anxiety from becoming overwhelming.

We know it isn't easy to begin to help yourself.

Even the best-intentioned people will probably suggest to you variations of, "Why don't you pull yourself together?" They may say this to help you, but what they may be doing is making you feel worse. What can you do? You can always tell them, "What do you think I'm trying to do."

Next, don't look at your depression as something you *should* be able to recover from immediately just because you know you are depressed. That's impossible—like expecting a person who's never before climbed a mountain to reach the top of Mount Everest on her first time out.

For now, say this to yourself: "Okay. I am depressed. There are reasons why I'm depressed, and they are valid reasons.

"My depression is telling me that something is bothering me about the way I am living my life. While it is very painful, it may help me to understand myself better."

When you feel "down" on yourself, tell yourself, "I'm going to learn something from this experience. And I *am* going to feel better." Say this to yourself as many times a day as you need to.

Here are some specifics to try:

1. Keep up your daily routine if it is at all possible. If you work outside the home, try to keep going each day. It is more beneficial for you to get up in the morning, get dressed, have breakfast, go to your place of work and go through the motions of working than to remain home in bed with your discomforting thoughts.

2. If your work is in the home, the same procedure may be followed. Consider your daily chores important. You may feel that "It doesn't matter what I do." But it does.

3. Try to get out, even for very short periods of time. Twice a day might be good. You might go out for the paper in the morning after breakfast, to a camera shop or the library in the afternoon. If it suits you, you might go for a walk and look at the sky and the trees.

4. If you can push yourself to do it, try to see family members and friends as much as possible, but for *very short periods of time.* Do not entertain in your own home. Try to visit others informally and briefly. End the visit anytime you want to. Don't make plans far in advance. Plan everything "by ear." Remember, you are hurting and you have to treat yourself gently and with care.

5. Deliberate physical activity is a *sine qua non* for overcoming depression. We do not mean calisthenics or vigorous sports—unless you want to try them—but involvement in any physical activity you ordinarily might like. For example, a singing group. It is almost impossible to feel severely depressed when you are singing! The same holds for dancing, swimming, bicycle riding, jogging, tennis, and so on. While there's no guarantee you'll feel greatly improved when you return home, you will at least have considerable respite from your depressed feelings during the duration of the physical activity. And you might feel better afterward too.

6. If you find it difficult during this period to talk to the people you live with, try writing a note. Explain briefly, for example, that it is of no use to you if they try to bolster your spirits by joshing or kidding you, however well intentioned they may be.

7. If your friends and family are the kind of persons who think that you will be strengthened by being scolded and criticized, tell them they are mistaken. Only your therapist—if you have one—should dare to try that. And if he or she decides to do it, it's always a calculated risk.

8. Let your partner know that it's really not "business as usual"—whether this pertains to routine chores, social activities, or marital obligations.

9. Try to remember that severe depressions usually end. If you can believe that you will not always be feeling this way, you might find each day easier to get through.

10. If you find the note technique useful, you might use it any way you see fit—even with children. Any

thought or wish you want to communicate can be written. For example, you can write, "Honey, I have a lot of laundry in the basket. It has to be folded. Would you please do that for Mommy and tell me when it's done. P.S. Please don't discuss it with me."

11. In all depressions, the best thing you can do is to have a person you can trust (this may not be a family member), to whom you can complain and to whom you can express feelings of anger. Find one— and let your feelings out.

12. If your appetite is poor and you are losing too much weight, try very hard to eat frequent, small amounts of food. It doesn't matter, at this time, if your diet is balanced or not. Anything will do—Cokes, milkshakes, potatoes, bread and gravy, ice cream, anything. But keep eating. Your depression might be alleviated by giving your body the nutrition it needs.

We recognize that these suggestions may be difficult or even impossible to follow, but to whatever extent you can follow any of them, to that extent you will be helping yourself more than you can possibly imagine at this moment.

Suggestions for the Partner of the Depressed Woman

1. Don't call up and ask how she is. If she's honest, she'll only tell you.

2. Do call and ask if there's anything she needs.

3. Do call and offer to take the bus home, if she doesn't feel like picking you up. If she insists, accept graciously; don't argue.

4. Help in any household chore that you know is being neglected.

5. Try to avoid asking what you can do. Remember that you live there too. You ought to have some foggy notion of what the routine chores are.

6. If you have children, don't be afraid to tell them that Mommy is not feeling well and that they must help as much as possible. Even a three-year-old can

pick up his room, put laundry in the hamper and fold it later, straighten up, set and clear off the table.

7. Try to remove the children at some time during the weekend. Arrange to have them visit overnight with grandparents, relatives, or friends.

8. Don't expect a meal until you see one. If you don't see one at a reasonable time, don't ask. Just make one yourself.

9. Plan a simple, brief, but *well-thought-out* outing (for example, dinner or a movie). However, don't insist upon it if she resists. Instead, arrange a little "party" with perhaps some ordered-in Chinese food in front of the TV.

10. Make every effort to avoid a slapdown, knockdown argument, but encourage discussion about anything she wants to talk about.

11. If she gives evidence of wanting to be alone, respect this, but don't "abandon" her. Remain available.

12. If she works outside the home, talk to her about her problems on the job. Everyone needs a sympathetic ear.

13. Try to find some way you can help her feel less overwhelmed by her double responsibilities. Can you divide the household chores more equally? Can you help her arrange to have free time that's all her own? Remember that there's much less free time when two people are working, so your planning has to be deliberate and done with foresight.

14. Does she feel her paycheck is a valuable contribution to the household? Work out with her an equitable dispensing of all monies so that she doesn't have to wonder each month what is going to be done with her money and so that she doesn't feel guilty— either that her contribution is not as large as yours, or that her contribution is larger than yours.

All of these are questions that have to be explored by two-income families. There are no rules, and there should be flexibility.

15. It's helpful for your partner to have money of her own that she does not have to "account" for.

16. If you can do it, a very brief discussion *before* spending your money often serves to bring you closer on this issue. It's unfortunate, but money still remains a great divider in human relationships.

17. You have to *deal* with such complaints as "I'm so depressed" or "I feel so awful." Try to remain optimistic. Try not to be sucked into low feelings yourself. She doesn't need that. Neither does she want to hear, *at that moment*, that her fears, or her disgust, or whatever, have no foundation. She will feel you don't understand and that you are putting her down. Later on, you can discuss why she feels depressed.

But for the moment, try to provide some TLC (tender, loving care). Do little things to make her physically comfortable. (Not sex—unless that's her particular interest at such times.) Help her take off her coat, take her by the hand, lead her over to the most comfortable chair, put a hassock under her feet. Do not ask, but say, "Now I'll fix you a nice ———" (whatever she'll like—a cup of tea, a cocktail, a snack). Don't pressure her into making any decisions. She may very well be hungry. A wafer and a piece of cheese, or some leftover cold spinach with a dot of mayonnaise on top makes a novel hors d'oeuvre. With a bit of wine, it can seem almost festive.

Then you can say something like, "You sit there for a little while now and I'll make a gourmet omelet for us." (It's always helpful to have at least one gourmet omelet up your sleeve.*) If you can't cook at all—learn. Set a place to eat right in front of her, unless she insists on going to the table. Eating at a different place might be more pleasant.

The ideas behind these points are: 1) Depression is contagious, but try not to be overwhelmed yourself. 2) Don't put her worries down. 3) Show your kind

---

*Our recipe for quick gourmet anti-depression omelet: Put a little oil or margarine in a skillet, heat, drop in some dry onion chips; add a few canned mushrooms, let simmer a few minutes. Drop in 4 beaten eggs, salt and pepper.

concern, not your worried concern. 4) Remember that she'll get over her feelings. 5) Keep things light, playful if possible. 6) Distract as much as you can. 7) Remember, you may very well get the VIP treatment yourself when you need it one day.

Please do not feel that these points must be followed precisely. They are merely open-ended suggestions which you should consider if you don't have a negative reaction to them.

Finally, the best advice that can be given: be kind —not mushy—but kind.

2

Cornerstones of Depression

"The individual who has lost contact with herself has to prove she is something she is not."
—KAREN HORNEY

DEBORAH IS in her middle twenties. She consented to be interviewed because she experiences periodic depressions and feels that "many people don't understand anything about those feelings." She is, in fact, just "coming out" of a severe depression. This is the first time she has left her apartment in over a week and a half.

Deborah sits forward in her chair, eager to be helpful. Her current depression began when she was fired from her job as an advertising writer. "I feel like someone who's been out of town for a while," she says, looking slightly ashamed.

Deborah was born in an affluent suburb. Her mother was obese and often sick in bed with a variety of illnesses. "I've never liked her," says Deborah. Deborah's father was a successful lawyer who was rarely home. Her childhood was an isolated one. "I did very well in school because my father expected it. But I had a lot of trouble dealing with my peers. I was aloof ... I didn't want anyone to bother me."

In high school Deborah majored in math and science and planned to become a chemist. However, during her college sophomore year, she began to have

25

trouble with chemistry. At the time, she felt she wasn't "bright enough" to continue with chemistry and switched to psychology.

"That's when I first fell apart," says Deborah. "When I'm okay, I have what can be called a bubbly personality. Like most women, even when I'm perfectly miserable, I keep smiling. But when this happened, well, I didn't feel sad at all, but I was tired all the time. I couldn't get out of bed. I lost interest in everything—my friends, my school activities. I went to the university therapist but he didn't know what was wrong. Doctors kept trying to find out if there was anything physically wrong with me—hypoglycemia, that sort of thing.

"Looking back on it, I think I felt that I had failed my father. He'd wanted me to be a scientist. But I see now that there was no one to help me. My professors didn't like girls in their classes. You could only get away with being a woman in science if you were brilliant, not average. When I began having trouble, instead of realizing I was good in math and science and that I just needed some help, I assumed I was inadequate—and this was backed up by the general belief that women weren't cut out to be scientists.

"I survived that depression, and after I graduated I got a job in an advertising firm. I moved up from secretary to copywriter. I found my own apartment and went to work with an organization for women. I learned how to relate to women for the first time. I had never been close to women before.

"This was a good time in my life. I had a good job and was getting known in my field. I'd done one clever ad that was responsible for a large sale of a new product. Then I was offered what seemed like a better job and I took it—and that was a mistake. The man who hired me was a con artist; he'd promised me the moon, but didn't deliver on anything. The work he had me doing was demeaning. I complained and I was fired. Before I was fired, when the problems of my job were getting worse and worse, I fell apart. First, I felt panicky and had to cut down on my activities—I stopped my meetings, began seeing less and less of my friends. I was so exhausted I'd sleep all day on Saturday. Then I'd sleep all day Sunday. Then I'd come home from work and go right to sleep. I was really spacy. One morning I found myself in a store but couldn't remember how I'd gotten there. My vision became very foggy, and I lost my period, too.

"I also let down my friends. One friend was staying with me until she found a place of her own, but I made her leave—I just *had* to be alone. Now I'm trying to get my friends back, trying to apologize and explain that my illness was responsible, that I *do* care about them. I'm not up to much yet. I'm taking one step at a time. I'm not ready to initiate projects yet— like look for a job. I'm just focused on getting through one day at a time.

"I think my basic problem is that my identity is wholly tied to my work—when I don't have that, I fall apart." She pauses. "Things have never been the same since I dropped chemistry," she says. "My father has no respect for advertising. He doesn't think it's valid."

What does she see for the future? "I can't deal with becoming over thirty—I just can't imagine it. I see myself as a young, single woman." As for marriage? Children? "Kids? I kill plants!" was her reaction. She adds, "I always want to work for someone else. I don't need a lot of money. Just enough to be secure and to have some freedom. . . . You see, I really don't want that much."

In this interview, Deborah puts her finger on the central factor in her depression. She can experience herself as a person only *through* something or some-one else. If that doesn't work, she does not feel that she has enough to fall back on in herself. She tells us, "My identity is wholly tied to my work. . . ." It's the word "wholly" that does her in because once the work goes, everything goes.

At first Deborah had used the image of being a

chemist as the center for her identity. This was an identity established by her father and it was clear to her that he would accept her on those terms. Therefore, when she decided that the science field was not for her, she was, in effect, cutting herself adrift from an inner anchoring force.

Had this interest been her very own rather than a kind of parental directive, she may have been more tenacious in working with it. We can suppose that there may have been resistances in her approach to the subject, however. If that is the case, her "failure" is all the more understandable.

Neither Deborah's nor any woman's identity is, in fact, tied to any *one* area of her existence. *Our identity is tied to everything we are, everything we feel, think or do, everything we have ever experienced, all the people we have ever related to.* By believing that her work spells out her identity, Deborah overlooks her personality, her friendships, her creativity, her intelligence. She puts herself down by seeing herself only as a worker. It's like saying a book is its cover, a person is her face.

But there's a double tragedy here. Even if she is working, she can't be satisfied with herself. Recall that she says, "My father has no respect for advertising. He doesn't think it's valid." If you remember how things "fell apart" the first time when she dropped chemistry and ostensibly "failed" her father, you can see how she continues to "fail" him by doing *anything* other than what she thinks he wants for her.

Let's put it another way. An undamaged child knows who she is, who she has been, and has some pretty good idea about who she will continue to be. A very young child will answer to the question, "Who are you?" with the response, "I'm me" or "I'm a little girl." While this child *is* dependent upon those who take care of her, she does not *feel* dependent or helpless. She takes the care she is given for granted, and knowing who she is, recognizes what she can or cannot do.

Without any sense of shame or fear, this child freely admits, "I can't read," if she hasn't learned yet. She will say, "No, I can't do that. I'm too little." Introspection is uncommon in the very young, unless they have reason to be frightened and uncertain of their small worlds. Even the question, "Are you married?" posed to a child of three or four does not confuse. "Wait, I'll ask my mommy," is a common reply, because they know they have never considered that question before, and therefore seek out the best authority they know.

Adults know that a child is dependent and helpless to some degree. And mature adults know to what degree *they* are dependent and helpless in their world. But neither children nor adults concern themselves with their helplessness unless it presses upon them in distressing ways. Thus the child naturally and gradually grows away from actual dependency and the helplessness of the little person if she feels secure in her family, if she feels she will not be rejected by them should she not toe the mark. For this security, she needs the experience of *unconditional love*.

Unfortunately, unconditional love is almost as rare as loyal friendship. Instead, many of you may have been subtly given the message that you had to meet parents' expectations in order to be loved. When you were "bad," you felt rejected; when you were "good," you felt accepted. It was not too damaging if your parents' expectations were reasonable and flexible. However, too many parents are often rigid and inappropriate in their demands.

In Deborah's case, her father set up an assortment of rigid standards for her. Since Deborah could find nothing to love or admire in her mother, her mother's influence was not as great as her father's. He became the primary person to help Deborah establish socially acceptable attitudes and values. Her identity was first with her father and through him with the standards he set for her. Therefore, she was compelled to follow those performance standards. Otherwise, she felt she had failed him—and herself.

Deborah was aware of these feelings about herself and her father. She was not aware, however, of the strong influence her mother had upon her. It is clear that when she recognized her "failure" to maintain a particular identity, she reverted to the only other role model she knew—that of a despised mother who was "often sick in bed." Certainly Deborah spent plenty of time sick in bed also. And in shifting from an "acceptable" identity that both she and her father sought, to the "unacceptable" one of being "sick in bed," Deborah, autonomous Deborah, is still nowhere to be found.

Nina was the first of three children. Her mother had wanted to "do something" with her own life, but instead married early. She thought she had given up a brilliant career and a glamorous life. "From the time I was very small," Nina says, "I can remember being terrified of my mother's rage. She would scream at me and my sisters for all kinds of things. Looking back on my childhood, I can see how anxious I was, *constantly* anxious. I had to live up to all kinds of demands: I must get the best grades in school or my mother will despise me. I must be pretty. Of course, I wasn't pretty then—I was awkward—and so my mother was always trying to 'fix me up' with permanents, bright red lipstick, rouge, anything. I was supposed to make her proud of me but I was skinny and bony."

Many mothers have a very strong impulse to help their adolescent daughters to look "prettier." And it would be futile to say that they might well let nature take its course, because most skinny, awkward, plain adolescents recover from those conditions by the end of their teens. In addition, girls are quite good at learning all about caring for themselves—mostly from each other and certainly from publications.

For those parents, however, who cannot resist the impulse to "improve" their daughters' appearance, two issues ought to be clarified: One, if the focus in the parent's mind is how to make the daughter less ugly, the parental message will include frequent "put-downs," that is, "I have to help you because you are so homely." This can convince a young girl, who may not be particularly concerned about her appearance at this time, that she is really a lost cause. She may then become compulsively concerned about her appearance, possibly for the rest of her life. And, most important, feeling an inner injunction to overcome her "ugliness," she may never achieve any measure of satisfaction even though she may later become a raving beauty. Two, if the focus in the parent's mind is to enhance what is already there without making the child feel she is in dire need of such enhancement, the outcome can be quite different. Then shopping can be pleasant excursions or "fun" together times for mother and daughter, unattended by any sense of grimness or rejection of what the daughter actually looks like.

To repeat: these efforts are most often unnecessary. Such positive comments as, "That color looks well on you," or, "I like your hair that way," are extraordinarily constructive for teenage girls. Just think for a moment how you feel if someone makes such a comment to you. Unfortunately, however, Nina's mother had little awareness of the value of positive input. Nina continues, "I was also supposed to be perfectly neat and I was always being called a slob. I was supposed to be bright and I was always being called stupid. I was supposed to be cheerful, and yet, I was always called secretive and stubborn. I was supposed to be pure, and yet, when I was a teenager, I was called a slut.

"I could keep going. I don't remember ever thinking about these things until much later. I know I was angry at my mother, furious at her. But I wasn't 'allowed' to show it and when I did, I was 'bad' and made to feel guilty and unappreciative for the way my mother had given up her life for me."

During her developmental years, Nina had begun to internalize her mother's demands and make them her own. Without being aware of it, she demanded of herself that she be charming, bright, that she always make the right choices, that she excel at whatever she did. When she failed to meet these demands, she became furious. "I found that I couldn't take criticism either," she says. "My husband once told me I didn't know how to make a lemon pie and I got into a rage and threw the pie in the garbage. Then I went into the bedroom and cried for hours. This would happen more and more frequently. Actually, *I* was demanding of myself that I be the perfect cook—but I never wanted to take the time to cook well. Maybe I was afraid I would fail at that, too. When he criticized my pie, I became furious, not only at him, but at myself. I can remember, while I was crying, feeling completely hopeless that I'd ever be able to cook anything perfectly in my whole life."

The feelings of hopelessness that Nina experienced are always found in depression. The hopelessness stems from her belief that she will never be able to live up to her perfectionistic demands on herself—her "shoulds." And when she doesn't, in her mind she becomes that person she was accused of being early in life—the slob who will always be stupid, stubborn, inadequate, inferior. Nina has taken these unwarranted accusations and turned them into self-accusations. When she fails to be her *Perfect Self*, she becomes her *Despised Self*.

When you are caught in this dilemma, you are subject to frequent and rapid oscillations between feelings of being perfect and feelings of being despicable. Each of these requires the other in order for it to have any existence. Since perfection can only be a goal, feeling that you *should* have achieved perfection always places you in the position of irrevocable failure. Then, as soon as you begin to feel the impact of your imagined failure, you immediately shift to the self-despising side—that is, hating yourself for this "failure."

PERFECT SELF ←——————→ DESPISED SELF

One side of this dyad is as fixed and rigid as the other. Either be Totally Perfect, or you will be Totally Imperfect—that is, totally despicable and unacceptable. Once in the latter, self-rejecting position, you cannot rest easily. In fact, most people in that position cannot rest there at all. And so you will use any defensive, protective maneuver to get away from those feelings.

To be on either side of the dyad always implies that there will be a shift to the other side. That is what creates the backs and forths, the ups and downs of the moods that so many women describe over and over.

Mary Ann provides a good example of this phenomenon. Her mother encouraged her to take ballet and tap dance lessons, drama and painting lessons. While her mother was seemingly giving her daughter anything a girl might want, she felt her mother's message to her was: "Excel! Make me proud of you—because you're really not good enough the way you are."

You can see how damaging that can be to a youngster's self-esteem. Here is a parent knocking herself out to be a "good mother" and "doing everything" she can for her child. Yet the message is repeatedly the same: "You are simply not acceptable as you are and I must make every effort to improve what you are and make you more acceptable to me and to the world." Poor self-esteem is generated through this constant and unwitting "putting down" through well-intentioned efforts of parents. This does not mean, however, that youngsters should not be presented with opportunities. What we are referring to is the spirit behind the encouragement. As described earlier, these activities should be regarded as fun additions to your children's lives, not activities directly essential to their present and future acceptability.

As an adult, Mary Ann began to see that she was the kind of person who started things but never finished them. She began a course in oil painting, then stopped. She took up yoga, then stopped. This pattern repeated itself again and again. She would start off with great amounts of enthusiasm and then "lose interest." During talks with a friend, she began to recognize her need to excel at whatever she did— quickly and with little effort. When it turned out that she was not instantly a good painter, or when other women in her yoga class did better than she, she would give up, rather than endure the humiliation of being "mediocre." When she was excelling, performing and living up to the way she felt she "should perform," she was in good spirits. When she was "mediocre," she hated herself and became her Despised Self.

A depressed woman doesn't always appreciate the depth of feelings of self-contempt that she harbors. While she may feel despised by others, it's actually *she* who despises herself. Friends and family members may criticize her, *but there is no one who will be able to "put her down" more critically and more devastatingly than herself.*

If this woman had not been damaged in her early life, she would have more of a sense of self-confidence. She would have a zest for life and would be able to accept both her strengths and her weaknesses, her assets and her limitations. However, the depressed woman finds it difficult to accept herself for the person she actually is.

Because she despises the way she *really* is—with shortcomings, limitations, imperfections—she has, as a defense against anxiety, built up an imaginary or idealized self, the Perfect Self. And she takes great pride in that Perfect Self. In a self-protective effort to avoid feeling self-contempt, she can turn her shortcomings into virtues. Thus, she can rationalize her fear of assertion as a wish not to hurt anyone's feelings. If she saw that she were actually afraid of asserting herself, she would be filled with self-contempt.

Her compulsive need to excel and beat out others becomes a precious characteristic rather than what it is, an attempt to overcome feelings of being despicable.

Beryl, an executive secretary to a corporate vice-president, sees her restricted personal life as a feature of her *perfect* dedication to her work. "I have to be prepared to work evenings, weekends, or at his home. He pays me very well and that's my commitment to him." She overlooks several factors which stem from her own needs. One, she finds it anxiety-provoking to try to establish personal relationships and to socialize with friends her own age. Two, she overlooks that she could not refuse any request her employer might make of her because of her fear of angering him. Three, she is unable to regard herself as anything but the "perfect" secretary. If she acted in her own behalf, she would feel that she was "selfish" and would be filled with rage at herself for not meeting what are ostensibly all of her boss's needs. In fact, they are her needs as well as his.

The elaboration of an idealized self, the Perfect Self, is an unconscious one, a process by which a person filled with anxiety tries to cope in any way she can. No woman consciously decides that she can *really* be glamorous, successful, beautiful, competent in *all* things. However, when she is confronted with the reality that she is not what she expects herself to be (nice all the time, self-sacrificing, likable, interesting, the perfect hostess or secretary, the brilliant writer) she may experience acute anxiety as well as abject hopelessness. Feeling there is no way she can live up to her expectations, her Perfect Self, she becomes despairing.

It is the attempt to keep these unwanted, terrifying feelings of rage, self-hate, anxiety and impotence (helplessness) from emerging that can result in a depression. In other words, these feelings are kept from reaching awareness, are kept "safely" within herself, by keeping them *de*-pressed. A woman may then be able to say, "I just don't feel well. I feel down. I have no interest in anything." Not, "I am furious. I feel like an enraged person who wants to destroy everyone who has ever hurt me. And, feeling that, I am filled with such self-loathing and guilt that I can't stand myself, and want to rip myself apart as well." You can see why the "safety" of a depression is preferred over the danger of potentially explosive rage and violence, and can even become addictive.

The act of depressing serves to keep feelings from tearing one apart with rage, grief, and hopeless despair. This is what a depression is mostly about. It actually serves a useful purpose in subduing the pain and suffering of conflict. The bid is made for a sense of inner peace. But it is a spurious peace and the price is too high. That is because depression depresses everything—not only the rage, the hopelessness, the pain, the conflict, but also interest, enthusiasm, affection, energy, stamina, resistance to illness, ability to work and play, sexual feelings. *The move toward depression is a move toward deadness*. It is true that you deaden your feelings, you feel less pain. But you feel less joy as well.

To state again, briefly: When your Perfect Self doesn't meet its standards of how you *should* perform, you become your Despised Self. When feelings that you are despicable, stupid, and unlovable become too painful, you may choose an automatic numbing process—*a novocaine reaction*—to relieve your pain. However, the "cure" may be as damaging as the cause.

Depression is a disease caused by emotional factors, by a group of feelings all of us may have at one time or another, but which are experienced in extreme forms in a more severe, full-blown, clinical depression. These feelings are: self-hatred, anger, guilt, helplessness, and hopelessness.

All feelings in depression are tied in with a pervasive hopelessness. A combination of these feelings may lead to changes in physiology. These changes are what contribute to the physical complaints—fatigue, insomnia, aches and pains, and a general feeling of malaise and lassitude.

Depression exists in different forms, from acute and transient to chronic and long-standing. Many of the physical symptoms can now be treated with medication. An improved physical status can lead to a feeling of optimism. However, any sense of improved well-being has to be supported by steps which are directed toward the undermining of the original psychological causes of the depression. In a severe depression, both approaches are probably mandatory.

(We might add here that some people find it difficult to distinguish between mourning and depression. These two phenomena often feel and look very much the same, but there are significant differences. It may be worthwhile to mention them briefly. An important change or loss, such as a retirement, an illness, a separation, a divorce, a death, can all cause mourning. When Lisa's husband died of a heart attack, she felt she was being torn apart with feelings of sadness, anger, grief, and despair. This was understandable—and common. Mourning was her natural reaction to a dreadful loss. Eventually, she came to terms with it.

In a true depression, there is seldom a similar catastrophic precipitating factor that can account for, or justify, the intensity of the reaction. In mourning, there is always some event that causes intense grief. Most people in mourning do not lose the ability to continue functioning, even though grieved. Another difference is the fairly rapid loss of the intense signs of mourning, followed by a more gradual lessening of the feeling of sadness and loss.)

Each woman has her own set of standards for what she experiences as her particular Perfect Self. For example, Jane gave a dinner party for several couples she'd recently met. She became anxious before the party, but didn't worry too much about her anxiety. Every woman gets nervous before parties, she thought, especially when she doesn't know her guests very well. However, as soon as the first couple came in, she felt "frozen" with anxiety. She couldn't relax, couldn't "think of anything to say" and she certainly couldn't enjoy the evening. The next day she was furious with herself and became depressed. She went over and over in her mind what she *should* have said, how she *should* have acted.

Jane had failed to measure up to her self-image of perfection. She wanted to be liked, admired, and loved. She expected herself to be charming, interesting, gracious, and most important, lovable. However, an inner voice was telling her that she wasn't so charming or interesting; she was—as her mother had told her—stupid and clumsy. Caught in this clash between neurotic pride (in having these impossible standards) and neurotic self-hate (in not living up to them) she experienced anxiety.

PERFECT SELF VS. DESPICABLE SELF ⟶ ANXIETY

When her anxiety reached unbearable proportions the next day, the *novocaine reaction* set in and she became depressed. What Jane would have to learn to do is the same thing you can do for yourself. When you feel anxiety or when you "suddenly" become depressed, ask yourself, "What impossible expectations or standards have I set up for myself?" If you can't figure out the answer right away, don't worry. Keep reading; your question will be answered many times over. In the meantime, you might want to start keeping a record of these occurrences in a journal or diary. You'll find that keeping a journal of your thoughts and feelings will be productive, creative, and fun.

The woman who is trying to be her Perfect Self is doomed to fail, for such a mechanistic molding of a person cannot be successful. That is because the human spirit, the inner self, or the real self, is remarkably antagonistic and resistant to an artificially imposed process. It will retain its eternal flame even though it may burn low and seem to be nearly extinguished at times by the vicissitudes of neurotic development.

It is that central self—the real self—that provides the strength to continue the struggle within. It actually stirs up the trouble that creates the pain that eventually has to be dealt with! It is that central force in you that will not be stilled and which cries out, "I am not a package! I am not a thing to be directed by somebody's checklist. I want to decide as I go. I want to see the world and myself in it. This is me in here. I will not be smothered by destructive directives. I am going to kick up such a fuss that attention will have to be paid to me."

We have personified the concept of the *real self* in order to emphasize our point. As Karen Horney uses the concept, it has a certain flowing quality, almost an elusiveness which is always difficult to define. She refers to "the *real self* as that central inner force, common to all human beings and yet unique in each, which is the deep source of growth." And further, ". . . there are forces which he [the child] cannot acquire or even develop by learning. You need not, and in fact cannot, teach an acorn to grow into an oak tree, but when given a chance, its intrinsic potentialities will develop. Similarly, the human individual, given a chance, tends to develop his particular human potentialities. He will then develop the unique, alive forces of his real self: the clarity and depth of his own feelings, thoughts, wishes, interests; the ability to tap his own resources; the strength of his will power; the special capacities or gifts he may have; the faculty to express himself and to relate himself to others with his spontaneous feelings." And then, she continues: "All this will in time enable him to find his set of values and his aims in life. In short, he will grow substantially undiverted, toward *self-realization.*"

A departure from one's essential human potential leads to neurotic development. Once the system of prides and disparagements is established, one is constantly subject to feelings aroused by the failure of the system. And the system always fails because there is no way that any person can fulfill all the DO's and avoid all the DON'T's. Certainly, Nina and Mary Ann couldn't. When Nina didn't DO the perfect meal, she was filled with self-contempt. When Mary Ann didn't DO outstandingly at a new hobby, she gave up to avoid feeling self-contempt. The DO for both Nina and Mary Ann is to excel. Occupied with this eternal struggle to find their way through their programmed DO's and DON'T's, they do not attend sufficiently to the details and experiences of a full life. Nina may not try to cook because of her anxiety. Jane may not entertain as often as she'd like because of her anxiety over not being the Perfect Hostess. Mary Ann will not stick to any new interest if she isn't instantly competent. She will work only in safe old areas in which she can feel proud of herself.

As a result, their experience in life becomes restricted and narrow. They always feel threatened by clouds of disaster if they do not perform according to plan. Yet, there is a simultaneous struggle taking place as well, the one between the Perfect Self and the person who might enjoy parties, cooking, new interests, new hobbies, new friends, without any unrealistic standards attached.

So your inner DO's and DON'T's do two things: One, they make you restrict your life. Two, they set you up for failure. And it is this failure that leads you to feel so worthless, so self-despising, and so ready to search for and receive, grovelingly, any crumbs of real or imagined approval and recognition from others. This desperate need for affirmation from without will lead you to prostitute any genuine need, feeling, or desire you may have. This need can be kept compatible with the image of your Perfect Self if you feel you will be the most *perfectly* submissive person around. One of your needs, in other words, is to meet the needs or demands of others *perfectly*. Thus, this type of woman *will* be glamorous. She *will* be charitable. She *will* be martyred. She will be anything she thinks you want her to be. She will please, please, please so long as you will identify her with a proper tag: This woman is competent. This woman is good. This woman is a box. Anything. You call the shot. She'll play it.

So now our formula becomes more elaborate.

LOSS OF PERFECT SELF ─────→ DESPICABLE SELF + ANGER
─────→ ANXIETY ─────→ REASSURANCE THROUGH APPROVAL
OF OTHERS

If the approval isn't forthcoming, the feeling of being despicable may increase and cause intense suffering. Any kind of criticism or seeming rejection will plunge the depressive woman quickly into despair and drive her to feel self-hate. It doesn't always matter who does the rejecting, a friend, an acquaintance, or a stranger. By and large, those who are prone to depression are more emotionally dependent than is compatible with well-being. Afraid of other people's disapproval because of the self-hating feelings that will follow, they feel they must *perform* constantly to live up to others' expectations.

However, DO's and DON'T's do not have to run your life. And other people's expectations don't have to run your life either.

Depression can give you an opportunity for greater awareness, for reviewing your goals and values, for evaluating your strengths and limitations, for coming to terms with your total self. Nina, for example, began to realize the impossible demands she placed on herself and was able to associate these demands with her bouts of depression. She had to review what *she* wanted for herself. Did she really care about cooking or was she demanding of herself that she be a good cook because she had a deep need to be perfect? She realized that she had options: She could accept her limitations with cooking, or she could take a cooking course and spend time learning to cook.

Those women who have been able to profit from their depression are legion. Some, as we'll see, have been able to document their courses of self-discovery and self-evaluation and have described, in dramatic terms, their climb "up from depression." Some, who have worked through the angry guilt, the hopeless despair, the vales of tears, have touched and released a flow of previously untapped compassion. When you stop hating yourself with such relentless passion, you open the door to that trapped "little me" waiting to take you by the hand to review and repossess some of the scattered treasures of a life lived under the heel of self-imposed tyrannies.

Let's return to the story of Deborah who went through a severe depression after she was fired from her advertising job. First, it must be emphasized that Deborah is not depressed because she disappointed her father, even though it was he who initially set her standards for her. Deborah is depressed because she has not lived up to her own image of what she feels she *should* be. The truth is that many men and women are fired, but they do not go into deep depressions for several months' duration. They may feel sad, angry, or frustrated, but they still feel confident enough about their abilities to look for another job. However, Deborah pinned all of her feelings of self-worth on the approval of others. If she had a job, she was somebody. If she didn't have a job, she was nothing.

Because she depended on others' approval, she felt she *should* meet their expectations. When she was fired, when she hadn't performed as the good and efficient worker as defined by her boss, she violated another "should." She *should* have performed well enough, been smart enough, to keep her job. She feels that she should always meet others' demands perfectly—that she should, in face, *be* perfect. She doesn't take into account the fact that her boss was an unethical and manipulative person. She doesn't take into account the fact that she didn't like the work she was doing. She doesn't take into account the fact that she had done very well in her last position. No. Because she hasn't been the perfect worker and the perfect employee, *every time,* she becomes her Despicable Self and goes into a deep depression.

However, Deborah can learn several things from her depression. She can grow as a person so that she doesn't have to experience depression again and again in her life. She says, for example, that while things were getting worse on the job, she became depressed. Her depression was a way of blocking out anxiety and the realization that she would have to do something about this worsening situation. Deborah "coped" by becoming depressed, thereby closing off any other options she may have had.

Many depressed women do this. They close their eyes (become depressed) and hope the problem will be resolved in some way, any way. Through their depression, they choose not to "see" the way other people take advantage or try to manipulate.

The next time Deborah finds herself becoming depressed, she can ask herself: What problem is there that I'm trying not to face? It would have been better, for example, if she had worked out a compromise solution with her boss: She would do certain jobs for him as long as she could do certain other things *she* wanted to do. She could have tried to combine his interests and goals with her own interests and goals. And in the meantime, she could have been looking for another job.

Or, she could have quit, thereby experiencing herself as the person in charge rather than the one being rejected. But Deborah closed her eyes to all these options by becoming depressed.

Deborah might have talked about her feelings with friends. Instead, she eventually alienated her friends by shutting them out of her life. Yet, her friends could have been a big help. However, by leaning on her friends, Deborah might have felt she was violating another "should": You *should* be able to handle your problems by yourself.

This kind of an isolated position can certainly lead to the road marked "depression." For, in addition to food, shelter, and clothing, people need a sense of relatedness to their fellow human beings. A continuity of relatedness must exist between child and adult.

Without adequate physical and emotional exchanges between them, a child may gradually waste away and die, or she may be subject to severe forms of emotional disorders, the extremes of which could be autism and/or schizophrenia.

Your relatedness to those about you fulfills an essential ingredient of healthful development. Emotional responsiveness gives you a sense of connectedness with your feelings, be they feelings of pleasure or pain. Contact with our feelings provides us with an on-going involvement with our actual experiences, our attitudes, our thoughts. These involvements serve as steady streams of input. You are as dependent upon those feelings as you are upon food.

Involvement with your feelings, thoughts, and activities, as well as involvement with the feelings and thoughts of others, composes the stuff of a sense of aliveness. All persons strive for this in one way or another. The school child who feels alive and involved with school experiences looks forward to attendance each day. She wants to make efforts and enjoy her work and play. Without such feelings, she will see no purpose to school attendance, and when she is older and more independent, she may stay away and become the truant, the drop-out, and sometimes, but not necessarily, the delinquent teenager.

A sense of aliveness fuels your efforts. Without this movement, activity and productivity come to a standstill. Feeling alive is essential to your well-being. Any diminishment of that feeling will impinge upon your relatedness to yourself and to others. *The opposite of this feeling of aliveness is a sense of deadness. This deadness is at the core of all depressions, mild or severe, chronic or acute.* Sometimes you don't realize that you are progressively feeling more and more dead. Depression can develop by *default*, a default in your efforts to maintain a quality of on-goingness in your life. To the extent that you restrict and deny yourself reasonable and appropriate involvements, to that extent you will feel less alive.

In the future, Deborah can try to build up other

areas of her life so that her identity is not so precariously built on one little island. She could find an interest—painting, gardening, studying, tennis—that absorbs her energies. She should try to build relationships with people she likes. In this way, she will be providing herself with insurance when and if her work doesn't go well in the future.

Lastly, instead of "giving in" to depression, Deborah has the option of trying to fight these feelings as soon as she can, before they completely paralyze her (as they did). This may be useful advice for any woman who is now feeling depressed. In fact, if you are depressed right now, the following exercises can help to begin to break the paralysis.

1. Try to exercise at least once a day. Jog, do yoga, or run around the block with your dog.

2. Focus on releasing your emotions. Loud crying is sometimes good. Pound a pillow in your home if you feel like it. Complain vociferously to friends who can "take it." This is a safe way to permit feelings of anger to surface. Anger, as you've seen, is one of the most important features of depression that has to be dealt with. All depressions are loaded with angry feelings, and unless they are relieved in one way or another, it is almost impossible to overcome feeling depressed.

3. Keep a journal or diary of your feelings, especially the times when you become anxious or especially depressed. Note what you said, what you did, how you felt, and what you now feel about what took place. Ask yourself, "When I became anxious or depressed, what impossible expectations or standards was I trying to meet?" Don't force your answers. Sometimes, an answer will come to you two or three days later.

3

Which Woman Are You?

COMPULSIVE STANDARDS, rigid self-expectations, or "shoulds," are established early in life. They are derived from composites of familial, parental, and cultural attitudes and values, together with conscious or unconscious input that you are continuously providing. *These standards become the masters of your destiny.* Because these standards call for a form of perfection, you must inevitably fall short, although you may not be aware of this; you just feel uneasy and dissatisfied with much of what you think, say, or do.

The way any woman develops throughout her lifetime depends upon her basic character structure. The child who does not feel safe, who feels anxious at home and at school, begins to elaborate neurotic defenses very early in life to overcome her feeling of anxiety and lurking danger. Whatever form her defenses take, every one of them is designed to relieve anxiety and to make her feel comfortable and safe. Because feelings of comfort, safety, and relief from anxiety are so essential to physical and psychological well-being, one is driven to feel that *any* defensive means justifies the ends.

In other words, a woman's energy and creativity are placed in the service of an elaboration of defenses that will keep her anxiety-free and secure. The tragedy in all this is that the safety she strives for is *never* actually secured. While it is repeatedly sought, it is only fleetingly grasped.

A depression-prone woman is like a seaman securing himself against each wave of a raging storm that strikes his ship. He cannot relax after any wave, for he must secure himself against the next and the next. A storm at sea will eventually abate, however. But without an incentive for change, the storm of neurosis is unending.

Even a baby can become apprehensive and tense in an anxiety-ridden atmosphere. The tension the baby experiences causes it great discomfort and it may feel insecure and uncertain. This state of insecurity is what leads to the baby's primary experiences with its own reaction of anxiety—that is, *basic anxiety*.

Basic anxiety results from feelings of being alone and helpless in a "potentially hostile world."* The little girl who has been brought up to feel unaccepted by her parents will mold herself in certain ways to elicit their approval. She will try to do what she thinks they want her to do. She will try to be the way they expect her to be. She will ignore her spontaneous reactions, and will behave the way she thinks she *should*. Eventually, her responses become automatic ones, geared toward the reestablishment of comfortable feelings. Her efforts in this task inevitably deprive her of her natural, spontaneous reactions.

For example, a little girl wants to express anger, but she becomes anxious because she knows her parents do not approve of it. When she gets older, she finds she can't express anger even when it is appropriate to do so. ("If I want to be accepted, I *should never* express my anger.") Because she doesn't defend herself other people can easily " put her down." A second child wanting to express her feelings has learned that she gets no response from her parents. She grows to feel that there's no use in trying to express herself or to make contact. ("If I want to be

*Karen Horney.

accepted, I *should never* express my feelings.") When she gets older, she wants to have a close relationship, but finds she can't—intimacy makes her uneasy. A third child wanting to be accepted finds that she is noticed only when she does something that is noteworthy. ("I *should always* be productive and achieve.") As an adult, she wants to be able to relax, but finds she has to be active, to keep working, to be "on top." Otherwise, she becomes nervous or depressed.

We note then that certain factors in childhood which make for the "good little girl," the one who adheres closely to her "shoulds," will give rise to the woman who becomes the "good big girl," the woman who is *still* obeying her "shoulds" in order to win approval. Her selfhood is determined not by her own wishes and needs, but through the acknowledgment she receives from another person. She is dependent on others' affirmation for a sense of self. This is the woman we shall call the *overcompliant, self-effacing, love-addicted person.*

Certain factors will give rise to the little girl who gives up trying to express her feelings. This little girl withdraws. Her very quietness ensures her safety. She demands little. ("I *shouldn't* cause trouble. I *shouldn't* demand too much.") She often becomes a dependable non-boat rocker, and one who keeps a distance between herself and other people in order to avoid entangling alliances. Her safety lies in freedom, in calmness, sameness, noncompetitiveness, and predictability. This is the woman we shall call the *detached, uninvolved, resigned person.*

Other factors may give rise to the girl who becomes an assertive, aggressive, competitive child, who needs to be "on top" all the time, winning and proving herself superior and the best—in *all* respects. As an adult, she experiences herself only by these means. ("I *should* always beat others out.") This is the woman we call the *domineering person, the one who wants to achieve mastery.*

These approaches to living, as described here, are examples of *compulsive living*, but are rarely found in "pure" form. There are usually combinations of these characteristics in most people. It is these combinations that provide the sub-strata for unconscious conflict.

Please understand that it is the compulsiveness —that is, the "shouldness"—of these approaches that make for their neurotic character. Without the quality of compulsiveness—or shouldness—they are common, human responses, which may be used selectively, and relevantly, depending upon the circumstances.

Each of these ways of developing has consequences for the rest of a woman's life. Therefore, before you read further, answer the following groups of questions. Your answers can be helpful to you as we continue.

Group I

1. Do you dislike competitive situations?
2. Are you often sick?
3. Are you very dependent on a partner?
4. Do you feel best when you are doing things for others?
5. Do you cry easily?
6. Do you feel very uncomfortable when criticised?
7. Do arguments upset you a great deal?
8. Are you afraid to be in control for fear of hurting others?
9. When making even a legitimate request, do you feel guilty?
10. Is it hard for you to express anger?
11. Do you minimize your capacities?
12. In spite of what people tell you, do you feel you are not gifted or attractive?
13. Is it hard for you to spend money on yourself?
14. Do you apologize when you give orders?
15. Do you feel misunderstood most of the time?
16. Do you feel other peoples' needs are more important than your own?

If you answer "yes" to any eight or more of these questions, you tend to be a love-addicted (self-effacing) person.

GROUP II

1. Do you prefer to do most things alone?
2. Do you dislike struggle?
3. Do you avoid being intimately involved with others?
4. Do you spend a lot of time fantasizing?
5. Do you avoid change?
6. Do you delay paying your debts?
7. Do you find you procrastinate a good deal?
8. Do you tend not to participate directly, but prefer to maintain a peripheral position?
9. Does making an effort anger or irritate you?
10. Do you feel that ambitious striving is not for you?
11. Are you opposed to planning and prefer things to happen "spontaneously"?
12. Do you feel you are not demanding and can feel content with very little?
13. Do you find that you are not likely to talk about yourself unless prodded?
14. Do you find that you sometimes tend to be indifferent about sex?
15. Do you react strongly against being influenced or pressured?
16. Do you sometimes feel that your life is "weary, stale, flat, and unprofitable"?

If you answer "yes" to any eight or more of these questions, you tend to be an uninvolved person.

GROUP III

1. Do you feel restless unless you are gaining some advantage over others?
2. Is it difficult for you to admit you're wrong?
3. Do you feel you should be free from criticism because you try so hard?
4. Do you dread feeling helpless or dependent?

5. Do you dread the humiliation of failure?
6. Do you have to be the leader, to take charge?
7. Is it difficult for you to take suggestions?
8. Do you usually feel superior to others?
9. Do you have trouble asking for help?
10. Do you believe that your criticism of others is motivated by your wish to help them?
11. Do you withhold compliments or praise because you think they will "spoil" others too much?
12. Do you feel you need to win when you play a game?
13. Do you often feel others are lazy or stupid?
14. Do you feel others do not appreciate you fully?
15. Do you believe in the doctrine of "dog eat dog"?
16. Are you bored by conversation with people you do not admire?

If you answer "yes" to any eight or more of these questions, you tend to be a domineering type of person.

Even if you have answered "yes" to more than eight questions on any one of these three tests, you are still in a position to help yourself in very significant ways. You may also find that you can answer "yes" to many of the questions on all three tests. This means that you have mixed tendencies. Remember, however, that it is a sign of health to have different needs under different circumstances. These needs are assumed to be neurotic only when they are *compulsive*, that is, choiceless.

It might be useful now to take each of your yes answers and ask yourself *how*, for example, are you letting others take advantage; *what* are you doing to avoid change; *when* have you had difficulty admitting you're wrong; and so on. Raising these questions for yourself is essential in order to understand yourself better. Why don't you write your questions and answers in the journal we have suggested you keep?

The Domineering Woman

Caroline was voted the "most likely to succeed" in high school. When her youngest child left home, she began her own jewelry business. Her many years of experience in leading others (in community activities) contributed to her success. That, together with her freedom from family responsibilities and her husband's encouragement, served her well. She was surprised at how "easy" it was. "As long as you have self-confidence, know-how, a little capital, and you're willing to work hard," she would say, "you can make it." However, she made one important error. She misjudged the people with whom she became involved. Their friendliness, hospitality, and compliments disarmed her, and she miscalculated by revealing too many of her plans.

Off they went, taking her ideas. Her rage and humiliation knew no bounds. She felt she had "lost face" and her fall into depression was rapid. Even though she was in no sense ruined, she behaved as if she had nothing left. Her family couldn't console her.

Caroline went to bed and refused to eat. After several days of anguished restlessness, she swallowed some sleeping pills. Now, months later, she regards herself as "foolish" for having made such a precipitous decision to end her life. She feels that she did not consider all the options open to her at the time. In Caroline, the outstanding feature of her depression was rage directed at herself and her "stupidity."

Caroline is an example of what we call "the domineering woman." She *must* be in control all the time. The key word here is "must." Many people are in positions of power and control. While they may prefer and enjoy these positions, they do not need to be there in the way that Caroline had to, nor do they fall apart if they fall from power.

However, the domineering woman dreads feeling helpless, or not in control. She sees herself (her Perfect Self) as the strong person who is easily in charge.

She needs to feel superior to others and succeeds to some extent by being well organized, energetic, and effective. But this superachiever must *constantly* compete, consciously or unconsciously, in order to maintain a superior position and ward off feelings of self-contempt, feelings she's not usually even aware of.

In other words, she feels safe only when she has a controlling or dominant position. She may achieve this through running her family, an organization, a business, dinner parties. It doesn't matter what the situation is. This woman is as commonly found in the PTA as she is in the business world.

Yet, because she *needs* to control, she is often manipulative with others. And because she needs to be in control, she cannot stand being criticized. She *must* be right. If she is criticized, or if she feels helpless or impotent, she may have to deny those feelings. If they give rise to strong feelings of self-hatred, as in Caroline's case ("See how easily I let myself be hoodwinked"), she may have to depress those feelings to keep them from flooding her with rage and guilt at not having lived up to her expectations (i.e., I *should* have been a shrewder businesswoman).

As a rule, the domineering woman is less likely to become depressed than other women. She is ambitious and competitive and is busy either with her career, community affairs, or family occupations. In some cases, however, a loss of pride—a calamitous fall from Perfect Self to Despicable Self—will cause depression. Caroline, for example, felt she *should* have been able to foresee the events that took place. She *should* have been smarter and more cunning. She *should* have seen through her colleagues. Because she didn't, she suffered a severe loss of pride which left her grief-stricken.

Despite her competitiveness and her need to be right, Caroline has raging self-doubts. Those self-doubts lead her to put down others whenever she can. In that way, she can feel elevated and less doubtful of herself. When she fails in this, and is on the losing side, she suffers a deep hurt to her pride, and it is the loss of pride in her perfection that can plummet her into depression.

The domineering person, in short, feels she must know and understand everything, be able to do everything and do it quickly. She feels she *should never* fail and *should* know better than anyone else. Failure, being wrong, is humiliating, so that there is always a great need to justify her actions.

The Love-Addicted Woman

Leila had always prided herself on being a "good wife and mother," always ready to put her family's needs before her own. When her husband told her that he wanted to make some changes in their marriage, to lead "more interesting" and "more fun" lives, she became severely despondent.

Because she felt she had always conducted herself as he might wish, she was devastated by his comments. She felt they pointed to an abysmal failure on her part. Furthermore, she was puzzled that she could not have known how mistaken she was in thinking she had done such a good job. She felt her whole married life had been predicated on a mistaken notion and that it had, therefore, been a total waste. She commented, "I thought I was doing such a good job and he throws it in my face. I did everything for him!"

Leila kept up a semblance of functioning. But she felt listless and lost interest in socializing and keeping up with her housekeeping. She knew that her husband hadn't meant to hurt her, but she became more and more hurt and angry with him. "Who the hell does he think he is that he can say this to me—that *I've* got to change!" This in turn aroused tremendous guilt. "How can I be so angry with him, when all he wants is a better life for both of us? What a horrible, selfish woman I am." The anger was then turned upon herself, and she felt hopeless about ever being able to change.

Leila is typical of the self-effacing woman who needs to be pleasing and submissive. She is more commonly found in our culture than the predominantly domineering woman.

The self-effacing woman needs to take a *subordinate* (rather than dominant) position to others; she is not consciously interested in being "first." Indeed, she may feel very uneasy in a leadership position. "Love" and "serving others" are the most important things in her life. Because of this, however, she is inordinately dependent for any personal satisfaction upon those she loves and serves. Therefore, her self-esteem rests on being affirmed by others. Because of her need, there is sometimes an indiscriminate quality in the choices she makes. Anybody and everybody must think well of her because she tries so hard to be lovable. Her need is so compulsive that she cannot direct her maid or secretary to carry out her wishes without feeling anxious or guilty. "Who do I think I am, giving orders to another person?" she thinks. If someone is critical of her, she will quickly agree with or try to appease that person, rather than stand up for herself.

Actually, she can't ask for *anything* for herself without feeling guilty. Not only can't she stand up for her rights, but she also feels it's presumptuous to express an opinion. ("What do I know?") Leila once disagreed with a point raised at a meeting. When she got home, she was "nervous" but didn't know why. The reason was that she had disagreed with someone, possibly incurring his displeasure. This went against several of her "shoulds": You *should* be nice to people all the time; you *should* not make a spectacle of yourself; you *should* try to understand others' points of view.

Basically, the self-effacing woman feels it's wrong to be "selfish." Joan is so "unselfish" that she can't spend any money on herself without feeling guilty. But she doesn't have any qualms about buying her son or her husband new clothes. She is constantly *busy* doing things for them. She easily becomes a slave to other people's needs, since she can't disagree, dissent, or refuse without feeling guilty.

Freida drove one hundred miles each Sunday to see her mother. She didn't really want to make the drive each weekend, for these trips left her no time to do what she wanted to do. But she felt guilty if she didn't measure up to her "shoulds" of being the all-perfect and dutiful daughter.

The extreme love-addicted woman cannot enjoy doing anything by herself. Says Elaine, "I just don't enjoy being alone. I like someone with me." This need deprives her of the sweet solitude most people occasionally need to confer with themselves, to sort and think things out, exercising only their own thoughts and imagination.

Finally, the self-effacing woman cannot express anger or criticism without feeling guilt. She may "like" everybody. She actually needs to be liked because she is terrified of other people's hostility. Veronica had a hard time in her new job because she had to tell several other workers what to do. She would give them their work with a smile, and sometimes apologetically. One day she became furious with a woman whom she felt had been taking advantage of her. She was able to reprimand her. But a half hour later she felt so guilty about it ("That wasn't kind of me") that she apologized and took the woman to lunch.

Veronica felt guilty because she had violated a "should": You *should* never get angry. Sometimes, if she becomes angry, she will become depressed rather than expose her anger. She is often not even aware that she is angry.

This is the woman who "doesn't hear" other people's put downs, who tries to "understand" others' criticism of her. She cannot be assertive. In fact, at times, she can be suffocatingly sweet.

As a child, Veronica was brought up to be "nice" and "good." She wasn't allowed to talk back. She now tries to live up to what she expects of herself as well as what she believes is expected of her: to be all-generous, unselfish, humble, lovable, saintly. These become her unconscious "shoulds." Having learned to feel safe by complying, by being what she believes others expect her to be, she gradually lumps most of her compulsiveness under the rubric of "all for the sake of love."

At the same time, her excessive dependence makes her feel helpless and incompetent. And because she feels so weak, she feels it's her right to rely on others. However, because her implicit demands for support are often more than most people can or will fulfill, she feels abused and neglected a good deal of the time. Here is the seesawing again. For as soon as she feels others are not appreciating her, she feels that she shouldn't feel that way, nor make any demands upon them if she is truly accepting of them. If she is not loving, then she is a "fraud" and a "hypocrite." (Remember, everything for love.) Her self-approach is aroused again. She feels she is "selfish and presumptuous," abusing herself much more than anyone else could or would.

In short, the self-effacing woman becomes a sufferer through and through—a first-class martyr. She does not realize she expects "brownie points" for her suffering.

The Uninvolved Woman

Jasmine, a nursery school teacher, is a gentle, orderly woman who is well liked by the people she works with. She seems easily satisfied with simple pleasures. Her friends remark that "Nothing ever seems to bother Jasmine." She can't ever remember having had an argument with anyone.

She lives alone and takes care of her needs quietly. She reads, watches television, and rarely plans a social outing unless someone calls her. Then she is ready to go, but she seldom initiates anything herself. Although she "likes" her friends, they sometimes get on her nerves and she "forgets" or "refuses" to make appointments with them. Later on, after weeks or months, she will resume the relationships.

Jasmine became severely depressed after her mother died. Her small, orderly, predictable world was rocked. She "didn't know how to react." She lost the one person who represented any rootedness for her, any contact with an ongoing, affectionate relationship. She was really alone.

Her usual detachment became more marked. She didn't want to speak to anyone, to see anyone. Since it was during the summer, and school was not in session, she hardly went out at all. Finally her friends became alarmed because she appeared so thin and pale.

It was a quiet, gradually developing depression. In retrospect, she says, "Although my friends said I was depressed, I didn't feel much different from the way I usually do. I just didn't seem to have any interest in anything. But that's not so different. I don't make a lot of noise over anything. The main thing was that the tears would just roll down my face. It seemed that I was sad. But I don't know what I was crying about. I didn't cry at the funeral. People thought I took my mother's death very well. My feeling was, Why make a fuss, it's all over anyway."

Jasmine is so removed from her own feelings that she says she "seemed" to be sad because tears are rolling down her face. This is a common response in the uninvolved woman who becomes depressed.

Jasmine has put a wet blanket not only on her feelings but on her wishes and needs as well. Above all, she must remain detached from others. Closeness is threatening to her. She was raised in an environment which threatened to engulf her individuality. In order to survive the terror she experienced, mostly at the hands of her domineering father, she had to pull away, withdraw into herself so that all of her wouldn't be "taken over." Moreover, her need to keep others at a distance keeps her from being aware of her need for affection.

Helga too lives alone and sees friends occasionally.
She has a job which she's not "crazy about" but which
"pays the rent." When asked why she doesn't try to
get a better job, she'll say, "I'm not ambitious. I can't
stand grasping, greedy people." Yet Helga often
wakes up in the morning feeling she can hardly get
up from the bed and dress.

Helga was reared by parents who were distant and
self-contained. Priding themselves on their self-
sufficiency and independence, they tried to raise
Helga with these same characteristics, overlooking a
child's need for ongoing closeness and warm exchange.

Helga learned her lesson well. This was apparent
when she became involved with a man who wanted
to marry her. She became anxious and panicked. Not
wanting to give up her freedom, she broke off the
relationship. Yet her "freedom" did not satisfy her
either, for she was undermining her healthy needs for
closeness with another person. She still woke up in
the morning feeling she couldn't get started, because
she was constantly pushing against her various resistances to involvement.

Uninvolved people are sometimes underachievers
because they have such an aversion to consistent
effort. They may, however, have an extensive fantasy
life, and dream of writing the great American novel,
becoming successful businesswomen. But that's usually as far as it goes and they settle for far less than
they might achieve.

These woman often have trouble talking about
themselves. They can discuss plays, movies, ideas,
other people, but they shy away from talking about
their own thoughts and goals. They seem to want
simply to be left alone.

Lois is afraid of closeness because that could mean
exposure. Exposure means recognition of shortcomings, and that can mean possible rejection. Rather
than suffer the pain of rejection, such a person main-
tains aloofness, thus relieving a possible onslaught of
self-hatred at the time of the rejection. Lois went

from one relationship to another, always finding some excuse to break it off when the man became seriously involved with her. She said that she wanted marriage, but she never did marry. Her inner dictate said: Remain free and that way no one can hurt you, criticize you, or reject you.

An uninvolved woman often feels too much anxiety about being *judged* by others. So she stays aloof. Her self-sufficiency and aloofness give her a secret sense of superiority and power over others. And again, she resists her natural strivings and yearnings, as well as her needs for closeness with others.

Basically, the uninvolved person cannot tolerate too much anxiety. If this person suddenly said, "I want this" or "I am ambitious," great tension would be generated. She therefore keeps her needs minimal; her uninvolvement, in short, protects her from anxiety.

Because of her need to remain free, the uninvolved woman is hypersensitive to any coercion. She may even see herself as a rebel against society's restrictions. Yet this need that she should not feel coerced, or pressured, often leads her to become passive, for as soon as she feels she *should* do something, she experiences tremendous inner resistance.

There are varying degrees of uninvolvement. There is the woman who lives alone, has a safe, predictable job, and keeps mostly to herself. There is the woman who follows the same pattern except that she may have one or more consuming intellectual interests. Then there is the woman who is in a relationship, who may have children, but who keeps a certain distance from those around her, and from what she herself wants. In every uninvolved person, however, there is deep resignation, a sense of hopelessness about change.

No woman, as we've said, is *completely* love-addicted, uninvolved, or domineering. Nor are many of the qualities described "bad" or destructive by themselves. For instance, it is not neurotic to want to compete sometimes, to please others sometimes, to be alone sometimes. These qualities are troublesome only when they become compulsive, when these needs become rigid self-expectations. Then you *must* win all the time or you might feel depressed. You *must* please all the time or you feel guilty. You *must* be a little withdrawn from others or you become anxious. In other words, these choiceless, rigid demands ("shoulds") prevent you from behaving freely and spontaneously.

There is even more trouble when you are trying to juggle two or more of these conflicting "shoulds." For example, a little girl may mold herself in certain ways in order to please her parents. Now suppose that her parents will not tolerate any dissent from her, but at the same time want her to excel in school. She may then develop both domineering and self-effacing tendencies: that is, when she is with people, she will be self-effacing, but at the same time, in her work and in school, she must be "on top."

Or suppose you have a need to "win," to be first, and also a need to please others. No matter what you do you can become anxious, because when you're winning you think you are incurring others' hostility, and when you're pleasing and complying, you may be annoyed with yourself for not dominating the situation. You can see what a terrible bind people unwittingly place themselves in. When their conflicting "shoulds" make them too anxious, too guilt-ridden, too self-hating, the Novocaine reaction, or depression, can easily take over.

Here are some examples of how your "shoulds" can set you up for anxiety and depression.

Laura, an assistant office manager, prided herself on working faster and more efficiently than most other people. Consequently, when her boss was out of town, she agreed to do his work as well as her own. She also agreed to throw a party for her sister's birthday ("How can I let my sister down?") and to show around a friend of a friend who had just moved to town.

It wasn't only that Laura couldn't say no. She felt she could do more than most people, and she could, up to a point. But even she couldn't stop the clock, and eventually time ran out. She was exhausted by the time the party came, and extremely anxious because she hadn't done all the office work she had said she would do. She also felt her boss had asked her to do more work than was possible in the first place, which made her angry at him. However, she couldn't tell him he'd asked too much of her. And she couldn't simply shrug and say to herself, "Next time I'll take on less." No, she became depressed for she hadn't lived up to her perfectionistic demands. She felt she *should* have been able to make more time, work faster, organize better.

Clara wanted to be a successful actress and "show the world" how talented she was. For a period of time, however, she stopped acting. When she went back to the theater, she finally landed an important role in a new play, but became torn with conflict. She was finally in the position she had "always wanted." Here was her chance for "success." However, involvement in this success required a measure of independence, and that collided with her wish to be "taken care of." Such anxiety was generated by the conflict that she had to muffle it somehow. This led her to her withdrawal, to the helpless position of the depressed condition. That way she need not confront her conflict nor assert her autonomy.

To be either compulsively domineering, love-addicted, or uninvolved is to possess a special set of directives or "shoulds." When a woman violates her "shoulds," she often becomes depressed, but for her own particular reasons. For the love-addicted woman, expressing anger (You *should* not be a bitch.) may make her feel depressed. For the domineering woman, not winning an argument or a top position may lead to depression. (You *should* not be a failure.) The uninvolved woman may actually be in a chronic state of mild depression, for she lives a basically flat life. However, her depression may become severe when she becomes dependent on someone or something, or finds her needs for closeness are conflicting with her needs for freedom.

Only by realizing what a cramping effect your "shoulds" have on your life can you begin to free yourself. Try writing in your journal when you become anxious or depressed. Ask yourself: What set of standards am I not living up to? What "shoulds" have I violated? Or, what clashing "shoulds" are waging war within me?

Suggestions for the Domineering Woman

1. Try to put yourself in a situation in which you'd normally dominate—at a meeting or party or a family discussion. See how you feel if you sit quietly or engage in conversation, but don't try to bowl people over with your personality. *Listen.* This is not intended to change you. It is to help you see that you can, with effort, be comfortable in situations where you choose to take a less central role. You will probably find that people will accept you even when you aren't being your most energetic, efficient, or brightest self.

2. Many domineering women find it hard to relax, even on vacations. Yet they *want* to enjoy their vacations. If this is characteristic of you, by all means bring along some work with you, and don't feel guilty about it. Do the work only when you feel yourself getting "edgy."

Make an effort, too, to pick a vacation spot that meets your needs. You may hate sitting on the beach for two weeks, for example, but might enjoy seeing art galleries in Florence, Italy. Pick a vacation where you'd be most comfortable.

3. When you become depressed, it may be because you are violating one of your "shoulds": I *should* not be inactive in any situation. I *should* always be accomplishing something or taking advantage of every opportunity. I *should* always be efficient. Write down your feelings and try to figure out which "should" you

are violating. If you can begin to see how hard you are on yourself, you will be making a first positive step toward change, accepting yourself with your limitations.

Suggestions for the Love-Addicted Woman

1. Your problem is that you will not assert yourself. So try small experiments in speaking up. Give your opinion whether you agree or disagree. If you are afraid to state your opinion, try asking a pertinent question. You can try this out first with people you know well.

2. Remember that you are "allowed" to express your feelings—even when you are annoyed. This is your right. You don't have to say to someone who's upset you, "You're a mean person." You can say, "I felt badly when you said that to me."

3. Practice giving an order or stating a wish without sounding apologetic. Practice until you have what you want to say down pat. For example, you have to return a blouse. How do you approach the salesperson?

You can actually write down what you want to say, look at it and read it several times. Or you can say what you have to say out loud and repeat it at least five times. You will find that when you are confronting the person with whom you have to deal, the things you want to say will come out of your mouth with much less difficulty. If you don't succeed in this the first few times, keep trying it because it's extraordinarily useful if you can get it to work.

4. Practice asking for favors if this is difficult for you. Don't sound apologetic and don't convey your guilt, even if you feel it. Follow the suggestion above about practice.

5. When you feel someone has put you down, speak up. Ask in your most courteous fashion if they have indeed done what you think they have. Make it a true question. ("Were you trying to put me down?") Even if it doesn't embarrass the other per-

son, he or she will at least realize that you're not such a pushover and will be less likely to try it again.

6. When someone asks for something, instead of automatically saying yes, tell them to wait while you put down the phone. Or say you'll think about it and let them know the next day. Ask yourself: Do I want to do what is asked of me? Don't automatically or compulsively comply.

Having taken the time, try to prepare in your mind what your reason is for not wanting to do the favor and then present that in as reasonable a way as you can. People aren't always ready to jump on you when you refuse them something. (For more tips see the section on assertiveness in Chapter 16.)

Suggestions for the Uninvolved Woman

1. Try to discuss your feelings with someone you trust. The more you can open up, the more alive you'll feel. Remember that you can select what you say and need not move to private or intimate matters about yourself. For example, you can discuss your feelings about a book or play.

2. Make the first step and call someone to plan an outing. Don't always wait for others to come to you.

3. Consider joining a drama or singing group. They can help you learn to express yourself and to get in touch with your feelings.

4. If there are any young children around, try a few minutes of active play with them. You may find you enjoy the childlike spontaneity that occurs.

5. Can you begin to see one area in which you can strive for something you truly want? Think about it.

4

The Lost Dream

LAURIE MARRIED at twenty-seven and had two children, Sarah and Billy, before she was thirty. "I grew up wanting to be a lawyer like my father," she says as she smokes a long cigarillo. With her red hair pulled back in a ponytail, outfitted in blue jeans and a blue turtleneck, she looks young and full of life. Yet the setting is somewhat discordant: a suburban home which seems to have little of Laurie's personality. The walls are off-white, the curtains beige, the furniture early American. From looking at Laurie, one would expect a bolder tapestry: huge bright modern paintings on the walls, multicolored shag rugs. She doesn't seem to be at home here. "I guess I wanted to please my father," she continues. "I know he wanted a brilliant daughter. But I couldn't bear law school, although I did marry a lawyer. I felt that law would stifle me, that I wouldn't be able to express the emotional side of my nature. Really, I always wanted to be an actress, to have people applaud me. I love the idea of being a star. Oh, I know that sounds childish. But I guess I need a lot of feedback from people. It's not enough having my family and friends love me." She pauses to check on Sarah who's taking a nap. When she comes back, her voice is softer, even more wistful.

"You know, when I look in at my baby, I feel like such a bitch complaining. I don't mean to sound discontent. Sarah is a beautiful baby. And really, work-

ing in an advertising firm, which is what I did before
I got pregnant, was not making me any happier.
Work wasn't the answer for me. But when I was
working, there was more of a hyped-up quality to
my life. I was busy. I always had to look good. Now I
feel so listless all the time. I have to force myself to do
things. I know my husband doesn't want to hear all
my complaints. Why should he? He wants me to be
happy. Isn't this nutty? I'm jealous of the fact that
he goes out to practice law every day, even though *I*
was the one who quit law school. But really, if I look
at my life, it's fine. I don't want to sound like I'm
totally miserable because I'm not. It's just that some
days I really feel down, especially toward the middle
of the week."

Laurie had not wittingly chosen to become a victim of what Betty Friedan calls "the feminine mystique." Actually, her life was filled with opportunities:
law school, advertising, acting classes. Laurie chose
to have children and says she doesn't regret that
choice. Yet she feels listless, almost as if her life were
over.

Sheilah would seem, at first glance, to be a very
different type of woman. Sheilah is thirty-nine, a
divorcee who owns and runs a small shop. She is a
controlled woman who seems to be cold and aloof.
Yet, the more she talks, the more this aloofness seems
like a façade. "My work supports me very well," she
says, "and I'm grateful for that. But it bores me, really. I'd like to be doing something else but I don't
know what. Sometimes, I feel I have so much inside
me that I'm going to explode.

"Because my work doesn't give me much satisfaction anymore, I try to do as much as I can in the
evening. I ice skate, go to concerts, go out with men.

"I hate the idea of marriage. I'm afraid to give up
my freedom. But part of me wants marriage—or a
lasting, deep relationship with a man." She shrugs.
"What do people want out of life, I ask myself. I
seem to be either in a frantic whirl or hidden away

listening to music. I feel restless a lot of the time—
and yet I know I do more than many people I know.

"Sometimes I find I'm in a rage—oh, if I see a married woman who is able to do what she wants to in
life because her husband is supporting her, or if I
walk past a magnificent piece of jewelry which I
can't afford to own. I love beautiful things. I have an
artist's sensibilities. I think I need to find some outlet
for that. But I can't give up my business; I like my
nice apartment and clothes, and, besides, what am
I going to live on when I get older?

"Sometimes I think I've been just a tiny bit depressed all my life. There are mornings I wake up
feeling so sad and listless, and don't know why. Sometimes I feel I was born to be a princess and here I
am struggling away!"

Sheilah's restlessness *seems* to be the antithesis of
Laurie's inertia. Yet both women are suffering from
the same problem: low-grade, chronic depression.
Because lawyers have the opportunity to be "on," in
much the same way that actresses have to be "on
stage," it is somewhat unfortunate that Laurie did
not seize the opportunity to be in the limelight by
practicing law. Law could have given her the "feedback" she says she wants and needs.

It might be easy to say that Laurie is afraid of success, or afraid of failure, depending upon where you
stand. But those are meaningless words unless one
can understand against what standard she measures
herself. A clue to that standard is revealed when
Laurie says, "I knew he [father] wanted a brilliant
daughter."

This is something so many parents inadvertently
burden their children with. Can you imagine what it
must feel like, throughout childhood and adolescence,
thinking that you have to turn out to be "brilliant"?
Even concert pianists who devote a lifetime to becoming "brilliant" artists have no guarantee that they
will ever achieve that brilliance.

At this stage in her life, however, Laurie is not suffering so much from failure to achieve her father's

goals, as from failure to achieve her own goals. It is true that parents may establish both possible and impossible goals for their children. But we have to remember that those children grow up into presumably responsible adults. They then have the prerogative of establishing their own goals. If Laurie makes her father's goals her own, then she, and not her father, becomes the one responsible for them.

When Laurie accepts and takes her father's goals for her own without evaluating them, she has not really exercised free choice. Nevertheless, she binds herself to a set of standards which may or may not be reasonable, and in which she may or may not believe. By doing this, she wraps herself in sticky plastic; no matter which way she turns, she cannot extricate herself from the rigid standard that she has internalized and made her own.

In terms of relieving guilt, it's helpful to be able to say, "Oh, that was my father's fault. He was the one who established my opinions, who made me the way I am." However, her father cannot be blamed for attitudes Laurie holds today.

Because Laurie *has* kept alive and has nourished a fantasy, a fantasy of brilliance in a profession, she must remain dissatisfied with any other work she does. It isn't that "work wasn't the answer." It's that no work which does not fulfill the fantasy will satisfy her.

Even Laurie's feelings about taking care of her baby are involved. She feels that any seventeen-year-old can take care of a baby, and discredits herself for "sinking so low" as to be *only* a housewife. Disliking herself for being in that role, she feels "bitchy" toward her baby. Ashamed of that feeling, and angry for having it, she becomes doubly dissatisfied with herself. This feeling, common in many young women, leads to a sense of having been "put aside" or "put on the shelf." They may feel there's no way they can unglue themselves from a "stuck" existence. Combined feelings of helplessness, hopelessness, anger, guilt, and deep dissatisfaction all serve to render

Laurie increasingly uptight. This spreads to other aspects of her life, and she feels herself being crowded in, more and more restricted. She can reach a point where she feels that some catastrophe might occur. At this point, her anxiety, which accompanies every stage of this process, will become greater and greater.

Laurie may not be aware of the progression of her anxiety. She might say, like Sheilah, "I feel like I'm going to explode." Or, "I don't know why, but I feel something terrible will happen." She will be aware of "listless" feelings, of being "miserable." However, if you were to ask her if she feels anxious, she might truthfully say "no," not recognizing her underlying anxiety.

Sometimes this anxiety reaches an intolerable level. Then a woman might seek relief by going to a physician, using medication, taking alcohol or drugs, indulging in any activity, including sexual, that might bring her a measure of relief. These moves may work for a time, but unless the causes for the tension and anxiety are dealt with, they become only temporary solutions.

Some people cannot tolerate the slightest anxiety. The very beginnings of anxiety can make them extremely uncomfortable. These are the men and women who feel anxious if they become angry with the grocer, who feel anxious if they have to make a phone call, who feel anxious about going out for a social evening, introducing people, planning a vacation, going to vote, asking for a bill to be paid, going to the post office, having a family argument.

So they must find solutions to cover their anxiety, to bind it, to keep it from rising to consciousness. In general, people who cannot tolerate anxiety tend to restrict their lives. They are the perennial "no wave makers." They narrow their involvements to the most simple, predictable elements, thus minimizing any experiencing of anxiety.

In this regard, depression serves an important function because it serves to bind the anxiety and other troublesome feelings. Especially for people who have no tolerance for anxiety, even those minor anxieties inherent in daily living, depression serves as an alternate feeling state to a state that includes anxiety. But very often, the anxiety escapes anyway, and one is left feeling *both* anxious and depressed.

Depression seems to reduce painful feelings. We see widespread, but often low-grade, depression among prisoners who have no way to express their rage, their feelings of continual frustration. They must subdue their feelings in order to achieve some relief from their pain.

Individuals who are chronically depressed are often referred to as "wet blankets." Consider the function of a wet blanket: it is used to throw over a fire, to contain the fire, to prevent it from spreading and causing damage. Psychologically, the wet blanket persons are continually attempting to cover the fires of their anguish. A serious consequence of the wet blanket approach is that it often spreads to other family members who are not strong enough to withstand its dampening effects.

There is another consequence. You cannot be selective. The following will explain what we mean. Let us label your troublesome feelings A, C, D, and G. If you depress those to bring yourself some relief, you inadvertently depress feelings B, E, F, and H also. They too are dampened, blanketed, diminished, covered, depressed.

What do we have now? No more sexual feelings? No feeling of enjoyment? No interest in work, play, friends, family? This was not part of the bargain!

Thus, we arrive at common features of depression: feelings of emotional, intellectual, and physical stagnation. Of course, these are found in different degrees and intensities, always depending on the severity of the depression.

The feelings of boredom that Sheilah talks about are an outcome of depression. If she weren't depressed, she might be able to look around and see how she could make her life more satisfying. Could she find some facets of work that could make her time on the job more interesting? Could she use the time she had on her hands to read or work puzzles? Could she plan her evenings more carefully so that she had more to look forward to?

Sheilah admits to having "so much inside her." But she cannot harness that energy. Through her depression, she has made it unavailable to herself. Both Sheilah and Laurie are trapped by their belief that they *should* be doing something they have little interest in. But there is also a conflicting "should"— they *should* be doing something else. It is this conflict, together with a deep resentment, that creates the resistance which feeds the boredom.

Laurie too is bored. She says she "chose" to have children, yet she feels her life "is over." One must then ask how much of a choice was her choice? Was it a choice dictated by traditional expectations of what a young woman is supposed to want?

There are choices and choices. There are those actions we really have no choice but to make, and those that our cultural and family backgrounds determine for us. Then there are those we make if we are willing and able to run risks and take consequences.

Laurie's entire background predisposed her to have children. Children, she was told again and again, were supposed to bring you happiness and fulfillment. A brief excursion into the world of men (law school) reinforced the cultural stereotype that identifies woman's place. Laurie didn't feel as if she fit in there. But Laurie was involved in a deep conflict, for her father had sanctioned this world of men while her social milieu pointed in another direction. The presence of this conflict was something Laurie had to keep depressed, for she could not bear the anxiety it generated. In this example we see once again how *conflict is always one of the cornerstones of depressions.*

Laurie's basic discontent relates to an inherent recognition that she will not achieve her dream of the brilliant career woman. As the years go by and she makes no attempt to develop herself, she will feel the loss of her dream more and more keenly. Her depression is partially grief, grief over the loss of her dream, a dream of an exciting life, a life she is making no real effort to achieve.

Laurie is leading the life she thinks she *should* lead. We can all understand this. Women are still being told, often by innuendo, that their place is in the home. And women know too that not all women are allowed to advance according to their capabilities in the work world. But in spite of this conditioning and oppression, Laurie feels her choice is not enough. Instead of making new choices in order to grow as an autonomous woman, she cannot, and even feels guilty that she has not accepted her choice. But she has depressed the guilt along with the conflict between her ambitiousness and her dependency.

It may surprise you that we have said women are still being told that their place is in the home. Nevertheless, like Laurie, millions of men and women still feel that. Although there has been much movement in the direction of real opportunities for women, this has only just begun. Laurie, like many women, remains extremely divided within herself about this direction. She is both influenced and confused by what she sees and hears. She both loves and fears the notion of freedom to choose.

The inner selves of many women remain in the home, even though they may have made, sometimes with the support and encouragement of their families, an intellectual transition to the work world. This is because the transition is not always an unequivocal commitment to a new attitude. It is in this conflict between traditional values and exciting, but anxiety-provoking, new possibilities where many women are finding themselves today. This ambivalence springs from many sources. Women are asking: Is work worth it? What can I do? Will my children suffer if I work? Why should I hold a job and then have the full responsibility in the home too? What

about the fact that women are discriminated against?
If I have to begin with a small salary, is it worth it
for me to work?

All these are good questions and women, together
and as individuals, will have to ask them, think them
through, and find satisfactory answers. This will be a
slow process. The process will occur gradually, with
surges of movement forward, and inevitable setbacks.

There is another factor operating here too, a factor
that operates in all depressions—that of *the lost
dream*. Because the dreams of Laurie and Sheilah
seem lost to them forever, they experience the sadness which is part of their depression.

Every woman who suffers from depression has a
lost dream. Yet you are often unaware of it. Sometimes, if you ask a depressed woman, "Do you feel as
if you have lost something?", she will say "yes," although she won't be able to put her finger on what
it is she has lost.

Each depressed woman will have a different lost
dream, but the dream is always connected with a
woman's image of herself. We have seen that when a
woman has conflicting "shoulds," or when her anxiety
at not living up to her "shoulds" becomes too painful,
the novocaine reaction can be triggered off and she
becomes depressed. Yet in her unconscious, her goals
and expectations persist, even though she has partially or completely blocked them from her awareness.

For Laurie, her lost dream concerns becoming a
brilliant career woman. She has, however, suppressed
her healthy needs for change and achievement because they make her feel too guilty. She feels she
should be satisfied. If she is not, she is a "bad person."
But as she suppresses her feelings and conflicts, to
block all of this from her awareness, she suppresses
and blocks *everything*—including her energy and
aliveness. *That* is why Laurie feels so tired, listless,
and bored.

Sheilah, whose lost dream revolves around being a
princess, is an example of the uninvolved, resigned

woman. She may have fantasies of being successful, fantasies of living a more creative life, fantasies of living with a man. But because she is torn by conflict, and because her uninvolvement is supported by inner resistances to making consistent efforts, she represses her strivings and the anxiety generated by her conflicts. But her anxiety escapes anyway, and she becomes restless.

Sheilah says she *should* be a princess. You can see how the idea of a princess in a tower fits in with what we know about the uninvolved woman, who is distant but superior, who lives more and more in her imagination, but who is awaiting rescue from the empty tower in which she finds herself.

The lost dream in many depressed, married women revolves around their husbands. They cannot accept their spouses for what they are. For if this woman is to be her wonderful, perfect self, she *should* have selected a wonderful, perfect husband. The woman who realizes her husband is never going to "measure up" to these expectations can become severely depressed. She knows he is *not* going to set the world on fire. He is *not* going to be the lover she wanted. He is *not* going to be rich. He is *not* ever going to become the life of the party. She realizes that what she wanted and expected just isn't there. Her Mr. Wonderful dream was all a fairy tale—a lost dream. She knows the situation is irrevocable, but she cannot accept this. She knows it's not there; she knows it will never be there. What she was looking for was her fantasy. She was looking for A, B, C, D, and he is H, I, J, K. She cannot reconcile herself to that loss. In her heart, she continues to insist that he be other than what he is. She is griefstricken when she confronts her loss. Her hopelessness becomes a cornerstone for her depression. Tears well and flow from her eyes; she is abject. She has accepted the inevitability of her lost dream, and yet she has not. Again she is in conflict; again she is in anguish. Her grief goes on and on and on.

The woman who can see this reality ("Okay, Joe is

never going to set the world on fire.") and accept it is in a better position. She, of course, is disappointed and she has to struggle with what we call her *marriage anger*. But she knows that if she continues to grieve, she will be damaging herself. This is why women who are able to accept such a loss experience great relief. They can put that problem behind them and get on with their lives. They will be able to relate to their partners in a new way, because they won't be constantly disappointed.

Other women's lost dreams often revolve about their children. The extreme example of this is the stage mother who becomes hysterical if her child doesn't do what she expects him or her to do. These are women who can only tolerate themselves through their children's successes. They keep the dream alive —and thus themselves elated rather than depressed —by pushing their children. If the child does not live up to their expectations, either because of lack of ability or desire or by deliberately resisting, these women can become inconsolable.

Most women, however, whose lives revolve about their children, do not fall into this extreme category. Nevertheless, they too have their fantasies of what they want their children to accomplish. When those children frustrate their mothers' expectations and drop out of school, postpone involvement in a career, run away, or involve themselves in unusual or bizarre lifestyles, these women can become very unhappy. Their profound disappointment with their children, and with themselves for their failure, often precipitates a severe depression.

For other women, the lost dream may involve success, fame, or fortune. June was a violinist who left her music to raise her family. She attempted to return to playing concerts after an eight-year hiatus. But she had repeated bouts of inertia. This is understandable considering the extremely difficult task she had chosen. Not only is there still much prejudice against women musicians, but there is also the fact that June hadn't been working in her field for eight long years. She was up against tremendous odds. After several months she said, "I'm a fool trying to do this. It's no use." And she became depressed. She had given up the dream of glory that she would ever become the exceptional violinist she expected to be. But she could not forgive herself for her failure to achieve this. She could not, therefore, reconcile herself to the challenge of the struggle to use her ability in a more realistic way. That loss is surely a greater one than the loss of her dream of glory.

In Chapter 2, we saw how Deborah became depressed when she was fired from her job. Failing to meet others' needs, she had failed being a "good girl," an efficient worker. Her lost dream was the loss of her view of herself as the perfectly dependable woman. In order for Deborah to recover, she is going to have to give up some part of that dream of perfection in order to become real, that is, to accept herself with her real limits as well as her strengths.

The despondent woman often doesn't realize that she is mourning for something that is lost, and that the lost dream is rooted in her "shoulds." All a woman may realize is that she is angry, either with herself or with someone else. This is understandable, because her pride has been bound up in attaining this dream, however unrealistic. This is what makes the loss so unbearable.

The grief persists because she sees herself at an impasse. If she believes that this is the *only* way she can live (having only the partner, or child, or job she feels she *should* have), she cannot possibly accept an alternative.

We must recognize the fact that our expectations, real and unrealistic, are also products of our culture. Living in a society which worships success, money, power, and prestige, as ours does, it is understandable that our expectations take on this cast. Thus, it is not enough for Laurie to be a lawyer, she must be a brilliant one.

The point we are making is that depression is usually tied in with a lost dream that involves perfection. However, this is not always the case. Phyllis Chesler, the author of *Women and Madness,* for example, has stated eloquently that women's depression often stems from mourning over the loss of a positive conception of themselves. How true this is, for, as you probably are only too aware of by this time, we live in a culture which has made women second-class citizens. This is why there is now a fight to gain for women equal pay and equal opportunities for equal work.

Let us return to Laurie's case in order to explain the difference between a real and unreal expectation. Laurie had an opportunity to go to law school, and she gave it up to become a wife and mother. She isn't satisfied with that choice. Now, the question is, what does she do? Does she become depressed? Or does she look around for a choice she can make that will use her energy and skills? *It is because she is in such conflict with what the culture expects of her, what her father expected of her, what her husband expects of her, and what she expects of herself, that she has blocked out this conflict by becoming depressed.* In this way, Laurie's lost dream is partially the loss of an achieving self that she has finally, but reluctantly, put aside. She cannot begin to rescue any part of that dream if she remains depressed, however. And if, on top of that, she still harbors expectations that, no matter what she does, she must be "brilliant," then she will make her struggle all the more impossible.

In June (the violinist) we find the same phenomenon taking place. She may not get the support and encouragement she wants and needs from her family, her friends, her community, the music establishment. But if June blames herself for her "failure," and harbors guilt because she is unable to overcome these obstacles and achieve success as she defines it, she is being unrealistic and unfair to herself. She is *demanding* the impossible of herself. This is what we mean by the lost dream being related to ideas of perfection.

Women are so used to blaming themselves for everything that goes wrong. You may want children, have them, but have to give up time in the work world to care for them. But then, when a woman tries to go back to work, she blames herself mercilessly because she is not doing as well as the men she sees around her, men who, all this time, were building their careers. It is this self-blame, rooted in our "shoulds" (I *should* be able to overcome all these obstacles) that feeds depression.

We believe that women must begin to define themselves and the values they live by. When you are depressed, you are often judging yourselves by a standard that *others* have set up—be they parents, teachers, media, society. Why should you feel "put down" because you are a mother? Why should you equate the making of money not only with status but with positive feelings about yourself? Why should you continually repudiate yourself for wanting something?

Can you not evaluate your dreams, any one of them, and see what is valid and reasonable for you? Can you select from your storehouse of dreams some that you feel you can take actual steps to realize? So much of the stuff of our lives has been started with dreams that they cannot all be rejected by us. But can we sift through them and take those which will not press us, will not frustrate us, will not immobilize us? Can we love a dream and deliver it, patiently and passionately, into the world of our real lives?

PART II

5

Love and Romance

"When I fall in love with a man, I want to take him inside me ... to fill me up."

"Yes! When my love left me, I was empty ... my insides gone ... that's love."

Conversation between two women at the National Organization for Women's Sexuality Conference, 1974

THE POET Lord Byron wrote, years ago, "Love is to men a thing apart. 'Tis women's whole existence." Unfortunately, it still holds true for many women that "love" is their whole existence. Not that these women don't have jobs, families, and friends. But in the deepest part of their emotional being, "love" is their major emotional value. Without being "in love," without having a relationship with a man, they often feel diminished, unhappy, unlovable.

However, in our view, those women for whom this holds true are not talking about love. They are talking about an *addiction to love*, a *morbid dependency* upon a partner, which drives them to forfeit an autonomous life, and to settle for *secondary living* through a man. For the most part, this kind of living through another person has been sanctioned, encouraged, upheld, and clung to for centuries by both men and women.

If we were to put the shoe on the other foot for a moment, how absurd it would sound to many people if we were to substitute "man" for woman in the statement: A *man* can find his greatest fulfillment in life through his role as child rearer and companion to his spouse, to aid and encourage her in all of her strivings as she seeks to fulfill herself in as wide a world as she can find for that fulfillment.

A man *might* find that role fulfilling, as many a woman has and will continue to find it. We are not arguing against that position at all, for that too would be an absurd position to take. We are only pointing to the unquestioned *compulsory nature* of the role that has led so many women to see themselves as reflections of, as secondary to, as dependent upon, and as living through, a man. Because in their minds their very existence has depended upon this view, they have had to believe it was all in the name of "love." Questions must be posed, however: Is this really how we see love? Is this really what we want in love?

The love-addicted woman might be regarded as the twin of the depressed woman, for the seeds of the depressed woman's destruction can lie in her *compulsive* need to give and receive love, and in her failure to succeed at this.

Julia might not understand being called a *love addict* for she is a teacher and "lives her own life." Yet she has had several depressions, all of them following break-ups with men. We spoke to Julia in a small restaurant. She is a thirty-six-year-old woman with straight blond hair and warm brown eyes. She wears no makeup except lipstick, and talks like a woman who takes herself seriously. One gets a feeling of strength from her. Her story, therefore, presents a paradox and raises the question: Why has she suffered so?

Julia's father was a salesman and her mother had been a beauty queen. Julia was an only child. Her mother, she says, was disappointed in her because she wasn't beautiful, and her father was disappointed because she wasn't a boy. They both let her know the way they felt.

"I can remember my father asking me to do things I was absolutely incapable of doing," she says. "For example, when I was ten, I was supposed to go to the library and take out Shakespeare and then discuss it with him! My mother couldn't understand why I didn't have ten boys asking me to the prom like she did. The point was, I was tall and gangly then. Nobody asked me to the prom."

As Julia's mother grew older, she became unhappy and bitter. The marriage ended in divorce. She never knew, Julia says, what had happened to the glamorous life she had been promised. Julia's mother remarried and now runs an occult bookshop. "She had beauty," says Julia wryly. "Now she has magic."

Julia says, "I was really brought up to get married to a rich man," and she did marry a rich man when she was in her early twenties, a man who was "powerful and wealthy," who had been married before, who was "incapable of fidelity." When the marriage began to run into trouble, Julia left a good job to take a less demanding position so that she could "work harder" at her marriage.

"I was going to a male psychiatrist at the time and I remember telling him I thought my husband was seeing other women. He kept asking me why I was so untrusting and insecure. He confused me and my husband confused me. Yet I was right after all. My instincts weren't wrong. I found out through my husband's diary that he *was* having affairs."

She and her husband divorced. Julia moved from a luxurious apartment to a smaller one. She asked for no alimony.

"After the divorce, I thought I was cracking up," she says. "I had gone to bed with two guys—up until my marriage I'd been a virgin—and I was confused. Because they slept with me, I expected both of them to take care of me for the rest of my life." She began going to a second therapist at this time, who told her, she says, that she would have to realize she was a "dependent woman" and that she'd "find a nice guy one day."

After a while, she stopped seeing this therapist. A few years went by. She was heading an important committee and had a job which meant a great deal to her.

When she was thirty-two, some friends introduced Julia to Paul, who "seemed to have everything. He was brilliant and successful."

They lived together for eight months. When they split up Julia went into the worst depression of her life. "I didn't go to work for ten days, I couldn't move. I didn't see how I was going to go on living.

"We were having problems because he was pulling the usual power trips men pull on women—we would only have sex when *he* wanted it, never when I wanted it! He could see other women, but I couldn't see other men.

"Looking back, I see I should have gotten out earlier, but there were good things in the relationship. I needed that closeness, that intimacy. I knew very few men who were as interesting as he was, as charming. Any woman would have wanted him.

"He does what a lot of men do, cause a little suspicion and uneasiness in your mind. Then, after you get uneasy, he screams at you that you're too insecure and dependent and he needs some space.

"The end nearly came one night—I was teasing him about something and he swung at me. For weeks, I wouldn't tell anyone; I was so ashamed and humiliated. Look what a victim I was! I should have left then, but I disassociated myself from the experience. I couldn't believe it had really happened.

"Later, we had another fight and he told me to leave. That was it."

Julia has analyzed her problems. She believes she sees her dependency clearly and must fight it in herself. "I see my troubles as stemming from the way I was brought up: dependent and submissive. I think because men have the power in this society they treat women abominably. That man I lived with could only be happy with a nineteen-year-old slave, not an assertive woman.

"I see a split," she continues, "between assertion and aggression. I see many women who are able to get it together and make a speech or be a fundraiser, but are unable to be assertive in their personal lives." Now, she says, she tries to "stand up" to the men she meets. "I'm not going to be a victim anymore." Yet Julia has little hope of meeting another attractive man in the near future. "How many unattached men do you know?" she says.

Julia says she could devote more time to her work, but states, "I'm afraid that power corrupts." She is happiest when she is with her friends, and finds Sundays the loneliest day of the week.

The worst of Julia's depression is over. She is not necessarily "happy" now, but she is functioning. "The way I got out of my depression," she advises other women, "was by doing two things. One, I had always wanted to go to Greece and I did. Two, I wanted to run a special program in my school and I did. Both accomplishments began to make me feel like my old self, which wasn't all that great, but it was an improvement. It's been eight months now and I'm just beginning to feel really okay."

Julia's relationship illustrates the point that Karen Horney makes regarding morbidly dependent relationships. The woman who sees love as the supreme fulfillment has compulsive self-effacing drives. She believes that to find meaning in life, she must have a partner and merge with that partner in order to have a sense of unity which she doesn't experience by herself.

The love-addicted woman involved in a morbidly dependent relationship is usually attracted to a man who seems strong and superior. This man often has the kind of expansive personality which she admires and desires. But because she is too self-effacing, she has a taboo on being assertive, demanding, and proud. Yes, she admires these qualities but she has suppressed them in herself. It is, therefore, *the man's pride and arrogance which win her over.* Even though she may be repelled by these qualities initially, she secretly admires them and finds them irresistible. She is looking for someone who will sweep her off her feet, for she wants to merge with this proud person in order to "master life" as she feels *he* has. It is something she doesn't feel she can do herself. It may never occur to her that she could make efforts to overcome her feelings of weakness. She believes she wants only the man's love, but she also wants his strength.

A man may also be morbidly dependent upon a woman, but usually the opposite is the case. There are good reasons for this. For the most part, only men have had access to the avenues of power, money, and status. Women who have felt helpless about achieving these goals by themselves associated with men who could provide them with what they needed and wanted. In the morbidly dependent relationship, the woman's compulsive need is so overwhelming that we feel we can justify calling her addicted.

"Insulting behavior," Horney says, "frequently precipitates a dependent relationship." Because the man knocks out the woman's pride—either by not needing her or not seeing her value—she is hooked into identifying with his pride. ("I'm nothing. He's everything. Only through him can I be anything.") This ploy works again and again. Its success is assured by the woman's basic disregard for herself. A self-effacing woman believes that she is unworthy and has little regard for herself. When she is insulted, humiliated, and degraded, it is only an external affirmation of what she feels she deserves. In other words, her partner's attitude toward her only confirms for her what she already thinks of herself. Such confirmation shatters whatever small shreds of pride she has clung to. This leaves her feeling weakened, naked, and helpless.

Yet, because that is so painful, she is frequently

obliged to distort an obvious put-down. In doing so, she can twist an insult into a kind of left-handed compliment. On one occasion, Paul said to Julia, "Those pounds that you've taken on make you look like a grandmother." She was hurt by his words but swiftly told herself that he was really saying that she looked like a loving, companionable mate. This lightninglike maneuver spares her from her self-contempt (not only because she allows him to speak to her in this manner, but because she has gained ten pounds) and restores her pride.

In describing these dynamics, it is often confusing to try to state what is conscious and what is unconscious. It might be more clear to say that there is a continuum back and forth, a flow between conscious and unconscious. Very often, such a woman behaves without a notion of what is driving her. Retrospectively and reflectively, however, she is aware of her repetitive behavior and its drive. Yet, the next time, she finds herself in the same destructive position again. Overlooking what she *knows,* she leads herself into the same position because of a promise she manufactures, a promise that this relationship will confirm her romantic dream of love. Her establishing of the promise and her movement toward its realization help to relieve feelings of anxiety, depression, or loneliness, which she cannot abide. It often becomes a matter of "the lesser of two evils": this relationship I know, somewhere deep down, might be destructive to me, but which I wish with all my heart and soul will rescue me; or to continue living the way I have been, lonely and frightened. And the choice is quickly, and often painlessly, made and vigorously supported.

The question can be raised: Isn't it better to have such a bad relationship than no relationship at all? There is, at least, *some* comfort in that, as compared with the abject loneliness that only those who have known it can appreciate. How can we answer "no" to that question? It would seem heartless to do so. But we are compelled to say that an ongoing search for the kind of "love" we are describing creates an inordinate distraction in terms of one's own self-development.

In the kind of relationship Julia describes, when Paul shows her that he doesn't care for her as much as she cares for him, he divests her of her feeling of pride in being lovable, attractive, charming, and interesting. She needs to have him accept her, on any terms, in order to restore her pride. Through his love, she feels restored. Her feeling is: If this fine man loves me, I am not as unworthy as I think. She may feel "reborn," as if she is "flying." No, she has no "fear of flying." But to what is she flying?

Terry says, "All of a sudden, I understood what all the love songs were about. I was so happy! I used to wake up every morning singing! But when he stopped calling me, it was awful. I couldn't get him out of my mind. I saw his face everywhere, even when I closed my eyes! There weren't five minutes that went by that I didn't think of him. And I was so depressed! I had to drag myself around. If I saw a man that looked like him or had a body like him, I'd feel sick. It was the most awful experience of my life."

Terry reveals a valid point about this kind of morbidly dependent relationship: It lasts only as long as the man permits. This woman is totally hooked onto her partner's whim. Overlooking that this man constitutes the most serious threat to her safety, she feels irresistibly drawn to him as her strength and her protector. For the maintenance of her addiction on him—which she needs to feel good about herself—she will pay any price. Submissiveness. Availability. Understanding. Sweetness. Sex. Meals on time. Anything he demands. We saw how Julia gravitated toward "power and wealth." These were the substantial qualities which provided the substance she felt she never had and which she feels she cannot achieve except through marriage to a "strong man."

In marrying the first time, she accomplished many things. She fulfilled a prophecy in moving toward an expected outcome. She won (perhaps) her mother's approval, even though she may have consciously denied that she sought it. Through this marriage she acquired "instant" respectability and substantiality, something she could feel proud of. She also alleviated a profound, inner sense of worthlessness. She thought: If I were so awful, he would not want to marry me, so there must be something redeeming, interesting, and attractive about me.

All of these moves take her away from the despair of depression. Her guilt at being a despicable person is relieved as well. Hope springs forth eternally: If he loves me, things can't all be that bad. *Over and over, we see in the depressed woman, in the love-addicted woman, a morbid dependency upon the partner, a dependency based on the need to restore pride in herself. As a bandage covers a wound, this pride serves to cover self-hatred.* As we've said, such dependency and the process we describe can be found as well in men, where these same repetitious patterns are evident, where the suffering is as intense.

A woman involved in a morbidly dependent relationship can lose interest in everything else that had formerly involved her. Now she is only interested in understanding her partner, in helping him, and in surrendering her life to him. She becomes so clinging and dependent that he begins to pull away, for he feels suffocated by the demands she makes on him. His pulling away makes her feel abandoned and makes her cling more. This rush to free himself is akin to the feelings a person has when he is rescuing a drowning person who threatens to drown him as well. The man in this relationship also has his neurotic needs. He is attracted only to this kind of self-effacing woman. Her subordination enables him to feel dominant and superior, feelings *he* needs in order to maintain his pride. Yet, in getting what he needs, he also experiences a withering contempt for her and begins to need to pull away.

Masochism is intimately related to the morbidly dependent relationship. Masochistic behavior (ex-

treme, hurtful subservience) is one form of defense
through which a woman tries to resolve her conflicts.
By giving herself up, so to speak, to the man, she
wipes herself out in order to become part of him.
This is why she will not complain, why she will take
any abuse. She is trying to get rid of everything she
despises in herself, and share in the glory she sees in
her man. But this is only one side of the picture. The
other side is the "pride" she restores in herself
through a self-sanctification that all martyrs enjoy.
(Even if you step on me, I will still love you. I am a
loving, giving woman.) Please remember that we are
not condemning here, only describing. Moreover, a
distorted notion of femininity has come to mean both
submissiveness and self-sacrifice. Severely love-addicted women can truly be called the Joan of Arcs of
love. In other words, the woman who is playing the
martyr is actually playing out a socially acceptable
form of behavior for women.

We did not see this extreme of dependency in
Julia. Except for the deepest period of her depression, she was able to continue her work, to go to
meetings, and to maintain her interests. As in all
neurotic behavior, there are degrees of neurosis. In
Julia, the strength she had developed during her lifetime constituted her health. It was with this health
that she was able to resist the ravages of her illness.
Thus, she was not immobilized except briefly, nor
severely incapacitated in her functioning.

Indeed, Julia knew that, in order to save herself,
she had to begin doing things for herself. Her relationship with Paul had been a solution to bring together the opposing forces of the conflict in her
personality: her drive to dominate and her drive to
efface herself for the sake of love. The relationship
actually put that conflict to rest temporarily. *He* could
act out for her her domineering "shoulds," and *she*
could act out her self-effacing "shoulds." That freed
her from that particular inner bind of two simul-

taneous yet opposing "shoulds," and thus relieved her anxiety for a time.

Even though Julia learns this, what can prevent her from becoming involved in another and then another morbidly dependent relationship? She would have to begin to replace her "shoulds" with healthy moves toward selfhood. More easily said than done! To begin to accomplish that, Julia would have to admit to, and accept her domineering drives as part of herself, and she would have to free herself of their compulsive nature. Domineering drives are self-destructive when they are compulsive for they deprive one of choiceful involvement. But without that quality of compulsiveness, they may contain elements of constructive living, i.e., willingness to expand and grow.

Julia says she doesn't want power because "power corrupts." Actually, power does not have to corrupt. The real reason Julia fears going after power is because, in her view of it, power conflicts with her image of herself, an image she sees as lovable, sweet, feminine, giving, nurturing, but which we see as self-effacing and love-addicted. At the same time, however, she *does* want the power and cannot be free of that wish. Although she keeps it deeply buried in her unconscious, this need still conflicts with the ideal of her ostensibly acceptable self-image—ostensible only because she is *not* aware of the stringent demands that that image makes upon her, and she can feel only dissatisfaction with her relationships. It is that conflict which leaves her feeling divided and torn. But if she can hook up with a man who has the power she covets (for it is more socially acceptable, in her view, for a man to want to have power), she has solved her dilemma. That is why with a strong man she can experience a sense of unity and integration which she cannot experience by herself.

Even though Julia is a competent teacher, in her heart she doesn't feel competent enough to receive the admiration and respect she sees Paul receiving. But if Julia is to achieve selfhood, she is going to have to work at taking risks, working toward the goals *she* wants—including receiving admiration and respect—by herself, and not through a man, a pursuit which keeps her in an addicting, morbidly dependent relationship.

For the less strong woman, that is, the more neurotic one, the more aggressive and demanding her partner is, the more she complies (for she is not a fighter) and the more she feels degraded. Jean Rhys' novel *Quartet* explores this theme beautifully. Marya Zollia, a pretty blonde, works as a chorus girl. After a while, she marries and becomes the petted, cherished child, the desired mistress, "the worshipped, perfumed goddess." However, when Stephan is thrown in jail for shady dealings, Marya has no means to support herself and unwillingly accepts an offer to live with an English couple, an older man and a younger woman, who have befriended her. Before too long, the male, Heidler, announces he is in love with her. She fleetingly remembers a sculptor once saying to her, "You're a victim. There's no endurance in your face. Victims are necessary so that the strong may exercise their will and become more strong." But she doesn't connect what he said to her present dilemma.

Marya decides to go away, but both Heidlers insist that she stay on with them. Besides, where can she go without money? Eventually, she and Heidler go to bed together. He is a strong, arrogant man. Once he takes her in his arms, she feels as if she's always belonged there, as if she's been lost until now. She begins to fall madly in love with him. Heidler's wife, Lois, learns of the affair, but she will not let Marya leave their home. Then, she says, people will talk. She tells Marya that she must go on acting normally.

Marya finds she is going places with the Heidlers against her will. Lois is cruel to her and mocks her. Yet when Marya complains to Heidler, he dismisses her complaints, telling her she is too excitable.

Eventually, Heidler books Marya into a hotel room. He pays the rent each week and gives Marya spend-

ing money. We see Marya becoming more and more
the Heidlers' victim. She fights back, but ". . . with
tears, with futile rages, with extravagant abandon—
all bad weapons." She begins to feel that she has lost
all self-control. She is obsessed by her need for
Heidler, yet she knows she has made a mess out of
her life.

Marya's "love" for Heidler would be more easily
understood if he were genuinely in love with her.
Yet beneath his façade of charm and kindness, she
realizes that he "despised love" and "didn't really like
women." Heidler was simply bent on having her obey
his will. He was intent on having her be his mistress,
to see her when *he* chose, to leave her for his wife
when *he* wanted to. He comes to the hotel, makes
love, goes home. In despair, she wants to see him
more and more. The more he eludes her, the more
she wants him. She begins to live with fear "that the
little she had would be taken from her."

Quartet is the classic story of a woman who is destroyed by "love." She becomes involved with a man
of whom she is afraid and upon whom she becomes
dependent. Marya has had no training in self-sufficiency, and it is because of this that Heidler's will
eventually become hers. In the process she is not
only degraded but lost.

As we have indicated, the love-addicted or depressed woman may see this degradation as proof of
her humility, of her love. This not only spares her
pride, but actually feeds it. ("What a loving, feminine,
giving woman I am.") Her self-effacement is a horrible way to collect brownie points for sainthood, acceptability, and even femaleness.

Since Paul can never satisfy Julia's endless need
for love and for the elusive safety she seeks in his
arms, and because he is not a considerate person in
the first place (she was attracted to him not because
of his considerateness, but because of his arrogance
and seeming strength), Julia begins to resent and
despise him, and to feel more and more abused by

him. At the same time, she despises herself for not having worked out the relationship. (I *should* be able to make it work.) This latter is always the final stumbling block that confronts a woman, even after she has actually seen her partner in clearer perspective. And it is this final block which is always her undoing: No matter how impossible he really is, if *I* were less stupid, if *I* were more loving and good, that impossibility would have been overcome; it is, in the very final analysis, my fault. Where do you stop!

Because the dependent, submissive, self-effacing woman will make a doormat out of herself, these other features of her motivations rarely stand out. The need she has to excel, to control, to master, all contribute to help her feel more self-accepting. It is only her methods that differ, not her goal. Her methods are the outcome of self-rejecting feelings which have also been fostered in our society. Having been denied equal access to the world outside the home, but nevertheless having learned to respect the values and rewards of that world, she feels less than competent, less than a full member of society. The method in her madness is based on her feeling that she needs a male's strength, for *she has been so long denied access to institutions that might have helped promote and encourage her own strength*. This woman has learned her lesson well.

Moreover, the dependent interchange is a mutual one. If Julia wants a strong man, Paul wants a self-effacing, submissive woman. So her submissiveness must be the finest, the most sensitive submissiveness in the world. If it is, it will achieve her goal of keeping this man bound to her. Her lovingness must be of this same "prime" quality for the same reason. When and if Paul begins to pull away (for remember, as much as he needs her, he also hates his dependency upon her and his hurtful treatment of her), she is enraged with herself, because her lovingness, her submissiveness, has obviously not turned the trick. She is a failure, not because she effaced herself in her efforts to pursue a losing dream, but because her self-effacement was not good enough to accomplish its purpose! (Again, a reminder—Julia is not aware of most of what we describe here. These feelings become only vaguely conscious to her, now and again.)

This is a two-sided attack on herself. On the one hand, she feels so despicable that she unconsciously feels she deserves nothing better than her partner's abuse. On the other hand, she is so driven that she believes she must and will succeed if she tries hard enough. When she doesn't, she hates herself for not achieving the control and safety she seeks. This second point is not one this woman is ever conscious of. For she sees herself only as loving and willing to submit for the sake of love. She can become instantly outraged if she is ever accused of wanting to control her partner. She may deny this vehemently, not seeing that she must control her partner to keep him in the position she needs to feel supported and loved. (Clinging is in fact controlling.) For her, it is all in the name of love. Actually, it's all in the name of safety and the alleviation of anxiety.

To understand this final point, that neurotic moves are all designed to protect, to bind anxiety, to establish security and safety, is to find compassion for one's self and one's neuroticisms. Only then can the morbidly dependent woman admit to her stringent need for control over her man, and, finally, to the futility of all her self-effacing maneuvers.

A less exaggerated form of dependency may occur in a marriage or a relationship in which the woman, on the surface, seems strong. In many cases she has been independent, has pursued a career. Yet after she marries, she gives up all interest in her work and seems to lose her zest for life. She may try to be the "perfect" wife or mother. Yet she becomes mildly depressed.

It is possible that this woman was not allowed to be a child when she was young. She had to grow up in a hurry, to ignore her own feelings in order to please her parents. She quickly learned to be independent for she had no choice. She is strong in many respects. However, she has repressed the common dependency needs which we all have, and she finally marries in order to be taken care of. With such a person, the burden of "being strong" to meet parental expectations has been overwhelming. Indeed, such a woman has fantasized all her life that she will find someone to take care of her so that she won't have to struggle anymore.

Marriage is the answer for her, and she is ready to "give up" her place as a self-directed person and, in the words of Dr. Alexandra Symonds, make her "declaration of dependence." She is prepared to live out her fantasy of peace and tranquility. But it backfires, because peace and tranquility exist only in bits and pieces. *To attempt to establish interminable peace is to move toward deadness.* Thus, she becomes depressed.

This woman actually deprives herself of her past life, of her strengths, her experience, her achievements, her health. To watch a woman persist in the actualization of this fantasy is to preside at a perpetual wake, as one hopes that the corpse will somehow rise up and resume living. Surprisingly, this *is* possible, for this corpse is not dead but only in hibernation, a hibernation that can be terminated when she has the thought and desire to recover what she had stored away, *when she relinquishes her child's dream of peace* through total dependency.

Some women take many years to relinquish that dream. Simone de Beauvoir's novelette, *The Woman Destroyed*, concerns a middle-aged woman whose husband, after twenty-two years of marriage, confesses he loves another woman. She walks through the streets thinking, "I have lived only for him." A friend advises her to be patient, that Maurice will tire of his affair.

Later she feels she ought to have put a stop to the affair in the beginning. She didn't because her "longings, wishes, interests, have always been identical with his." Here is the typical response of the woman mentioned earlier, who needs to see herself as the most loving in the world—here, even to the point of not interfering with his affair. How more "loving" could anyone be?

Throughout the diary, the reader senses that Maurice is becoming more and more attached to his other woman. While he and his wife have numerous scenes, nothing is resolved. She tells him, "The worst thing you did was to let me lull myself into a sense of false security. Here I am at forty-four—empty-handed, with no occupation, no other interest in life apart from you. If you had warned me eight years ago, I should have made an independent existence for myself." She chastizes herself for not "keeping up," for not going to the hairdresser, for letting her intelligence wither away.

She then becomes severely depressed and stays in bed all day. Finally, she goes to a psychiatrist who encourages her to write down her thoughts. "He is trying to give me back an interest in myself, to reconstruct an identity for me. But the only thing that counts is Maurice. Myself, what does that amount to? I have never paid much attention to it. I was safe, because he loved me."

In the end, Maurice leaves her. She is alone. She must begin a new life. Her mistake has been to live for (and through) others. Now she must learn to live for herself.

The love-addicted woman's self-esteem rests on the affirmation, approval, and affection she receives from others. She needs this affirmation in order to contradict her feelings about her despised self. Moreover, Western culture has hammered it home to women that being loved and needed is their *raison d'être*. Shulamith Firestone, in her book *The Dialectic of Sex*, says, "In a male-run society that defines women as an inferior and parasitical class, a woman who does not achieve male approval in some form is doomed."

Because she needs proof from males that she *is* lovable, her choice of partners is often indiscriminate.

This indiscriminate choice renders her emotionally, intellectually, and sexually seducible by any person who will give her a feeling of acceptability. A woman reared in these circumstances will be attracted to a man who makes her feel that she is important to him. She finds that sense of importance completely irresistible. Feeling so unimportant to herself, so insignificant, she is a "patsy" to anyone who offers her the opportunity for respite from the cowering position in life that she abhors.

Some men are aware of this particular susceptibility in certain women. While they may not understand the underlying dynamics, they know how to approach such a woman to ensure success with her. It is almost uncanny how these men are attracted to and can pick up the signals of such a woman.

Sally, a well-educated young woman, is this kind of person. Feeling lonely and depressed, she had gone to a political rally. There she was approached by a handsome young man named Jim who introduced himself as a block worker. As soon as he began to speak, she mentally "wrinkled her nose" at his manner, his speech, his self-important gestures. Later she said, "I was almost repulsed by his coarseness at first. But very soon, I found him fascinating." He told her several times that the candidate he was backing needed "refined people" like her to give the campaign "some class." She thought this amusing, and she laughed merrily each time he said it.

She had come to the rally to be part of something worthwhile. And here she was almost immediately being asked to make a unique and significant contribution to the campaign. What a lift for someone burdened with feelings of loneliness and depression.

Jim became the instrument for a sudden change in Sally's feelings about herself. As low as she was when she was alone, she was equally as high when he was with her. They became lovers, and she remained excited by that, as well as by their involvement in the campaign. Jim spent a lot of his time in Sally's apartment because he was unemployed. She overlooked his manners, his general slovenliness, his passionate interest in sports and in the racing sheets. She felt that she should not permit her personal preferences (she did not like sports) to intrude upon her love for this man. To do so would have been to indulge her "snobbishness," she felt, and to be less than a loving partner.

Finally Jim moved in with her. When Sally returned home from work each evening she was greeted with hugs and kisses and sighs of "Oh, how much I missed you all day." What a change from returning to a quiet, empty apartment where she would begin to feel teary and anxious in the elevator and to have a lump in her throat by the time she put the key in the lock.

Sometimes his greetings were so passionate that they fell into bed immediately. She often thought, "What a wild way to start the evening!" Sometimes he would inquire sweetly if she had brought anything home for supper, even though he could see that she had not. He might mumble something about taking a shower and then going out to "pick up something." But Sally would quickly offer to do so herself. She knew that he had no money to pay for groceries, and she wanted to spare him any embarrassment. She also felt that the feeding of her lover was an essential feature of being a loving person. All of this was small payment indeed for something she so valued and wanted.

Things went fairly well for several months. Much later, Sally admitted that she felt the way she thought some men must feel when they returned home to find the "little woman" waiting for them. However, at the same time she felt completely dependent on Jim for her new sense of well-being. She was so grateful for what he had done to change her life that she overlooked her usefulness to him and the actual power she had in the relationship. (She had the money, she cooked, she washed his clothes, etc.)

As time went on, Jim became less agreeable, and

less thoughtful in his demands. He began to be arrogant and mean. Shocked and humiliated by his behavior, Sally nevertheless continued to comply with his demands and to meet his needs. Her compulsive need for approval and love left her no other choice. She felt that anything was worth putting up with for the sake of "true love."

When Jim accused her of not loving him enough (if she didn't make something special for dinner, if she came home late from work), she denied it vehemently and had to go to great lengths to prove her love. But secretly she agreed with him, and because she was becoming angry with him, felt she was incapable of love. Moreover, she not only felt deficient in her ability to love, but in her ability to be a spontaneous person. She could never do or say the things he did. She couldn't be as arrogant as he was, as demanding, as relaxed. He accused her of being "uptight" and she agreed with him. She did not see this as merely a difference in her way of being, in her pattern of living. She saw it as a deficiency in herself and began to feel depressed again. This time, her sense of hopelessness was even deeper than before, for she could not blame her feelings on her loneliness. Yet she *was* terribly lonely. It was the loneliness of living alone while living with someone else. She could not recognize it for what it was, and she berated herself for her "coldness, prissiness, aloofness," all terms Jim repeatedly threw at her.

She continued to cling to him in order to reestablish the old high feeling. But like any addiction, she needed larger "doses" from him, and he was giving even smaller ones. Because her craving went unsatisfied, and because she couldn't permit her anger to emerge, she became more depressed, and at the same time, severely agitated. While she fantasized that she might walk out on him, or that he might drop dead, not once did it occur to her to ask him to leave.

One evening she paid her family one of her infrequent visits. They were appalled at her weight loss and her anxious state. She met their inquiries with

"I'm all right." But when they continued to show their concern, she broke down sobbing and told them enough for them to piece the picture together.

Sally agreed to stay overnight at her parents' home. Her brother, who had previously met Jim, went to her apartment and told him to leave. Jim complied, although promising himself to "give her the business" when he saw her again. When Sally heard of what her brother had done, she was extremely upset, but she permitted her family to "baby" her for a few days. However, when she returned to her apartment, she became even more deeply depressed. It was at this point that her family persuaded her to seek treatment.

Sally went through a period of relentless self-recrimination that she had permitted herself to "sink so low" because of a man. The outcome of her affair had exacerbated her feelings of emptiness and despair; however, those feelings had been there all along.

Often these feelings of emptiness create an exaggerated need for romance. One of the great novels to deal with this theme is *Madame Bovary* by Gustave Flaubert. Emma is married to a simple man, Charles Bovary, a small-town, unimaginative doctor. She is not satisfied with her husband or with her marriage. She believes in her schoolgirl dream of a "heavenly lover," and yearns to be in the grip of strong emotions. She has no other goal.

When her marriage doesn't live up to her dreams, she is disconsolate. "She could not believe that the calm in which she was now living was the happiness of which she had dreamed." She is totally dependent on men, and therefore constantly disappointed in them. She relentlessly peers at her husband's faults. "But a man should know everything, shouldn't he? Excel in many activities, initiate you into excitements of passion, into life's refinements, into all its mysteries?" Charles doesn't toe this mark one bit.

Emma goes to a ball and, jealous of everyone else's seeming happiness, becomes more depressed. "She now spent entire days without dressing, wearing grey cotton stockings. . . ." She had become "difficult and capricious. . . . Some days she would talk with feverish abandon. These moments of exultation were suddenly succeeded by sullen moods in which she remained silent and motionless . . . she lost her appetite completely." Full of self-pity, she thinks, "she certainly deserved as much as all those women who were living happily."

It is almost predictable that Emma will "fall in love." When she does, she wallows in the pain of never achieving what she wants. ". . . the memory of Leon was the focal point of her boredom." At one point, Emma does attempt to expand her mind, to learn Italian, to read books on history and philosophy. "But her readings ended like her half-worked tapestries . . . she would start them, drop them and move on to new ones."

Then she meets Rudolphe and begins an affair. "She was entering into something marvelous where all would be passion, ecstasy, delirium . . . ordinary existence seemed to be in the distance, down below, in the shadows, between the peaks . . . she was realizing the long dream of her adolescence, seeing herself as one of those amorous women she had so long envied."

Rudolphe becomes the focus of her life. Yet, after the headiness of their initial passion has worn off, he gradually becomes more and more indifferent to her. She becomes unhappy and afraid. Impulsively they decide to run off together but he changes his mind and she takes to her bed.

When she recovers, she meets Leon, her first "love" and, again predictably, she tries to assuage her despair and rejection in his arms. This affair, too, runs downhill. "Emma was finding in adultery all the banalities of marriage." To conquer her wretchedness, she dreams of yet another man, "a phantom fabricated from her most ardent memories, her most beautiful literary memories, her strongest desires."

For Emma, the fulfillment which she sought in romantic love eludes her. In despair over the bills she has run up and over ever achieving her fantasies and hopes, she commits suicide.

In Emma Bovary, we see a woman who has been brought up without any sense of her own capabilities. She puts all her hopes on men. Her affairs are a means to escape her depression, her feelings of desperation, and her noninvolvement. Yet she learns nothing from her disappointments. She sees no way to gain excitement in her life except through a man who will sweep her off her feet.

Although Emma Bovary lived in the nineteenth century, many a modern woman can sympathize with her. For a woman who feels she has few, if any, options, for a woman who sees her marriage as a similar trap, the romantic illusion can still be a compelling one. Indeed, how many women yearn for romantic love in order to escape the dreariness of their lives? At the same time we must ask, how many women have been disappointed in the romantic promise?

Consider Micki, who is married and has three children. She works as an interior decorator; her husband works as a stockbroker. To outward appearances, she appears to have a marvelous life. But after seven years of marriage, she is increasingly restless, dissatisfied, and depressed. No matter how good her work is, she is certain that instant disaster is around the corner. She is terribly impatient with her husband who, she feels, suffers from depression but doesn't realize it. She is furious that he is constantly in front of the television set and that he doesn't "do" enough with the children. She is also dissatisfied with their sex life. Micki has many, many anger points to feed her marriage anger.

So what does she do? She responds by having affairs. First there was Tom, who is a stockbroker in her husband's office. Tom made her feel like "a woman." However, he was too afraid his wife would find out and he ended the affair abruptly. Next, she had an affair with Larry, a man with whom she had worked. He was charming, fun and "very good" in bed. She enjoyed being with him and felt "renewed." However, he was also involved with another woman and Micki became more and more jealous. When he told her he was considering marrying this second woman, she was despondent. So again she looked for another man whom she could have a "crush on" and with whom she could "feel alive."

You could say that Micki is a *romance junkie*. She needs the excitement of an affair as a sick person needs a blood transfusion. When an affair ends, it is on to the next. In between she is depressed. Micki is using "romance" to cover up her anger with herself and her feelings of deadness. She already has had several affairs and none of them made her feel permanently better about herself. If any of them had, she would not be suffering so. But in her case, her vision of romance offers false promises and hollow dreams.

The last man she had an affair with was Bill. He was charming at first but later became sadistic. He told her he wasn't really attracted to her, that he had other women whom he liked more. He rarely called when he said he would and she was often left feeling anxious, waiting for the phone to ring. Some part of Micki knew she should give Bill up. But she wouldn't and couldn't end the relationship. It was not Bill she was clinging to; it was a promise of love, a dream of love. She was addicted to the fantasy of romance because it was the only thing she thought could make her life exciting.

Not in touch with her strength and the many opportunities she has to live a good life, she is hooked on men, romance, and the dream of love. Each time she tries for this brass ring she is hurt. Yet she continues to try. One day, hopefully, when she has been disappointed enough, she will look to something else and to something more substantial, perhaps herself, to feel alive.

We must add here that we are not denigrating romance, per se. Romantic trips, dinners, evenings, are fine. But what we are talking about here is a compulsive need for romance that is never satisfied.

Consider the case of Marjorie, who comes from a loving family of four daughters. "I was allowed to be a child," she says. "I never had any chores to do. I've always been very close to my parents. In college I wrote them every day. I now talk to my mother every day on the telephone. I want to have as happy a family life as my family had.

"I need to have someone to do something for. I'm always happiest when I have a goal. I always got A's, for instance, to please my mother.

"Last year I had a boyfriend and for a time it was serious. I was so happy I was bubbling like a kettle. I think he got scared of all the attention I was focusing on him because he ended the relationship. Now, not having a boyfriend is really depressing. My life is fine in every other way except that I don't have a man and that seems to take the fun out of everything else.

"I think of marriage as like having a permanent date for New Year's Eve. You're part of a pair.

"In the evenings I fantasize a lot about having someone around. I have taught myself how to entertain myself alone. But there's nothing to look forward to on the weekend. I'm depressed because I'm lonely.

"My sister was always brought up in my shadow. I was the achiever. Yet I cry easily. Outwardly, I'm the strong one, but I am the one who would crumble."

One does not get the feeling of self-rejection from Marjorie in the total way we have seen in so many of the other women we talked to. Marjorie describes an ongoing, loving relationship with her family. Not only was she loved, but she was regarded as someone rather "special." Surely this could provide her with a sense of selfhood that could withstand the loneliness in adulthood. Yet she suffers too. Perhaps not so greatly, but she is certainly not content. She admits to depression.

Although there is not a great deal of evidence that Marjorie gives us, she seems to have been "allowed to be a child" too long. She was admired for her intellect, but not especially needed as a responsible member of the family. Her "closeness" to her parents is to be questioned too. How many college girls write to their parents every day? How many young women call their mothers every day?

We could answer by saying a great many, but those who do are usually very dependent upon that primary relationship. When did Marjorie develop long-standing relationships with her own peers? Why hasn't she built other close relationships for herself, apart and separate from the family? Has she only one way of relating to people—with feelings of overwhelming happiness? She appears impoverished not only in the number of people she feels close to, but also in the manner of her closeness. One gets the feeling of perpetual girlhood, with adequate intellectual development, but little else.

Marjorie speaks of needing goals. It sounds as if they have to be established by someone else. Like self-effacing women, she is always ready to perform, and perform well, but someone else has to "start her engine." In fact, her attitude about herself and her place in life seems lifted from the attitudes of her mother: A young woman finds an eligible man, marries him, loves, cherishes and cares for him, and builds her life around him. Here it is again, the cultural and familial programming that has gone on generation after generation. Unless Marjorie follows this program, she has none of her own.

Marjorie feels empty because she *is* empty. She has moved through the first part of her life in a crazy bunting that her parents provided. She apparently had no opportunity to strike out as a child, as an adolescent, as a young adult, with her own opinions, her own values. And here "striking out" is not meant literally, but refers to the process of moving away from parental attitudes, of exploring other values. This seems to have evaded Marjorie almost completely.

After all, this is what adolescent rebellion is about.

It's not just making a lot of noise and driving parents up the wall. It's risking a departure from the known and familiar into new, sometimes exciting, often anxiety-provoking avenues. It's finding out whether you agree or disagree with parents, with teachers, with other adults, with your peers. It's finding out what it feels like to be on your own, without Mommy there *every day*. It's worrying, fretting, suffering. It's taking chance after chance, doing things Mother should never know about because she might have a fit if she did. Being "close" can be wonderful, but it can be smothering.

Marjorie simply switched mothers in giving all her "bubbling," all her "attention," to her boyfriend. It might be more accurate to say that *she tried to take on another parent, in the form of a husband, and perform for him, live for him.*

We are not knocking close and harmonious family relationships. That is not the point. In fact there are not nearly enough of them around. But we are questioning the kind of "closeness" that results in the friendly, cheerful, undeveloped, non-person we see in Marjorie. She is so completely convinced that she is incomplete without a "boyfriend" and that doing things on her own is not any "fun." How is that possible? What a bore it would be if we had to do everything we enjoyed *with* someone else. How could someone else always *want* to do everything we wanted to do?

Marjorie says she learned to entertain herself alone. Yet she contradicts herself when she says, "There's nothing to look forward to on the weekend." What does she think weekends are? What can one expect of weekends? Aren't weekends days like any other? Nothing happens on weekends unless we make something happen through our own efforts. There are no magical weekend fantasies that materialize like genies out of bottles from the Far East.

Marjorie is still living with romantic fantasies usually found in the adolescent years. She believes weekends are special, invested with some magical quality.

She believes boyfriends make everything worthwhile. She believes marriage is a permanent New Year's Eve date. Although it was said somewhat tongue in cheek, it still reveals she is in for some disillusionment if she ever does get married.

In some respects, Marjorie has established a particular set of standards, her "shoulds," for life and living with people. These have been mentioned throughout. You *should* always: be bubbly . . . be close to your parents . . . marry when you grow up . . . do what parents and husband want you to . . . cherish your husband and live for him. *These are not destructive ends, in and of themselves, but Marjorie adheres to them so rigidly that she closes herself off to other options.* Therefore, when these standards aren't attainable, she is left with nothing to fill in the gap.

Despite Marjorie's lack of development, she has many assets and strengths that will be available to her if she'll just stick one toe in the cold water of the world-at-large. She is young, bright, cheerful, optimistic, loving, is loved, and actually has many satisfactions although she doesn't quite appreciate them. She is healthy, and while somewhat undeveloped, she does not give the impression of being severely neurotic. These features are all to the good in supporting her journey, if she chooses to make it, into a rewarding adulthood. Many of her fantasies will probably go. Many of her preconceptions about men, marriage, and life will probably go. But she needs to achieve selfhood. For if she does marry with these fantasies intact, she will be in for a rude awakening.

The question is: What will trigger Marjorie's desire to set off on this journey of self-exploration? Possibly a full-blown depression? Sometimes people have to strike bottom before they understand that climbing up is accomplished by putting one foot in front of the other. Possibly a wise and patient friend who will tell Marjorie what she has been about? Perhaps her parents will see that their "little girl" is still just that, and help her to grow into womanhood? Perhaps all of these. We certainly believe Marjorie can mature.

For if the Marjories of this world cannot manage to free themselves of ridiculous, outmoded retardants to full womanhood, who can?

How does a woman go about breaking her romantic addiction, her morbidly dependent preoccupation? There are no fast and easy rules. But we did speak to two women who had overcome such relationships. Here is what Ann had to say.

"The man I was involved with didn't call me for several days and I felt so awful that I thought I was going to die. I had a panic attack on the street and thought I was having a heart attack. Then I became extremely depressed and couldn't leave my apartment for several days. It was the worst experience of my life.

"This happened again and again and I was in such bad shape. Then he stopped calling me altogether, and I was calling him and crying. I joined a rap group and they all urged me to get out of the relationship, that it was destroying me. And I did. I had to fight each day not to pick up the phone and call him. Sometimes I would hear his voice at the other end, but I would hang up. I would talk to myself, tell myself to stop destroying myself. When I fantasized about him, I would force myself to think of something else. I was fighting tooth and nail all the time, but I couldn't stand the way I was living. It finally worked. When I didn't see him for six months, my fantasies about him lessened. I wouldn't let myself think about him. And I began to study Italian, something I'd always wanted to do, so that I could keep my mind occupied. It's been two years now and I feel much stronger. I would tell women to fight. Not to give in to their weakness. Fight, fight, fight!"

Elissa says, "I had just broken up with a man and I was lonely. Some nights I thought I would go out of my mind. I remember searching frantically through the phone book for someone, any old boyfriend, to call. I entertained thoughts of going into a singles bar, except I really didn't feel comfortable in that atmosphere. But luckily, I could talk to my sister, and she urged me to try to cool men for a while. She'd been through the same thing and had come out of it smelling like roses. She thought I could too. That first week I felt so lonely. I really wanted a man around. But you know what? After the first week, I felt stronger. I could do it. I didn't need someone as badly. I wasn't happy, but I could function. And the most important thing of all—I felt much more self-respect. And the self-respect enabled me to cope. That's what I would tell other women. No matter what, fight, fight for your self-respect."

Elissa and Ann both went through great pain in learning to become stronger. If you are trying to become less love-addicted, you may find what they have to say of some use. Fighting to change your behavior is a day-to-day, minute-to-minute process. You will find that you *can* change your fantasies, that you *don't* have to pick up the phone when a compulsive need overtakes you. And the more you are able to find this strength, the stronger you'll feel tomorrow and tomorrow.

Remember too what Julia did. One, she went on a trip. Two, she began work on a project that was important to her. Both steps were important, for *developing yourself* is the best thing you can do when you want to feel better.

Love-addicted women have to give up their outrageously distorted views of femininity and will have to learn to embrace those parts of themselves, the assertive, competitive, achieving parts, which they often despise—and which many men despise in them too!

The love relationships we have been describing have not been mutually supportive or growth-promoting. They have been destructive and have brought great pain and suffering. However, as women can become proud of their skills, strengths, and assets, as women begin to demand an equal place in society, as the myths about femininity and masculinity are exorcised from our hearts and minds, one would hope that women and men will learn to see themselves differently and will be able to develop freer, less exploitative relationships.

Suggestions for the Separated or Divorced Woman

1. Whether you want the separation or divorce or not, you are probably going to experience some degree of depression, from low-grade to acute. Our point here is: Don't be surprised if you are depressed and don't look upon it as a personal weakness. Depression, because of your anxiety and still-buried anger, is to be expected.

2. One of the best things you can do is to find someone with whom you can talk. (If you and your husband think your relationship has any chance of surviving, you should obtain professional help if at all possible.)

3. Express your anger. You had better believe it's there, perhaps deeply "underground." Trying to keep it from your awareness will contribute to keeping you depressed. As we have seen, depression is a way of muffling the anger and guilt which seems to threaten to tear you apart. It is better to cry, to complain, to express your rage to someone, rather than depress it.

The way *you* express your anger depends upon your personality, your style. If you feel yelling is self-destructive, find another way—perhaps some physical outlet. If you have never yelled at anyone in your life, you're not likely to start now. Maybe you can release your anger by pulling up crabgrass or bicycling for three hours. You decide how. All we can say is that it is useful and necessary to do so.

4. As soon as you can, try to have a plan for living alone. Get the best legal advice you can and make sure your needs are being considered. There is no need for self-effacing behavior such as "I should not ask my husband for anything" or "I won't ask. He should know what I need." Don't be timid. Ask, get

it in writing and, in some cases, expect to fight. You may not succeed; you may have to expect failure as well as success.

5. Rebuilding your life can be very exciting. Do not expect to meet a new man right away, however, even if that's what you want. Try to relate to all kinds of people.

6. Divorced mothers are often terribly overworked. Try to arrange it so that your ex-husband has the children at least one day a weekend and perhaps one or two weekends a month if you have the children during the week. Fathers know they have responsibilities toward their children after they're divorced. Don't hesitate to let them exercise that responsibility.

7. Try not to dwell on the past, but to look to the future. What are your plans? Your goals? A job? A new hobby? New friends? There are no "shoulds" concerning how you live. If you have children, you have their welfare to consider, but you have your own needs to consider as well. Keep in mind that a happy mommy makes for happy children most of the time. We know you won't feel *happy* happy for some time, but a few scraps of whatever contentment you can glean will go a long way in this period of your life.

8. Form a rap group with other women in your situation. You can share experiences, problems, solutions.

9. Consider living with another woman who's in the same situation you are. Your money will go further, you'll have company, and you can share baby-sitting.

10. If you can, especially when you feel harried, try to take time for yourself. Treat yourself to a movie or a lecture. If you don't have time for that, take thirty minutes all for yourself—without interruption.

11. When trying to get a job, present yourself as having your problems under control. For example, say you have a housekeeper for your children in the event that they become sick. No employer wants to take on a new set of problems. Present an optimistic front

regarding unexpected minor catastrophes, i.e., "I can work them out."

12. When your ex-husband has the children, plan in advance how you will spend your time. Don't simply sit home waiting for them to return. This happens more frequently than you might suppose. Try to avoid that trap. It's a real downer.

13. If you have stopped working to raise children, or worked at a low-level job to put your husband through school, can you arrange for him to pay for training in a field you're interested in? Remind him that you did the same for him if you did.

14. Because many women do not have the opportunity to earn enough money to support themselves and their households adequately, there is often justification for alimony. The fact that women are working today does not mean that they are immediately able to make the money they might be worth.

Begin to Marriage

more tired. She sleeps ten hours on
and Sunday. Billy begins to feel her more

6

Women and Work

YES, OUR "SHOULDS" ORIGINATE from our parents' expectations of us and from our reactions to those expectations. However, *cultural expectations* also have a major impact on our development. There are so many cultural "shoulds" that we can only enumerate a few here: A woman *should* be giving and loving. A woman *should* find satisfactions in the home. A woman *should not* be aggressive. A woman *should* be understanding. A woman *should* have children. Etc., etc., etc.

To understand these "shoulds," we have to look at our society. Man has traditionally been considered the breadwinner, even though today about 50 percent of all American women work. Masculinity, then, has been equated with breadwinning, with qualities of aggressiveness, competitiveness, independence, and autonomy. These are qualities that are highly valued in the work world.

These so-called masculine qualities often did not fit in with woman's role as homemaker. It is not hard to see that competitiveness and aggression, for example, might interfere with domestic life. It was because of her role that a woman's emotional makeup was seen to be basically a nurturing one.

While nurturing behavior is to be valued (and we are certainly not denigrating the crucial importance of nurturing children, friends, families, lovers, animals, and plants!) some women have *exaggerated* this behavior. *They have gone to extremes in nurturing others, thus depriving themselves of essential self-nurturing.*

In doing this, as we saw in the last chapter, a woman places her happiness on precarious grounds, for she becomes overly dependent on others to give her satisfaction. Of course, she may get the satisfaction she wants. But if she doesn't, she may feel it is her own failure and wallow in her guilt. ("I'm not good enough." "I'm not pretty enough." "I'm not loving enough.") Moreover, the woman who rebels against this traditional submissive role, by being too independent, too assertive, too unwilling to boost a man's ego at her own expense, runs the risk of being called "unfeminine" or "castrating."

What a bind this places a woman in! What unending conflict she is subject to! What does she do? Forget about her needs to realize her abilities? Withdraw from competition? Lead the life she has been told she *should* lead even if she finds it unsatisfactory? What if the dream she was told to expect doesn't appear? What if marriage doesn't materialize? What if she has to support herself? What if she needs to add to the family income? What then?

For the most part, woman's role as homemaker was a lifetime one. Dr. Horney addressed herself to this matter when she said, "A woman lived for centuries under conditions in which she was kept away from great economic and political responsibilities and restricted to a private emotional sphere of life. This does not mean that she did not carry responsibility and did not have to work. But her work was done within the confines of the family circle and therefore was based only on emotionalism, in contra-distinction to more impersonal, matter of fact relations . . . love and devotion came to be regarded as specifically feminine ideals and virtues. . . .

"Since her relations to men and children were her only gateway to happiness, security and prestige, love represented a realistic value, which in man's sphere can be compared with his activities relating to earning capacities. Thus, not only were pursuits outside the emotional sphere factually discouraged, but in woman's own mind they assumed only secondary importance."

However, today woman's traditional role as a homemaker may no longer be a lifetime one. Moreover, there may be stringent economic reasons for a woman to work. But here you are penalized again. You may have raised your children, done the job that society prepared you to do and expected you to do. But where are the jobs which take into account your unrecognized but extensive skills, derived from your experience in running a home and raising a family?

A woman who feels she has few options available to her may turn against herself. This may be the young college graduate who is not offered work commensurate with her abilities, the high school graduate who has potential but is not encouraged to tap that potential, or the mature woman who is returning to work. She may berate herself for "not doing things right." However, this is not where the responsibility can be placed. Society has yet to make a broader place for women. Women are still being offered lower status and lower paying jobs. So far, we have emphasized that feelings of unlovability and inadequacy have been fostered in an ambivalent home environment. But it is necessary to understand that these feelings are also engendered because of the low status women, by and large, have had in our society.

The woman who has the most difficulty in finding the work she likes and in advancing on that job is the woman with a predominantly self-effacing personality. If we think about what we have learned about her so far, it is easy to see why this is true.

First of all, she is compulsively humble. That means that the minute she has an idea that she can do anything, an inner voice tells her, "Who are you to think that you can do that?" She puts herself down before she even gets started! She is, therefore, very different from the predominantly domineering woman who believes that she can pretty much do anything once she sets her mind to it.

Already, as you can see, this places the self-effacing woman at a tremendous disadvantage. She may have many areas of potential within her, but they remain locked away because she can't even begin to take them seriously. She is like the five-year-old boy who says, "I can't" even before he attempts to ride a bicycle or hold a bat.

More than that, because she is so dependent on others, it is hard for her to be alone. However, in order to do creative work, she must have solitude. In order to find a job, she must work at it by herself. So again, she is at a disadvantage, fighting her compulsive needs for companionship even when they can do her the most harm.

Even if she can get to first base and line up some job interviews, she is going to have a difficult time "selling herself." Remember, she thinks it's presumptuous of her to speak up, to express an opinion. So on an interview where it is necessary to portray her strengths and abilities she may "forget" to tell the interviewer what her skills and experience are. She does not evaluate her own worth realistically. Deep down she may have some inkling that she could do the job. But she is not adept at saying, "I can do this job because . . ." or "I would be very valuable to you in this area because I have worked with . . . in the past." Moreover, the minute an interviewer seems to be putting her down, even in the slightest way, she actually aids in her own destruction. She cannot assert her position. She has to be agreeable or she becomes uncomfortable. So when the interviewer says, "You're really not very qualified" or "You're too old," instead of thinking through his remarks and responding appropriately, disagreeing if necessary, she gives in without a struggle. She may try a few feeble "yes, but" remarks, but basically she *has* to agree with this person. The domineering woman would say, "I don't feel I'm too old. I have much valuable experience and

is nothing she wants, there is nothing she
ve for. Feeling that there is nothing she
ere is nothing she has to offer anyone.

to overcoming these problems may lie in
y to see which "shoulds" are operating in
The next step is trying to break the power
over you. It's very useful to reach out to
support in your endeavors. Elizabeth, for
had had some theater experience and
try her hand at writing plays. However,
to tremendous work blocks when she was
e. Finally, with the help of some friends,
le to do two things. First, she signed up for
playwriting at a local college. By doing this,
aking seriously her own need and desire to
s. Then, she was going to learn more about
g. Thus, she was placing herself in an en-
in which she could talk to others who were
same frustrations and problems as herself.
the end of the course, she would probably
e writing accomplished.

cond thing she did was to join a group of
men who were interested in doing work but
also "stuck." They would meet at a different
home one night a week. A woman might dis-
progress she was making in owning her own
tore. Elizabeth would read from the play she
ing on. A third woman would read her poetry.
und rules were: support each other; give
uggestions; avoid criticism and put-downs.
eth says, "I found both of these things ex-
supportive for me. I think we all need feed-
vasn't capable then of writing my play in my
e vacuum. I needed to feel that my work was
at's what I did when I took that course and
these women.

I also learned one other thing. I may not have
idea before I sat down at my typewriter.
e I sat down and started to work, even if it
y for a half hour, ideas and words would come

wisdom to contribute." A more experienced woman
would say, "This is why I believe I am qualified," and
then go on to tell the interviewer why.

Again, even if she gets a job, and even if some part
of her wants to advance in that job, she is consistently
at war with herself. She will feel that it's not "nice"
to be competitive. It's "selfish" to want to get a raise,
to get a promotion. She (again, compulsively) puts
others' needs before her own (e.g., "I'd like to have
more than twenty minutes for lunch, but Nora said
I really should get this report done.").

Her supervisor or her co-workers may take advantage of her, but she does not know how to state her
own needs. Besides that, she needs their good opinion
of her too much. God forbid that someone dislikes
her! God forbid that a colleague is annoyed with
her! That would cause her too much anxiety. And so
she doesn't protest in order to avoid feeling this anxiety. If she does say (and she probably can't), "I'm
sorry, I have too much work on my desk. I can't handle another piece of work today," she will feel
ashamed. For by saying this, she goes against one of
her basic "shoulds." You *should* always meet the expectations of others. More than that, *she is so afraid
of other people's hostility that she complies again and
again rather than risk their anger.*

Moreover, this woman may not be able to put her
heart into her work. Some part of her is awaiting
rescue, awaiting the man who will save her from having to work so hard, from having to endure the difficulties and adversities which she feels helpless to
face. She doesn't realize it, but in waiting for that
rescuer, she is also waiting for someone to "rescue"
her from exploring her resourcefulness, creativity, and
growth-potential.

We see much of this taking place even in women
who want to work and who have taken steps toward
an involvement in painting, music, writing, or any
other work. When an interesting man comes along,
"the work goes." This phenomenon is what the novel-
ist Doris Lessing was referring to when she said, in

effect, "I don't know of any man who would give up his work for a woman. And I don't know of one woman who wouldn't drop her work in a minute for a man." In this type of woman, it is the conflict between her strivings toward selfhood and her dependency needs which still has to be explored. In other words, this woman's healthy strivings for independence are at war with her compulsive "shoulds."

What the self-effacing woman has to do, first, is recognize the many, many ways she hurts herself. She is not able to, or going to, change overnight. She will feel anxious when she asserts herself, when she says, "No, I won't do that" or "I really am very good at proofreading. I would like to work on that project." But she has no other choice but to learn to withstand her anxiety as she tries to become more assertive. (If this is your problem, see our section on self-assertiveness in Chapter 16.)

This is not to say that the changes the self-effacing woman might make in her behavior are going to necessarily win her the presidency of a corporation. Because, despite all the constructive changes women will make to prepare themselves for the work world, they are still going to face discrimination because they are women. Besides that, and even more central to the problem, these women may remain limited in the actual shifts they will be able to make away from self-effacement. Furthermore, some men cannot stand women who aren't submissive. To deny this would be incompatible with the facts.

But a woman will be better able to cope with this injustice if she learns how to fight in her own behalf. She will then stop collaborating, not only in her own self-destruction, but in her own oppression. Fighting one's oppression is the beauty in learning to be assertive, in learning to *use* and be proud of one's assets, talents, and skills.

One last word about the self-effacing, or love-addicted, woman. We have talked about the special problems she faces in the business world. We should also say a word about her problems with her own

creativity, whether it be
take a trip, or take up ten
herself down. ("How pres
can paint a room.") Just
she cannot determine her
many inhibitions against d
man asked her to write a
could probably do it. But fo
her own growth? Probably

The domineering woman
growth, but in a different
from inertia unless she is s
prides herself on her abilit
forts. Her advancement in
interfered with, however, be
she tends to induce in her
willing to work hard, she de
equal her in that respect. Be
and creative, she has no tol
ties. Because she is competit
energetic, she ridicules peopl
characteristics. Unless she's in
she can be undermined in he
others who aren't willing to pu

The uninvolved woman als
comes to creative work, but fo
may want to explore a new pi
to fight her inertia and resist
volved. New efforts elicit an
from following through. Thus s
rising interest (in the new p
remain free from the exertio
prides herself on her effortless
doesn't immediately do what sh
she might give up, moving on t
out even beginning to explore h
particular field. This can cause
is not only ability but consisten
for *any* kind of work.

It is characteristic of this w
life by suppressing her ambitio

that there
has to st
could do,

The key
your abili
your life.
they have
others fo
example,
wanted t
she ran
home alo
she was a
a course
she was
write pla
playwriti
vironmer
facing th
And, by
have son

The s
other wc
who wer
woman's
cuss the
antique
was wor
The gr
helpful

Eliza
tremely
back. I
own litt
real. Th
met wit

"And
had on
But on
was on

to me. I was astonished." Elizabeth is now working on a second play.

Women who are interested in working can adopt Elizabeth's methods by taking the first step: learning about the fields they might be interested in, reading books and articles about that field. Talk to as many people as possible. Find out who can help you.

Many women are immigrants to this new land of work, and they will have much to learn before they will be able to function as well as they do in other areas of their lives. But as women learn more, they can pass this information on to their sisters. This is perhaps one of the biggest challenges women face as they may get little support from society, from family, from friends. The goals may never be reached in one woman's lifetime. Equal pay and equal work may not come soon. But we can all struggle together. In that struggle lies our hope.

Suggestions for the Depressed Working Woman

1. If your problems are on the job, and you are frustrated, it will be wise to keep in mind that many other women suffer from the same problems you do. You can try meeting with other women to discuss common problems and solutions. Can your YWCA or community center set up a career counseling program? Is a union a possibility? Can your Human Rights Commission or the National Organization for Women help you?

2. Find a successful man or woman with whom you can talk. His or her experience may be invaluable in solving your problems.

3. It will be helpful for you to realize how certain "shoulds" ("I should always be nice" or "I should not be selfish and ask for a raise") keep you locked into a less than satisfying position. Can you find a role model on whom you can pattern new behavior?

4. If you are married and are depressed because of the conflicts and overwhelming burdens you feel caused by working outside and inside the home, you

are going to have to explore new solutions with your family. You cannot hold a job and have the full burden of the home. Your husband and children must assume responsibility too. You need not feel guilty about this. Make a chart, if you like, to divide up the work.

5. You must have time for yourself, an evening a week or a Saturday or Sunday afternoon at least.

6. One group of working married women arranged that on Saturdays, five women would go to each home and clean. Husbands took the children while they cleaned. The next week the roles would be reversed. This may seem like a "way out" idea, and it is, but if you are depressed, remember that *new* solutions must be devised.

7. While anyone can feel lonely, the loneliness of the single working woman has a quality all its own. There can often be an unmitigated, hopeless loneliness; it is the hopelessness that makes it so self-defeating. This hopeless loneliness is perhaps one of the most difficult features in a depression to overcome. Suggestions for quick, temporary relief will do little here because the ultimate cure for loneliness is companionship. And companionship has to be cultivated. Time then is essential here, taking the time to cultivate friendships. Our best advice is offered in Chapter 16, where we discuss the problem of loneliness in some detail.

7

Anger in Marriage

THIRTY-NINE YEAR OLD Kirsten had been divorced for several years and was teaching when she met Joe. Joe's wife had recently died. Joe was fifty-four.

"The first time I saw Joe was in a restaurant," Kirsten says. "I was on vacation and was sitting with a group of friends at a long table. Joe was alone and there wasn't an extra table in the place so he asked if he could sit with us. Right away, that shows what kind of a man he is. You looked at him and you knew that here was a man who could take complete charge of the entire place in two minutes.

"After that, he asked me out. During the whole vacation, he sent flowers, notes, took my daughter and me to lunch, dinner.

"We were married four months later and we moved into a beautiful home.

"Joe was a top-notch lawyer. His first wife was a teacher. She refused to socialize with his clients. He was determined to have a completely different life with me.

"Let me describe my husband—my ex-husband. . . . He is a very big, impressive-looking man who dresses immaculately and expensively. He is able to manipulate almost everyone, to have them eating out of the palm of his hand. He needs constant attention, he must be the center of the party.

"In order to understand him, you have to understand his upbringing. He was brought up in the only

127

Jewish family in a small town. He was fat—and had no friends. He was ashamed of his family. They were the butt of everyone's jokes there. Humiliation was a big part of his childhood.

"His mother always told him—because he was bright—that he would make good. And he did. He decided he was going to be Somebody and he is.

"I, on the other hand, had such a different upbringing. I came from a distinguished, artistic family. Beauty and art and culture were part of my upbringing.

"Right from the beginning of our marriage, he took charge of everything. The whole show was run by Joe. We had the best of furniture, and he bought me the best clothing.

"We went on trips to practically every country in the world. We gave big parties and went to them. Yet the marriage was a terrible one. We fought each other in every hotel and in every country we were ever in. That lasted nine years.

"Joe would ask me, 'When are you going to be my wife?' He resented the fact that I insisted on teaching. I am very gifted in teaching and reaching children. I can always reach a child, even if it takes months. I would answer him, 'When are you going to be my husband?' For he would never let down his barriers with me. He wouldn't discuss his feelings. I think he felt that he was so humiliated in his childhood that he had built up these defenses, and if he let a woman break down his barriers, he would lose something, he would collapse.

"During my marriage, I kept going from seven in the morning until one or two in the morning. I had a lot of nervous energy: Now I think I pushed myself to keep going so that I wouldn't collapse.

"I met all of his friends, but I knew that 90 percent of them didn't like me. I think I was too refined for them. I couldn't bear many of their habits—their taking off their shoes in your home, their asking you how much a painting cost, their using the telephone to make long distance calls without asking. Much later,

Joe told me, 'My biggest shame is that I married a Gentile.' When I told this to my friends, they were embarrassed—for him. They were shocked that anyone could say this to me.

"But what a show it was to be with Joe! You always had ten waiters hovering around your table.

"Toward the end of the marriage, we were on a boat to Bermuda. Now I know that he was trying to get me to leave him and that is why this happened. He didn't like being on a boat—he felt closed in. So he was up in the bar drinking, this was about two in the morning, and there were all these women, all of whom were alone, flirting with him.

"I was tired and I felt the whole scene was cheap and I wanted to go to bed. He didn't want me to. He came into the room we had and took my thumb and bent it all the way backward.

"When we got to Bermuda we had to get a taxi and drive thirty miles to the hospital. I was in terrible pain. He told me not to tell the doctor what had happened, but I refused to promise that. When we arrived at the hospital the doctor asked me if the man sitting there in the waiting room had done that to me. I said he should ask him. The doctor called him in and showed him the X rays and told him how painful it was going to be for me. My thumb was dislocated. The doctor was shocked.

"He made Joe admit the whole story—or he threatened to call the police. That was the first and only time I ever saw Joe humiliated. On the boat back to New York he didn't speak to me for four days.

"Later there was another incident. We had gone to a fancy restaurant with a client. Afterward, Joe had gotten in the car and I was in but I hadn't closed the door yet. When he pushed on the accelerator I almost fell out of the car. Then he was driving at ninety miles per hour and calling me every name in the book, 'bitch,' 'cunt.'

"He was seeing another woman, a woman older than he and I guess he wanted to be with her. But by this time I had gotten a good lawyer who told me not to move out because then I would get nothing. So I stayed until he was willing to sign the separation papers my lawyer drew up.

"During all this time, he was always seeing other women. He wouldn't stop himself.

"The whole time I was married I was never allowed to be by myself. For example, we'd be on a trip and I'd want to sit on the terrace and read, but no, I had to put on my bikini and go down to the hotel pool and be shown off by Joe. That was the way he was.

"When I moved out, I withdrew from everything for three months. I rarely went out. I spent Thanksgiving and Christmas and New Year's alone. I knew I couldn't work, I was afraid that I would begin to cry in the classroom and I couldn't do that.

"I lost about twenty pounds.

"Being alone was the only way that I could pull through. When the crying came to an end, realistic thinking began.

"I think now I am so depressed because I had never invested so much of myself in anything as I had in Joe. It was an endless amount of work, of supporting and trying to help him, without accomplishing anything. I had fought so much for the good things I believed in and I had absolutely nothing to show for it.

"After three months, I began to feel I was beginning to understand what had happened to me. Now, one of the things I do very fast is to open up a window and get some fresh air and put music on right away to get my mind off things. There is just this absolutely incredible loneliness. Then, I walk the dog to get out.

"I have forced myself to go to parties, but I don't like men anymore. A man talks to you for a half hour, then he tells you that he's unhappy with his wife, and can he come home with you. Even though I want love and affection, I'm not going to compromise by being with a married man while his wife is sitting home. Temporary relief is not for me.

"I went to visit some friends in the Midwest, but

I was so alone as a woman. I was so resentful of men.

"I had decided that if Joe wanted the divorce, he was going to pay for it. And I did get a nice settlement. Now, my feelings of revenge have moved to compassion. Now there is space inside me to allow for compassion. I think he sensed an independence in me which made him terribly resentful of me. He couldn't humiliate me.

"My depression is less troublesome now. I felt very low for only a half hour this morning. I know that you have to go out to people, you can't wait for the world to come to you. And I will go out. But I think the time of thinking and thinking, of being alone, was good for me. I couldn't just run out and begin life again. I had to figure out why my marriage had gone wrong."

Kirsten's story, while not a typical one, does point up certain realities about separation and divorce. After a break-up, even though there may be feelings of great relief, there is usually anxiety and depression. The body mourns the loss of the relationship.

Kirsten had kept fighting for her autonomy all alone. Yet, because she had married such a forceful and neurotic man, her struggle seemed to be a losing one. She could not keep enough of herself to maintain her individuality, and build a satisfying relationship with her husband. That being the case, Kirsten's wisest move might have been to leave. She suffered because she could not accept the fact that this was not the man she had expected and wanted. She always had the option of leaving, which she chose not to take. Furthermore, she was in a particularly advantageous position because she did not have any children with Joe.

Her depression was brought about mostly by her pride. She was determined to maintain and to impose her refined qualities on Joe and his friends, even though they didn't share her interest in them. It is quite appropriate for a person with high standards to try to maintain them for herself in a realistic way. But to try to impose them on others who are not interested is another matter, and only encourages repeated disappointment and frustration.

There is no way to control people's taking off their shoes or asking the price of objects, except by refusing to have them in your home. Kirsten couldn't realistically do this, but her pride in her unrealistic standards (unrealistic under the circumstances) kept her from being able to tolerate offensive, yet relatively insignificant, behavior.

In asking Joe when he was "going to be her husband," she was again imposing upon him a set of standards which she maintained in her head—*standards for husbands*. When she married Joe, she had assumed she could impose those standards on him. Her expectations of a husband is that he "discusses feelings" with his wife. When she failed to get him to do so, she didn't give up. She felt he was continually depriving her of what she badly needed.

That Joe would not accept the one thing about her, her teaching, which provided her with a sense of purpose and wholeness was the signal, par excellence, that he could never accept her interests, her standards of behavior.

If a woman reaches the point where she clearly recognizes her husband's position in these critical areas, she usually has several options. After making every effort—forthrightly, honestly, assertively, and gently—to convince him of her need, and after failing in this, she has to decide if she wants to leave, or if she can make certain compromises that will maintain harmony and yet permit her to keep on with her work and her continuing growth. Then she has to accept her compromises so that she does not build up resentment.

This may sound like the old-fashioned admonition, adapt to your husband's ways and organize your needs around his. However, we are not making that kind of statement. The former adapting role of the wife (which many women today still choose to follow)

was usually her only option. In the case of Kirsten, she had other options.

The question of why she did remain in the marriage so long has to be raised. She had her reasons, her own needs. Perhaps overriding everything was a need to win—quite apart from what was being won. In that respect, she was a good match for Joe, who also had to win. That mutuality explains the impasses they repeatedly reached.

Besides her need to win, Kirsten also wanted to maintain her position as the wife of a rich and powerful man. However, if Kirsten decided to stay, she would have to decide first whether she could make the compromises that would insure her staying.

All of this might take several years to explore. But it rarely takes nine years. Kirsten took so long because she kept trying to do something that could not be accomplished. She was trying to change her husband into the person she felt she wanted for a husband. She wouldn't accept defeat, even though it was clear much earlier that she could not succeed. The only changes a husband goes through (and the only changes a wife goes through) are those he or she makes, not those the partner insists upon.

Sometimes a partner will change if he or she wants to please the other person. However, if a person fails to get his or her partner to accept reasonable demands, and cannot be content without some effort to compromise, he or she is likely to know this before nine years have elapsed.

Even if Kirsten's ideas, when practiced, could produce a good relationship is beside the point. Since they could not be practiced in this case, they were of little use. Such an absolute stance, just because you believe in the value of your own cause, is like any other absolute position. If you want it, it's all right for you, but not for anyone else.

This is what is meant by Kirsten's being defeated by her pride, her pride in a rigid view of what a good marriage *should* be. *That pride blinded her to*

the impossibility of her goal to change her husband.
That's why it took her so long to admit what she considered failure.

And that's why it took so much out of her. She couldn't tolerate her inability to succeed in a task that was doomed from the start.

Kirsten is another example of a woman who has both domineering and self-effacing trends. She chose a man who was outwardly more domineering, but then became locked in a battle to change and control him. Because she valued her perfectionistic "shoulds" so compulsively, she set them up for Joe to follow as well, not realizing that their compulsive character was rooted in her intolerance of her own limitations. She may have felt that she would be a better person if she demanded perfection from others. But in choosing a clearly less-than-perfect partner, indeed a man with severe neurotic problems of his own, she insured his failure. She then became the superior, triumphant one.

Joe, for his part, had to have her stop teaching, or he felt humiliated. That made him hate her: She wasn't submissive enough. Finally, he had stored up so much rage that he wanted to kill her.

Kirsten may or may not re-marry. Whether she does or does not, she can still have a full life of friends, interesting work, travel, hobbies—if she works at it. So many women don't realize this is all possible for them. In clinging to the idea of marriage as the only way to give meaning to their lives, they are often cheating themselves of their own development.

Unmet "shoulds," as in the case of Kirsten and Joe, can be and often are the reason for the continual struggle that takes place in so many marriages. Stanley and Harriet provide a further example. They went for marital counseling because of the continual accusations and counteraccusations they threw at each other. He complained she was a "nag" who was strangling him with her demands. She called him a "bum and a good for nothing."

Stanley was a passive and depressed man who was the only child of an alcoholic father. In his father's eyes, he couldn't do anything right, so that a positive image of himself as a male was almost nonexistent. He used drinking to get back at his father and his wife.

Harriet ostensibly had less severe problems than her husband. But she was an anxious woman whose mother had been extremely domineering. As a teen-ager, she had been engaged in a long struggle with her mother, and when she married she adopted the same domineering role her mother had taken. Harriet saw her husband as a weak and ineffectual male.

She said she wanted Stanley to stop drinking. However, she also needed to feel superior to him. Not feeling worthwhile herself, she defended herself against her feelings of inadequacy by accusing *him* of inadequacy. He was the bad guy. She was the perfect, suffering wife. (Blaming the other person relieves one of self-hate.) Yet she was constantly en-gaged in competitive battles with everyone—her mother, her brother, her children, her husband—be-cause she *had* to be right. She felt that her husband *should* be a different kind of person from the one he actually was.

Susan and Fred were another young couple who fought all the time. Susan's mother was also a domi-neering woman who had worked throughout Susan's childhood. Susan's father was a passive man and a "nothing" in the family's eyes. From the time Susan was little she had to act like an adult. She had to be responsible for herself—cook her own breakfast, take care of her own clothes. She grew up with a life script which read: "I have to do everything for myself. Nobody will ever help me."

Even though she said she wanted her husband to take care of her and assume a more "masculine" role in the family, she couldn't allow it to happen. (We are not saying that this is what he should do, but what she said she wanted him to do.) She had an image of herself as an independent person, and was terrified that if she allowed her husband to do things for her she would be a "nobody." She took great pride in her self-sufficiency, one of her primary "shoulds."

Susan openly said that she could live with or without her husband. This is a very safe position (she doesn't risk being hurt or rejected). It is also a lonely one. As is characteristic of the detached person, Susan was afraid of intimacy. In her marriage, she had placed herself in the same position she'd been in as a child: responsible and angry.

Fred, on the other hand, had been catered to as a child. His mother and father had tried to "give him everything." He knew how to take; he didn't know how to give. He defended himself against his wife's onslaughts of criticism by being "above it all." Naturally this upset her.

Here was a couple who rarely talked to each other. Fighting was their way of communicating. Each held up his and her own "shoulds" as models for the other and insisted upon their being followed. Fighting allowed them to keep their distance from each other and it also provided them with a little excitement. Without their fights, they were like two zombies, going through the motions of living, acting according to the "shoulds" they had learned to rely upon early in life. They had yet to negotiate a relationship which both of them could accept.

Mary and Steve had been married for eighteen years. He enjoyed his teaching and she enjoyed her bookkeeping. Their jobs were real strengths for both of them. However, he was an impulsive person who needed to explode occasionally and vent his feelings. She was more controlled, and withdrew when she was upset. They didn't share many of their worries and anxieties, because both were afraid of being shamed or humiliated, and both were afraid the other would use any "confessions" at a later date.

For Steve, Mary was supposed to be the stabilizing, calming figure in the family. Yet he also interpreted her stability as coldness. Mary needed Steve to provide some warmth in her life. However, his emotionality terrified her. At the same time she enjoyed his rages because they enabled her to experience some of the emotions she had repressed in herself, and which she couldn't allow herself to express.

Mary said she wanted her husband to be in charge and be the boss. She wanted him to handle the finances, for example, but at the same time *she* kept control of the checkbook. Actually, she had a need to maintain control. She was afraid that otherwise he would dominate and ignore her. Mary and Steve would have to see how their "shoulds" (I *should* remain in control, but he *should* be the man of the house) kept them from working out a better life for themselves.

Steve and Mary had sexual problems also. She wanted to be courted while he wanted to be sure there was an invitation there before he approached her. Both had a real fear of intimacy and cooperated in avoiding it: either he was shy or she was tired or he was feeling neglected or she was angry.

As their marriage was set up, their mutual insistences were repeatedly frustrated. Mary insisted that Steve *should* behave in certain ways, and when he did not, she maintained an ongoing cold anger toward him. Steve did exactly the same thing, insisting upon his set of "shoulds." So we have a relationship principally built upon various intensities and forms of anger, which we shall call *marriage anger*.

Steve was apparently better able to express his anger upon occasion, so ordinarily he would not be the one to become severely depressed. But Mary admitted that she could not express nor even be aware of her marriage anger. (Remember, his emotionality "terrified" her.) Therefore, she would be the one to have to repress her anger and feel guilty that she felt so angry in the first place. Here we have two necessary ingredients for the existence of a depression: anger and guilt.

Depression is one of the main factors underlying marital problems, and *marriage anger* is one of the main causes for this depression. If a woman (or a man, for that matter) is depressed, it will be almost impossible for her to have a satisfying marriage. Angry with herself, angry with her husband, and probably angry with her children, she will be locked, through her marriage anger, into a position which can only be destructive to the marriage.

Many more men, by the way, suffer from marriage anger and moderate depression than one supposes. Because a man usually goes to work each day, because he has to get out of bed to hold his job and has to function on that job if he wants to keep it, his symptoms of depression may not be as evident. But the depressed man will suffer from inertia, may not be interested in sex, may complain of feeling restless or bored. If you are not sure if your husband is depressed, go back to Chapter 1 and look over the questions we've raised.

Mary Ann says, "I knew that I was depressed because I cried a lot, although I couldn't explain why I was crying. It was only much later that I realized that my husband was depressed too. He didn't realize it either. I wish someone had told me then what I know now! He didn't have any outstanding symptoms. But he seemed angry with me a lot, or just plain angry in general. And he never seemed to want to do anything but sit in front of the television. That made me furious. I wanted to take the TV and throw it out the window."

Mary Ann corroborates that *depression is contagious* —especially in a marriage. As we've seen, two of the main ingredients in depression are anger and guilt. The anger can be anger at oneself, and/or anger at one's partner. Many women are furious with their husbands for not being the men they had fantasized, wanted, and expected. Many men are furious with their wives for not being the wives they had fantasized, wanted, or expected.

John may be furious with Mabel because she isn't as cheerful as he expects her, wants her, and needs her to be. And Mabel is furious with John because

John is angry with her, and she is also furious with herself for not being cheerful. But then she thinks, Well, John isn't cheerful! And so she becomes more furious with him. At the same time, John knows that Mabel has many nice qualities: she is not a bad cook, not a bad housekeeper, and is nice to the kids. So he feels guilty that he is so furious with her. This too, is true for Mabel. Why is she so furious with a man who holds a steady job and is reasonably nice to the children? So she too feels guilty. See how they go around and around and around!

To see how much marriage anger you have, take the quiz at the end of this chapter. Think about your answers. Are many of your anger points reasonable or unreasonable? For example, you may be furious that your husband doesn't make more money, but if he doesn't and isn't going to in the near future, what are you going to do? Remain furious? Can you perhaps think about going to work? Can you cut down your living expenses? What can you do?

Suppose you don't feel you have enough freedom? What do you do? Take a stand? What specifically would you like to do? What could you arrange? How can you bring it up to your husband?

Suppose that your problem is that you are bored with each other. A rather common complaint. Again, what can you do? Plan your weekends and evenings more carefully? Develop an interest of your own so that you don't have to depend on your husband for your happiness?

We are raising these questions because, as we saw from Kirsten's story, insisting on something that will never take place is both futile and destructive. You must ask: What changes can you make in your marriage which your husband can go along with? What compromises can each of you make?

One of the most common reasons for marriage anger comes from feeling that you are being coerced by the other person. Mabel is furious at Joe as she gardens. She hates to garden. Yet she feels Joe wants her to do it and if she doesn't do it she'll feel guilty. However, while Mabel may be responding to Joe's implicit or explicit demands, she is also responding to her own "shoulds" which tell her: You *should* meet all your husband's demands. You *should* do what is expected of you. A good wife *should* garden. Etc. etc., etc.

The rage resulting from feeling coerced by others is one of the main causes for inertia. Again, it must be stressed that much of inertia stems from one's own demands on oneself, although these demands may be experienced as coming from others. For example, suppose Mabel didn't garden? Can Joe understand? How can they work out a way to get the minimal gardening done? (If Mabel gardens because she wants to please Joe and that doesn't bother her, that's another matter entirely. But if she is adding points to her marriage anger, she had better call it quits.)

Unfortunately, many marriages are run by lists and lists of "shoulds": You *should* be together on weekends. The man *should* putter around the house. The woman *should* cook all the time. A man *should* be strong. A woman *should* keep busy. Couples *should* sacrifice for their children. Couples *should* do something special on Saturday nights.

These "shoulds" keep you from experiencing authentic and open living. Why can't a woman spend Saturdays away from her family if that won't upset the applecart too much? Why can't a man go to the movies alone if his wife doesn't like the movie? Perhaps the most constructive thing a couple can do for themselves is to examine their "shoulds" and investigate the ways they can change their patterns, routines, and anger-making expectations.

Consider Jane and Billy. Jane is a secretary, Billy is a policeman. Billy expects Jane to be home on time every night to cook dinner. She *should* be around on the weekends. She *should* stay home while he goes out with the boys. First Jane begins to feel bored, then she begins to feel angry. Then she begins to think she should have married someone else. But then she feels guilty because Billy is also sweet and nice. So she begins to feel more tired. She sleeps ten hours on Saturday and Sunday. Billy begins to feel her anger and depression and reacts to it, whether he realizes it or not. So he too either becomes angry or depressed.

What can they do? Why can't Jane develop an interest apart from the home? Why can't she become more involved in her own development? Why can't two people define their relationship according to their individual needs? Who says togetherness *should* be satisfying all the time?

If your husband is depressed, what can you do about this? After all, he too needs to express his anger. Is there someone he can talk to? Can you take his anger? Can you respond without being vindictive, but by being honest? Can you work out areas in which you can compromise so that he's not so angry? Can you help with some of his pressures so that he doesn't feel so harassed? Can you relax your expectations of him? Can you encourage him to be more active, to exercise, to take part in some sport?

Men as well as women have conflicting "shoulds." There are domineering, self-effacing, and uninvolved men, just as there are domineering, self-effacing, and uninvolved women. Men, too, can't feel dissatisfied and guilty because they aren't living up to their "shoulds," or because they have conflicting "shoulds."

Just as depression is contagious, so is aliveness contagious. If you begin to help yourself, your changes in attitude and expectations may help your husband to change. If he does, fine. If he doesn't, what can you do? Do you want to end the relationship? Or, can you lead your own life within the marriage? Too many women feel their happiness depends upon their husband's moods. This is unfortunate. You don't have to suffer even if your husband is depressed and can't seem to help himself right now. You can still find satisfaction and pleasure with your interests. You are not shackled to your husband, and it is relieving to acknowledge this.

Because marriage anger is so common and so corrosive of the marital relationship, it may be useful for you to read through the following:

Do You Suffer from Marriage Anger? A Quiz

Are you angry because you feel your husband should:
1. Make more money
2. Spend more money
3. Save more money
4. Spend less money on himself
5. Be more generous
6. Be more ambitious
7. Be less ambitious
8. Work fewer hours
9. Work more hours
10. Be less competitive
11. Be more competitive
12. Travel more for his job
13. Travel less for his job
14. Want you to come along on business trips
15. Want you to stay home on business trips
16. Want you to entertain more
17. Want you to entertain less
18. Want to change jobs more frequently
19. Be willing to stay with one job
20. Talk to you more about his job
21. Talk to you less about his work
22. Conduct himself with more dignity at work
23. Be friendlier at work
24. Enjoy outings more
25. Want to stay home more
26. Stop spending time in front of the television set
27. Play more with the children
28. Play less with the children
29. Plan outings with you
30. Consult you less about outings
31. Be more social
32. Be less social
33. Pay more attention to you
34. Let you have more time to yourself
35. Take a greater interest in the children

36. Take less interest in the children
37. Do more around the house
38. Keep out of your way around the house
39. Take care of the garden and yard
40. Have a gardener to take care of the yard
41. See that the car is kept in good condition
42. Spend less time on keeping the car in good condition
43. Be able to drink socially and mix drinks
44. Stop drinking so much
45. Be more cheerful and optimistic
46. Be more serious and contemplative
47. Talk to you about his feelings
48. Stop talking so much about his feelings
49. Be more interested in sex
50. Be less interested in sex
51. Improve his appearance
52. Spend less time on his appearance
53. Talk more at parties
54. Talk less at parties
55. Be charming and vivacious at parties
56. Stop flirting with women at parties
57. Be well read and informed
58. Be quiet about what he knows

You also may find it helpful to show your husband this list:

Are you angry because you feel your wife should:
1. Keep a neater home
2. Not be so worried about the neatness of her home
3. Go back to work
4. Stop working
5. Be a better cook
6. Not spend so much time in the kitchen
7. Be more devoted to the children
8. Be less devoted to the children
9. Talk more
10. Talk less
11. Spend more time on her appearance

12. Spend less time on her appearance
13. Spend more money on clothes
14. Spend less money on clothes
15. Make more money
16. Make less money
17. Provide more of a social life
18. Provide less of a social life
19. Spend more time decorating the home
20. Spend less time decorating the home
21. Be more helpful to you in your career
22. Stop interfering with your career
23. Be more economical
24. Be less penny-pinching
25. Be more social
26. Be less social
27. Be more involved in community activities
28. Be less involved in community activities
29. Be more interested in sex
30. Be less interested in sex

If either of you have answered "yes" to 20 or more of these questions, you are probably storing up *anger points* for your treasure chest of marriage anger. You may feel that it would be impossible to live with someone without being angry about these things. Clearly there is no area that could not give rise to marriage anger. And we would agree with you. But the *excesses* of marriage anger can harm you. For anger points *are* collected, *are* stored, *are* used in dead seriousness to destroy any possible beauty, comfort, and solace that any two human beings can experience with each other.

8

Myths about Sex

"As far as the sexual basis of self-confidence is concerned, certainly the puritanical influences, however one may evaluate them, have contributed toward the debasement of women by giving sexuality the connotation of something sinful and low. In a patriarchal society this attitude was bound to make woman into the symbol of sin: many such allusions may be found in early Christian literature. *This is one of the great cultural reasons why woman, even today, considers herself debased and soiled by sexuality and thus lowered in her own self-esteem.*"

KAREN HORNEY

WHILE INFORMATION REGARDING sex is useful, it can sometimes be used as just another "should." For instance, do you believe any of the following? Couples *should* have sex several times a week. A woman *should* have sexual fantasies. She *should* be multiorgasmic. People *should* be monogamous. A man *should* always satisfy his partner. A woman *should* have sex with her partner whenever he wants it.

Have you answered "yes" to any of them? These "shoulds" can interfere significantly with your sexual spontaneity. The best use you can make of sexual information (and there is plenty of it available these days) is to feel you can accept or reject it according to your own wishes.

As in all aspects of living, there are ranges of taste, making it possible for individuals to make selections from a wide variety of choices. This is true for food, clothing, dwellings, cars, and even styles of intimate relationships. It is certainly true for sex. Selections can be made from no sex to a great deal of sex, from one partner to several partners, from simple sex to gourmet sex. Each range can contain many varieties and combinations.

No choice is right for all persons. It is important to establish a rhythm in your sexual activity which *you* are comfortable with. You may, for instance, have intercourse once a week, once a month, or every night. There is no need for you to feel you *should* be behaving any differently from the way you are, unless you want to be behaving differently. Unfortunately, however, sexual "shoulds" can be tenacious. They can dictate changes in your sexual behavior, even though you may really be satisfied with your established pattern.

Marcia was worried because she did not have the kind of sexual fantasies *other* women had. "I don't understand why I should be fantasizing about another man when I am holding Jack in my arms," she said. "But that's what my friends do. There must be something wrong with me."

Marcia had no difficulty with sex, except when it came to this area—worrying about what was "normal" fantasizing and what wasn't. Here, she had a need to go along with the crowd. Because she was so used to agreeing with others, she was afraid to be "different." Her natural, first assumption was that she was "wrong" and everyone else was right.

Such women are usually susceptible to their partners' suggestions for different forms of sexual behavior, including group sex and exchanging partners. They have great difficulty in expressing preference about what *they* would like to do in bed, or expressing their reservations about expanded sexual behaviors

They may feel they *should* have "open marriages" which, to them, means involvement in extramarital sex. But what they prefer doesn't seem to matter.

What about open marriage? Certainly it differs from the traditional closed marriage in which the man and woman had clearly defined and different roles. These roles often led to a man's being chained to a routine existence where his main function in life was to be the breadwinner. (And woe betide him if he shirked that duty!) The woman was chained to the routine existence of child care and home maintenance. In the past, these roles have had the sanction of society and of the couple as well. Options for departing significantly from these roles were few, and few attempted it.

In contrast are the two main features of the open marriage: an increase in the number of options available to both partners and the willingness of couples to explore and to avail themselves of those options. Sexual experiences outside the marriage are not necessarily one of the options that must be practiced. While the term "open marriage" has sometimes become synonymous with extramarital sex, it was not originally meant to connote that. Open marriage might be better understood as synonymous with *open living*, as opposed to fearful, constricted, closed living.

The principal premise of a more open way of living has to do with developing yourself in a continuum, realizing that there is no end point until death. However your sexual relationships develop in that context depends upon your own needs and interests, and not upon some new (or old) standard of sexual behavior.

Cassandra, for example, didn't receive any information about sex until her late teens. She was active in school and was a good student. She enjoyed the company of boys, but wasn't "panting after them" as some of her classmates were. In college, she fell in love with Roy, but didn't want to have intercourse with him until they married. However, she says, she felt it was hypocritical to say she loved him while at the same time refusing to sleep with him.

Here again, a need to adhere to a *standard* of proper behavior for a woman in love (i.e., a woman in love *should* not refuse her lover) made Cassandra behave in a way that was inconsistent with her beliefs. This led to Cassandra's feeling resentful toward Roy. Many young women are having this problem today. They feel they *should* be sexually active, yet it goes against the values with which they have been raised. The conflict is painful, and *can* lead to depression.

Sometimes, unconscious, destructive needs are played out on the sexual couch. Anastasia, a divorcée in her thirties, says "I feel that David is only interested in me when he wants something—sex or some favor. After he gets what he wants, he becomes indifferent."

Despite her feelings, she continues to sleep with David, for she wants to believe that having sex with him is evidence of their "love." Because she feels lonely and depressed when she doesn't have someone around, she is not prepared to risk losing him. She'll lie to herself, ignore her feelings, ignore his behavior. She can make no move toward a resolution of her problem, for she is bound to keep safe what she has. Her anger at being a sex object for David has to remain obscure, so that she can cling to her adolescent, romantic dream of love. Here, again, is an example of the self-effacing woman who clings to "love" no matter what the cost to her self-esteem.

Some women who cannot enter into close relationships without feeling anxious use their sexuality only as a link to others. When Dolores was twenty-five, she had been feeling depressed for several months before her first love affair. The excitement of the affair made her feel "high." This "high" was in such contrast with her "lows" before the affair that she couldn't "keep away" from George. However, when he proposed, she suddenly "remembered" she hadn't been to see her family for some months and she left the city abruptly, staying away for several days without calling him.

During her visit home she again felt depressed. But rescue was around the corner! She met a man she'd previously known—and slept with him. Now, she felt "better." She remembered thinking, "This isn't so bad. I don't have to have sex with only one person. I'm free. I'm liberated. I can do what men do. I can have sex with anyone I want to."

When she returned to the city, she had a series of what she called "one-night stands." "There was no need to get involved with any of them," she explained. She had her work, and a few women friends, most of whom she could "take or leave." Her "highs" consisted of sexual encounters.

Some years later, she began a relationship with a married man. This relationship lasted ten years. While they talked about marriage, she admitted that she did not believe he would divorce his wife. Actually, she had found the perfect lover for herself. Through this relationship she could satisfy both her need to relieve tension and her needs for companionship and affection. Yet she was not threatened with the relationship becoming too close.

Dolores's safety was predicated on her keeping a certain distance from people. It gave her a sense of power and superiority—feelings she needed to have in order to combat a deep sense of inferiority. She told herself she was not dependent upon anyone. She could be self-sufficient. She could have lovers when and if she wanted them. What more could anyone want? She had a nice place to live and modest material needs. She was not required to work too hard, because she felt she was neither ambitious nor competitive. She had established a cozy little cocoon in which she called all the shots.

Dolores kept a certain distance between herself and others. This is a choice many detached women make in order to avoid feelings of anxiety. By keeping needs and wants down to bare minimum, the possibility of suffering seems to be minimized. Yet this is an illusion, for depression is often associated with this kind of resigned living. Perhaps the final indictment of such an unlived life is seen in old age, where one is left without family, without friends, without interests, without involvements, without anything.

Dolores is an example of what we are calling the uninvolved woman. She differs from Zelda, a predominantly self-effacing woman, who combats her wretched feelings by clinging to someone who will protect her from these feelings. Zelda will go to any lengths to keep Anthony's love. As long as he is there, even if the relationship is a destructive one, she can believe: I am loved; because he loves me, I am not a wretched person; I am desirable and good.

Being left alone is hell for Zelda because she lacks the capacity to be comfortable with herself. She becomes terribly lonely and believes that sex will relieve her. That loneliness, plus her predisposition to feel unlovable, often leads her straight to the abyss of depression. Without help, she frequently perpetuates the cycle of loneliness and dependency. Zelda's underlying motive, however, is different from Dolores's. Zelda uses sex as a bridge to self-acceptance.

Women who need to feel dominant are sometimes also submissive and self-effacing in their love lives. And when these women *are* submissive with their sexual partners, they are often extremely so, sometimes being what we call masochistic. Vivian, an assistant buyer, played an entirely different role with Carl from the one she played at work. She catered to his personal and sexual demands so completely that her friends were always astonished at the change from her personality in business. Although Vivian was confident of her abilities in business, and was assertive and aggressive when she had to be, she lacked self-confidence about her ability to attract and hold a man. Moreover, because she felt she was so aggressive on the job, she had to prove to herself that she was still "all female." So she played out her domineering drives in business and her self-effacing drives in her personal relationships.

However, in her sex life too, the domineering woman often needs to dominate and control, choosing the time and place for lovemaking, for example, rather than allowing her partner to do any choosing. Such a woman is much more active in selecting her partner than, say, the detached woman, and she is also more demanding of her lover, which *can* be healthy up to a point. However, this depends on how compulsive her domineering drives are, for she could easily make her partner feel inadequate. (Remember, the domineering person *has* to put others down.)

Yet this presents a dilemma, for while she wants to do the picking and choosing, she too is in conflict and also wants a man with visible strengths, one whom she can admire. She can have only contempt for a man she can control and manipulate, just as the domineering man in a morbidly dependent relationship has contempt and disdain for his self-effacing partner. Yet very often this weak man is the only one with whom she can have a relationship so she has to delude herself into believing he is "strong." When she is presented with repeated evidences of his submissiveness, she develops a towering contempt for him and may accuse him of "tricking" her into thinking he was "more than" he was. This prevents her from seeing how she, in fact, selected him.

Such women, like such men, are often so driven by their general competitiveness that each sexual encounter becomes a kind of battle in which someone wins and someone loses. Intellectually, they know that a sexual encounter cannot be satisfying under these circumstances. Yet it is difficult for them to separate themselves from their compulsive competitiveness. An unconscious concern about "winning" or being "the best" in bed may result in impotence or an inability to experience orgasm.

The domineering woman is not the only woman who has orgasmic problems. A self-effacing woman may be unable to experience orgasm because of her deep resentment and anger at the humiliations she feels she experiences at the hands of her partner.

These abuses are often real, for she is a "patsy." Yet she also has such an exaggerated need for support, love, and affection, that she can often feel too easily abused. Anger, especially suppressed anger, is probably one of the greatest blocks to sexual gratification.

The uninvolved woman, because of her very detachment, may also be unable to experience orgasm. However, she doesn't suffer so much from it, because she can keep herself away from sexual involvements if they present any problem to her. A detached woman is often surprisingly successful in her sexual encounters, however, and uses sex to satisfy her need for human relationship.

A woman's inability to experience orgasm, however, may also be the outcome of her partner's lack of sophistication. Sexual researchers have found that many women do respond once they are able to express their needs, or once their partners have overcome their own sexual problems. Says Fiona, "I was extremely self-conscious. I wasn't that experienced, although I had slept with several men. I didn't have orgasms and I began to be very upset about this. I began to resent my husband—actually have contempt for him. Our sex life deteriorated. Since it was so unpleasant and we were both so anxious, we'd put it off until the tension was too high. Then we'd have sex and go through another cycle of frustration and resentment.

"Finally, I took a lover and I had my first orgasm with him. I was able to relax my inhibitions with him. I was able then to take the experience and transfer it to my relationship with my husband. After that, two things helped. One, I learned what *I* needed. For example, I don't have orgasms during intercourse. But I can have them afterward if I'm stroked and petted.

"Two, I like to lie in bed and touch after sex. I can't bear it when my husband jumps out of bed to read the paper or watch a TV program. We were both so anxious about relaxing. But relaxation to me is what love-making is all about."

Relaxation—the ability to be more or less free from

anxiety—is one of the keys to enjoying sex and one's sexuality. The woman who has not been subjected to parental antisexual attitudes or taboos early in life is the woman who will be most likely to develop an easy attitude toward her sexuality and her sexual activity when she is ready to be active. Whether or not she is well informed is not a crucial issue. For sexual activity is a normal activity and actually takes very little "on the job" training when one comes to it unburdened by *conflicting* preconceptions, tensions, and inhibitions (e.g., you *should* enjoy sex, but you *should* be pure). A woman who is comfortable with her sexuality will see to it that her lover is respectful of her needs.

On the other hand, the woman (or man) who has inhibitions and a list of sexual "shoulds" will have difficulty in being at ease with her partner. Many women do have these inhibitions, because of their upbringing and because of the way our culture has regarded women.

A woman who is depressed may simply not be interested in sex. She may be unable to "feel anything" because she has suppressed all her feelings—her anger, her dissatisfaction, her guilt—as well as her sexual feelings. However, this does not mean that she will always remain disinterested. As depression is overcome, her sexual feelings will return to what they were—and perhaps be more satisfying than before.

When sexual inhibitions are too painful and debilitating, professional help may be needed. You can investigate new sexual therapies at reliable facilities. You can overcome inhibitions that aren't too severe, however, by courage—the courage to approach your partner with your needs. Your sexuality can be a source of pleasure and esteem once you establish your own rhythms and your own preferences.

9

Motherhood Without Guilt

" 'Christ!' they would say to each other,
clutching small wailing babies . . . wandering
dully round the park. 'Christ, if only we'd
known what we had to go through'—but in the
very saying of it . . . they had smiled at each
other, and laughed, and had experienced happiness. Life has been so much better, and so
much worse, than they had expected. . . ."

—MARGARET DRABBLE, *The Needle's Eye*

"When things go wrong, and they always do,
she [the mother] bears the burden, the responsibility and the blame."

—FLORENCE RUSH, *Women in Sexist Society*

"I've known few mothers who haven't suffered from tension, depression, or emotionally
induced trauma in varying degrees. Nearly all
the mothers I've talked to rely on something
external to help them cope with the difficulties
of raising children. For some, it's alcohol, for
others, it is tranquillizers, and others use food."

—SHIRLEY RADL, *Mother's Day Is Over*

OF ALL your idealized self-images, that of the all-
loving, all-sacrificing mother is perhaps the hardest
to bury. Before you have children you may think, "I
won't make the same mistakes my mother did" and "I'll

155

always be a loving, cheerful parent." However, when and if the children actually do arrive, you can find that you are not a superwoman! Here you are—sometimes feeling frustrated, bored, resentful, and depressed.

Says Annette, "Boy, motherhood was different from what I expected it to be. I really had visions of myself being totally content with my child. And I was going to have free time to do all the things I wanted to do. I didn't expect to feel as bored sometimes, and as hassled other times, as I do."

If you've ever felt like Annette, many of your expectations about parenthood are probably out of proportion. You may have expected parenthood to make you feel "happy" or "fulfilled." Well, that can happen once in a while, but not every day, nor all day long.

Perhaps the "happiest" or most exciting time with your baby is just after its birth, when everyone is still dewy-eyed over the advent of the miracle. The hospital room is filled with well-wishers, flowers, and other goodies. Mother is Queen. You can see your baby as much as you like, or as little. You have no real responsibility for it, unless you are trying to breast feed. If you really want to and can, fine. If you really don't want to, but think you *should* try, there is, hopefully, someone around to relieve your unwarranted guilt. In any event, your child will not be permitted to starve while you are deciding, or readying yourself.

When bottle feeding is decided upon immediately, it is often easier all around, and there may be much less tension for your baby to put up with. This tension is, unfortunately, sometimes present in the mother who feels she *should* want to nurse her baby. Actually, there are many women who cannot feed their babies or who do not enjoy the tranquility of spirit that is desirable in the nursing mother. More important than a mother's milk is the person behind the breast. "Uptight" mothers ought not to feel *obliged* to breast feed their babies unless they find that it soothes *them* as well as their babies. If you breast feed under duress, you can become only more tense.

On the other hand, your decision may not be an

unequivocal one, but may be made nevertheless. You may be one of those women who just can't be *sure* about breast feeding. That is workable, too, unless you feel you *should know* whether or not you want to breast feed. Remember, any decision only needs 51 percent of your vote. So if you feel 51 percent you want to breast feed and 49 percent unsure, go ahead and breast feed. It's not an irrevocable decision in any case, and if you decide against it, you can always feel that you really tried.

One woman tried to breast feed for several days when her child was born, but eventually decided on bottle feeding. But she derived great satisfaction from being able to answer her daughter's question later, "Mommy, did I drink milk from your titty?" She answered, "Yes, for a little while." The child beamed.

Even though your doctors and family members may give you a hard time pro or con, let us say emphatically that for those women who want to, breast feeding can be wonderful.

A reasonable compromise exists, however, for the woman who doesn't really care to, but who would feel guilty if she did not breast feed. That is: There's no reason why breast feeding cannot be *combined* with bottle feeding. This releases you from being "on call" all day and all night long. And, unless the baby cannot thrive on cow's milk, there is no practical reason for insistence on breast feeding.

Those first few days in the hospital can be quite joyous ones for you. But not always. There is something that happens to a great many women, especially after the birth of their first child. It usually occurs almost immediately after arriving home, but it may occur in the hospital two or three days after delivery. It is a gradually deepening sadness, associated with inexplicable crying jags. Apart from any hormonal factor, there are other contributing factors for this, which may differ from woman to woman.

In many households, a wanted pregnancy is a time of optimism and expectancy. The birth and activities surrounding it are exciting and unusual. But there comes the time, sooner or later, when all the excitement and novelty fall off and you feel let down. This is a common reaction, occurring after events that have been important to you or after periods of great stress. You usually recover from these let-down periods, and they are often beneficial in that they allow you to rest and recover your strength. Many mothers experience this let-down feeling initially. But the busyness of caring for your child usually overcomes this sad feeling.

Another factor is the sudden shift of attention from the pregnant woman to the adored baby. That can be difficult to accept. You can feel left out, unimportant, and even a little jealous of the baby's position as the center of attention and recipient of all gifts. Even if you're aware of these feelings, you may begin to wonder about the "joys" of motherhood. Your sadness usually results from your disappointment over your "loss of status." "Before I had the baby," says Babs, "my husband was so sweet to me. He was always asking me if I wanted anything, needed anything. But now that our baby daughter has arrived, all he does is coo at her. He seems to feel that I'm a big girl and can take care of myself. This makes me furious—and I'm jealous of her, that poor little thing. I want him to pay a little attention to me too!" Obviously, an understanding partner can be a big help here.

Probably the most difficult thing you have to accept is the full and total responsibility for another human being. Every mother confronts this, when she is finally at home, alone and in full charge of this little person who is totally dependent upon her for its daily survival. This is a sobering responsibility, and one which parents-to-be might discuss at some length *before* any decision is made to have children.

But talk is talk, and it's often impossible for you to imagine what parental responsibility will be like—a responsibility that may seem overwhelming. "This is it," you may think. "This is *my* baby! Whether it lives or dies depends entirely upon me." We know that this is not entirely true because there's a father, grand-parents, other relatives, friends. And, some younger couples with less rigid role definitions are sharing the responsibilities of parenting. But unless you live in a commune or in an extended family situation, the re-sponsibility for the child is pretty much yours.

The fears this responsibility arouses are under-standable, for there is no preparation for this kind of total commitment. Not only that, parenthood is a *permanent condition*. Once a parent, always a par-ent. Even if a child is abandoned, a parent is still a parent, and is subject to a unique set of attitudes and feelings, usually alien to a non-parent.

Confrontation with this kind of responsibility is unique. In any but the most self-confident woman (and which young mother is so confident?) it can be frightening. It is not the fear of physical care, although that can be a factor. It is fear of inadequacy over the long haul. "How can I be so competent, so knowl-edgeable, so persevering as to take responsibility for this other person, every day, all day long? Suppose I decide I don't want to? Suppose it's just too much for me? Suppose I'm really inadequate?"

These are all good questions. And if you've ever asked them, you show some comprehension of the enormity of your job as a parent. The fact is that no one is that competent, that knowledgeable, that will-ing, that dedicated, that responsible, all day and ev-ery day. But you may not have learned that yet. Neither recognizing nor accepting the *natural limits* of your ability to be a parent, you can feel over-whelmed by what you believe are your duties.

We are *not* describing a neurotic process. This is merely a reaction *many* mothers seem to have to go through, more or less intensely. Sometimes, there is sadness and sudden tears. "I don't know why I'm cry-ing," you might say. "I'm so happy with the baby. But I somehow feel so weak, so helpless. How do *I* know how to raise a baby?" The reply to that is that you don't. And there's no reason why you *should* know how to raise a child if you've never done it before. That knowledge doesn't spring forth full-blown. It's acquired daily, bit by bit, piece by piece. You'll have to listen. You'll make many mistakes. But that's to be expected.

All of these feelings mirror minor signs of depression: the crying, the sadness, the feeling of inadequacy, the guilt for not being stronger, or not wanting such a burden, the slight feeling of hopelessness. But these are usually quite short-lived and hardly merit the label of depression. They are realistic concerns which a mother has, and while she can be overcome by them, this is usually only for brief periods of time.

However, when these signs intensify and become prolonged in duration, and when they combine with other causes and more intense symptoms of depression (great fatigue, sleeplessness, anxiety, loss of appetite, helplessness), we have what is called postpartum depression, the depression that can follow soon after the birth of a child. Says Francine, "I was really looking forward to being a mother, but when the baby finally came—I didn't *feel* anything. I looked at my son and I thought, 'Hey, I don't love that little, red crying thing.' I became really immobilized. I couldn't take care of him—my husband had to hire a nurse."

Francine is putting her finger on what caused her depression. She didn't feel immediate love for her baby—but felt she *should* immediately love this "little, red crying thing." Suddenly seeing this baby made her realize how confined she would be by her new mothering role. Her feeling was: "I'm trapped. What am I going to do?" In a sense, she *is* caught. She has done what has been culturally expected of her and what she felt she wanted to do, and now there's no way out. Francine's dismay at being in this situation, and the guilt she feels for not "loving" the baby, are all too much for her to accept. And so she becomes depressed.

A less severe form of postpartum depression resembles low-grade, chronic depression. The motions of caring for the baby are gone through, but you feel little satisfaction and almost no joy. You may not even be aware that you are depressed, and may attribute your feelings to "not enough sleep."

Now, it is true that you probably have not had enough sleep. The new mother has a twenty-four-hour-a-day job—unless she gets help. And let us say emphatically here that if you can possibly get help, get it. You can certainly use it—especially for the first days or weeks. Until you "learn the ropes," you will feel uncertain and expend much more energy than is necessary. If you have other young children underfoot, in addition to your newest family addition, you will probably feel continually hassled, unless there are others around to share the burden. Moreover, when we say help, this includes not only help with the baby, but help with the cooking and housework. Your husband can share the cooking and housework. It's his house and his baby, too.

Yes, as a new mother, you *are* tired. To begin with, you don't sleep very well with a new baby in the house. Says Laura, "My baby would make these gurgling noises all night and I was sure he'd strangle. So I would only half sleep—this went on for a long time." Moreover, the mother of a young child has few, if any, snatches of rest, or time for herself, during the day. Let's say you've played with the new baby, fed him, diapered him, and given him his bath. The baby is ready for a nap. "Good," you think. "I'll just put in a load of diapers, straighten up the kitchen, and then take a little nap myself." What happens? More often than not, you do the diapers, clean the kitchen, and are just ready to lie down when the baby wakes up. Contrary to myth, most babies *don't* sleep for six hours straight.

Any person who has slept as little as the new mother does would end up (even without a baby to care for!) feeling exhausted, irritable, and weepy. Because many men, including many male pediatricians, have not experienced this day-in and day-out routine, they find it difficult or impossible to empathize. Their lack of understanding may only add to your guilt and you'll probably feel, "I *shouldn't* be tired. What's wrong with me?" Rest assured that you have more than adequate reasons for feeling exhausted.

What other debilitating "shoulds" can be pulled out from a new mother's basket of "shoulds"? Well, here are a few: I *should* be more organized and efficient. I *should* have more time to myself. I *should* not resent the baby's constant demands. I *should* have a cleaner house. I *should* be cheerful.

It is the feeling that you are not living up to a cultural image, and your own image of motherhood, that can lead to depression. Laura continues, "I had one child and was vaguely depressed. Well, then I had another child because I didn't think it was right to have an only child. So now I have two kids and I'm so tired and discouraged I can barely get anything done. I really feel like putting a bullet through my head somedays."

Is this the way *you* feel? Perhaps you're trying to be a supermother. A supermother is always trying to live up to impossible demands; and she can become terribly depressed when she does not receive an "A" for her efforts. She *must* cook well, have a perfect home, raise admirable children. This is her role and she had better do it well! You can feel as if you're under tremendous pressure all the time, and you're never satisfied with what you have done. *Nothing* is ever enough.

Many supermoms live for and through others—most often, through their husbands and children. However, some supermoms have careers too and indeed may be super-working-mothers. To find out if you're a supermom, take the quiz that follows at the end of this chapter.

The supermom has a rigid set of standards for herself, and when she makes a mistake—when dinner doesn't turn out right, or when her children don't do well in school—she feels guilty. By now, you know that *anger* coupled with *guilt* is one of the cornerstones of depression.

Different women will have different notions of what supermom is all about. The woman who has the need to dominate must feel that she is "right" and in control all the time. This means that she will not be able to take any show of anger or criticism from her children, although she can dish it out in large doses. She takes great pride in self-sufficiency and feels she can do everything by herself. Pride prevents her from ever feeling hurt. ("Nobody should hurt my feelings. I'm strong.") However, since she *does* have great stores of self-hatred (never being able to completely live up to the image she has of herself as the all-wise and all-capable woman), she will project her disappointment onto her husband and children. When something goes wrong, she'll call her child "stupid" or berate him or her unmercifully. She is the woman who can have terrible rages one minute and be all cheery self-sufficiency the next.

The compulsively domineering woman will humiliate, exploit, and frustrate her children—perhaps just by being a killjoy. This is not intentional on her part. She really believes that her behavior is in the interest of raising "strong, self-reliant" children who won't blow away when they encounter a little adversity. This is her way of "toughening them up." The intention may be admirable, but her methods are sometimes not justified and are often destructive rather than constructive.

The love-addicted mother is more of the martyr. She may even iron the towels and permanent press sheets for her family's comfort. She is constantly overworked, engaged in doing things for others. This kind of mother feels safe only when she is being indispensable. Therefore, any kind of leisure is difficult for her. She is most deeply hurt when she feels unappreciated. The only time she may be able to stop serving her family and others without feeling guilty is when she becomes sick.

The uninvolved woman will need to remain separate and aloof. She may resent it when too many demands are made on her. At the same time, she justifies this by saying she is teaching her children to be "self-sufficient." Because of her own needs, this woman may appear to have less trouble trying to be a super-mom. She will not "fuss" and "do" or "demand" as overtly as the self-effacing or domineering mother. But she has her own individual set of standards which may relate more to the intellectual growth of her children, to their individualistic, perhaps liberal, development.

She is the one who will be the first to "drop out" of the parenting role when her children become teenagers and do not want to share their lives with her any longer. She will be hurt, but her best defense is withdrawal. That's how she keeps herself from "feeling upset." This is the parent who overstresses decision-making for her children. But she goes to an absurd extreme in telling them, while they are still far too young to make wise decisions, that they have to decide whether or not they will drink alcohol, smoke pot, have sex. We have already seen, to our great dismay, how destructively youngsters handle decisions with which they are in no way prepared to deal.

If you are a domineering mother, your children usually know where you stand. You are often an effective parent. But you are too critical and probably too rigidly demanding of your children. What can you do about this? You might begin by *listening* to what your children have to say, without judging what they're saying while they're saying it—and before they finish.

When you find you are going to say something critical, don't say it. Wait! Think: Am I justified or am I demanding that my child live up to some unreasonable expectations I've set for him or her? Or, am I really angry with myself—and taking this anger out on my children?

Even though we're trying to help you be aware of your tendency to be overcritical, please don't feel guilty about it. You deserve sympathy because you are as hard on yourself as you are on others. But a healthier life lies in learning to accept and enjoy what is, rather than consistently insisting upon some fantasy standard of perfection.

If everything is going well, perhaps you can leave things as they are. But if you find that you're never satisfied—with your children or yourself—and if nothing you do ever seems to be quite enough, you're going to have to face the fact that you are causing yourself a lot of suffering—needless suffering. It is fine to have high standards, but impossible standards—standards of perfection—are something else. Can you see how they put a damper on your life?

If you are a self-effacing, or love-addicted mother, you are too much of a pushover, and secretly you're pretty angry about it. But because you have a taboo on expressing anger, you cover it up, depress it. No wonder you often feel listless and tired. Besides that, your child isn't stupid. He or she knows something is wrong—but is never sure what. This can make your child feel uneasy.

You must begin, as we've said in previous chapters, to learn to feel your needs are as important as your children's. Express *your* wants, needs, feelings. Let your children know where you stand.

A warning. You may, in fact, have an especially hard time when your children are teenagers and when they are not at all reluctant to show their ungratefulness for your persistent services. This is the time that your expectations of them must undergo extraordinary shifts. This is also the time when external influences (i.e., peer pressure, media influence) exert their greatest impact. It is well to know this because you will have an especially hard time thinking that your children don't love you, never have, and never will. Since love is your stock in trade for maintaining a good feeling about yourself, be forewarned. This period of adolescent reaction comes to an end—sometime. But since it may take years, this is a good time for you to look around and try to find other interests with which to occupy yourself.

If you are an uninvolved mother, you know you don't come on too strong. You keep yourself separate from your child, which has some advantages. Your child has a chance to develop without feeling overwhelmed by parental needs and demands. *Many parents really devote too much time and attention to their children.* However, your remoteness may convey lack of interest and lack of pleasure, and your child can get the feeling of being adrift. Of course, you are not being physically negligent. But there's a kind of *emotional negligence* which makes it difficult for a child to thrive. The child can feel unconnected, insecure, and may withdraw from you.

What can you do? As you've seen, part of your problem is not that you are a cold or distant person, but that you have pressed down your feelings in order to avoid experiencing conflict and anxiety. The more you can do to express yourself in a rational way, the more you may benefit your child.

You might try, too, just sitting quietly and talking with your child for a half hour or even ten minutes a day. Ask what the school day was like. What would he like to do after dinner? That will reassure your child that he or she is, indeed, part of a concerned family.

All of a woman's conflicts will clearly emerge in the arduous task of mothering. But these problems will be even harder to deal with if you accept the image of mothering which our culture offers. For example, in the advertisements on television, we see a woman smiling cheerfully as she re-washes the kitchen floor even after her children have just gotten dirt all over it. Who smiles when this happens? Think about your own internalized set of rules and standards about what a mother *should* be. For since perfection can *never* be achieved, women who attempt supermom status are secretly and continuously dissatisfied and disgruntled with themselves, their families, their lives. This can result in bitterness and disgust—both of which are forms of deep anger.

Men have their parental standards too, but they are not as extensive and insistent as the woman's. This is because *fatherhood has not been regarded as the pri-*

mary focus through which a man can experience himself as an adequate human being. Men have their own area that exerts as powerful an influence upon the elaboration of *their* Perfect Selves. This area pertains, of course, to success in their work. Until recent years, women have not had to contend with a similar measuring rod. They have had to deal particularly with their role as wife/mother and it is there that they usually exert the full pressure of their "shoulds."

Today, however, a new mystique is emerging which includes the working mother. This woman is supposedly so energetic and so organized that her home runs as efficiently as a well-oiled machine. However, contrary to myth, many working mothers report they often feel overwhelmed and depressed. This is because they have unwittingly added the role of working woman to their existing ideas about supermom, which means two stringent sets of "shoulds": You *should* be able to hold a job and earn money. You *should* still be a supermom. By doing this, women only add to their guilt and run a race that is often doomed from the start.

In her book, *Mother's Day Is Over*, Shirley Radl reports on what it was like for her as a working mother.

I went back to work full-time at a job I found consistently interesting and challenging when Adam and Lisa were in nursery school a couple of days each week. My daily routine consisted of getting up at six A.M., making breakfast, making the beds, doing the dishes, getting myself dressed, leaving a list of instructions for the sitter, talking to the sitter, and finally leaving for the office. When I got home at about six P.M. (if I ran errands during my lunch hour), I would spend a few minutes with my sitter . . . then with each child. Then I would change my clothes, start dinner, and because Cal didn't get home before seven, feed the children and get them ready for their baths—a ritual I did not delegate to our sitter because I felt I did little enough mothering.

We would eat dinner, and afterward I would do

the dishes, and Cal would work on whatever projects he had brought home. Then I'd do some laundry . . . and finally fall into bed.

Even women who *think* they may have rebelled against their standards still often find themselves unwitting victims of these standards. Listen to what Eunice, a thirty-five-year-old woman with one son, has to say. "I *was* a supermom," Eunice says, "in addition to holding a good job selling real estate. But I was getting more and more resentful of my family, more and more depressed.

"I had to change. Let me tell you what I do now. I do not serve elaborate meals every night. It's chopped meat or tuna fish, fruit for dessert. I never do any work on Sunday—not even cook. It's cold cuts or a pizza. Sunday is *my* day to enjoy my life.

"The house is not as immaculate as it should be. I bought everyone extra underwear so that I do laundry only one night a week. And on that night, my husband makes dinner."

Look at what is revealed by Eunice's statement. Ostensibly, she has relaxed her "standards." And, insofar as this goes, it is good for she is less anxious and more content with herself. However, she says that "Sunday is my day to enjoy life." We must ask: Why only Sunday? Why doesn't Eunice enjoy every day? She has an interesting job, a nice family. Why does she feel that only the freedom to do nothing is enjoyable?

Eunice also says, "The house is not as immaculate as it should be." Maybe she doesn't mean immaculate —but she said it. It is often in our statements that we reveal our true attitudes. Why should Eunice's house be immaculate? Actually, it is not possible to have an immaculate house—except for about a half hour after you've just done spring cleaning. Why are we brainwashed that our houses *should* be immaculate all the time? For, at the same time, we also feel that we *should* have houses in which our husbands and children can relax and enjoy themselves. How can they enjoy themselves and relax in a house that has to be kept immaculate? You see what an impossible conflict of standards this is. You experience guilt if your family can't relax in the home, but then you're furious at your kids for not keeping an immaculate house. By accepting these "shoulds," or any "shoulds" for that matter, women set themselves up for constant frustration, disappointment, and yes, we'll say it again, guilt.

Let us state emphatically that, more important than an immaculate house, more important than gourmet dinners (kids have a lifetime to become gourmets), *the most important thing you can do for your family is to have a relaxed atmosphere in the home*. But please—please—don't make that another "should." If you need help in order to be relaxed, try to get it.

Says Nora, "My marriage changed completely after we had a child. I used to fix lovely dinners, have them on the table by seven, give my husband a cocktail before dinner. I kept to that routine after the baby, but found I was beginning to resent my husband's sitting around waiting for me to mix his drink. Now he gets his own drink while I have a nap before dinner. I have a young girl come in for about three hours to play with the baby and generally help with the dinner and dishes. You don't know what a help that is."

Shawna helped set up a day-care center when her son was four years old. "It was so good for him and so good for me," she says. "I had occasional days I could look forward to that were almost totally mine. We worked out a system that we would each put in so many hours a week. Working mothers who couldn't put in the time paid what they could so that we could get extra help. It took a lot of work to get the center working. But it was worth my time and energy—every bit of it."

Shawna realized that she would have to help organize a day-care center if she wanted one to exist. So that's what she did. Perhaps this idea doesn't interest you. But if you are unhappy with the status quo, it is important to look beyond the standards and structures you have set up for yourself. (e.g., "I am the only one who can take care of my baby well!") Otherwise, you may feel hopeless about *ever* feeling like an adequate mother.

Hopefulness can be fed by making efforts in thinking up new solutions for your problems, and for coming to terms with those new solutions. Perhaps they will not be everyone's cup of tea, but they can be yours. Hope also lies in telling yourself that your life is just as important as your children's.

As Shelley says, "I am not from the cracked plate school of motherhood—your kid gets the good plate and you take the cracked one. I never thought it was healthy to give up my comforts and pleasures, to sacrifice everything for my child."

Five "Shoulds" to Be Rid Of—Forever

I should not get angry with my children

Why not? You're a human being. You're entitled to feel angry. And you will get angry anyway. What's important is to be clear what you are angry about. Then, try to bring it to a conclusion. Try not to call names. Address yourself to the particular issue about which you're angry. Don't castigate the total person.

I should meet all my children's demands

No, you should meet only those demands which you feel you want to meet and can meet without doing harm to yourself or your child. Trying to meet all your child's demands would almost invariably lead to overindulgence and overprotectiveness and could encourage passivity.

I should be able to work at a job and still run my home the way I always did

Not unless you have help you won't. If you try, you will probably be putting extreme pressure on yourself. Working mothers are entitled to divide household chores among paid help, husbands, and children.

I should be happy with my role raising my children

Well, maybe you should and maybe you shouldn't. The point is: are you? If you are, that's marvelous. If you're not, why beat your head against the wall telling yourself what you *should* feel? You'll be better off trying to find outlets to feel satisfied with how you spend your time.

I should be with my child all the time

It's wonderful to be involved with your children. And if you enjoy those times, great. However, if you find you are resentful or bored, try some of the suggestions we make on the following pages.

THOUGHTS FOR MOTHERS

1. Arrange to have at least half a day or an evening a week that is entirely free of any duties and responsibilities. If you can't take that, try to get at least two or three hours. Plan what you want to do with that time. It doesn't have to be cultural or athletic. You may choose to sit in the sun with bare feet, go antique-hunting, go to a movie, or sleep it away. It doesn't matter. But try to plan the time carefully, or it will come and go without your fully savoring it.

If you get a longer time to yourself on a more regular basis, then more elaborate plans can be made—but only if you want to make elaborate plans. Find out if there are any dance groups, discussion groups, ceramic groups, or the like in your neighborhood and join one or form one. Find quiet, beautiful places to be in for a little while and just sit, and read, or do whatever you want.

2. Help set up a babysitter pool or day-care center with parents in your area. Or make an effort to get your place of business, or your husband's place of business, to set up a day-care center for working mothers.

3. Get together with a group of mothers in your area to discuss common problems and worries and how to solve them. The less isolated you are, the better you'll feel.

4. If you are at home, begin making plans now for your future after your children are in school. *Do not* give up your interests while your children are young. Take courses. See if you can become involved in some field, reading, talking about it, or doing it.

5. Plan one day a month to be out with your husband *without* the children. Try to plan ahead for the activity and include him in the planning. If you can't do it every month, do it at least twice a year.

6. If you live in a city, get information on free or low-cost entertainment and activities around town. This information can be found in newspapers, or by calling the Chamber of Commerce.

7. Take this time to investigate volunteerism. It can be a wonderful outlet for energy that refuses to be expended in more mothering. Remember, however, to do volunteer work not because it is the thing to do, or because you feel you *should* do it, but because you want to do it.

8. Deepen your friendships with other women by doing things together on a regular basis. Get to know people *of all ages*. Don't restrict yourself to your own age group. Many an older woman's wisdom has been used by a young mother.

9. Try to find one or two couples who will be compatible with you and your husband. This isn't easy. It takes some shopping around to find a couple you both feel comfortable with.

10. When you go on a vacation with your family, make sure everyone (including yourself) realizes it's your vacation too. Have a plan before you go which gives you free leisure time to do anything you want to do—alone or with your family.

11. Find friends whose children get along with yours. Then try exchanging weekend baby-sitting with them so that you and your partner can be completely free of child care for an entire weekend. You don't have to leave town. You can stay in your own home and just loll, or play, or go out to dinner, or anything you fancy that your financial status can

tolerate. On the weekends that you have the child-care duties, a little planning goes a long way. In addition, you'll find that your own children are often easier to cope with when there are other children about.

These suggestions are predicated on the principle that you must have pleasurable, relaxed time for yourself. The time element can be very flexible. The activity itself can be anything at all that removes you from the tension of your usual routines. This is a time to replenish your inner self, a time to recharge your batteries. This kind of thing is needed by everyone, but it will not happen by itself. It has to be planned for and time set aside.

THOUGHTS FOR FATHERS

Do you feel the weekend is the time for you to relax? Fine. But it's also the time for your wife to relax!

As we said before, it's your home and your family too. Do try to help with meals, errands, picking up. You'll find it can be fun because the children will want to help too, if Daddy is doing it. This is one of the easiest and best ways to teach children to be cooperative in the home, but remember your goals: *They are not to do a perfect job but to help out a little and have some family fun.*

Plan an occasional family outing where Mommy is *invited* to come. Don't involve her in the planning. Have the children work with you in making all the arrangements.

It's also a nice idea to take the children for a couple of hours so that Mommy can have time for herself. This will be time for her to do something different for herself. In return, why not take several hours of uninterrupted relaxation from time to time to do anything *you* want to do.

Are You Trying to Be a Supermom? A Quiz

1. Do you feel guilty because you don't spend enough time with your children?
2. Do you flare up with rage without "any reason"?
3. Do you find yourself nagging a lot?
4. Do you try to give your child "everything"?
5. Are you resentful when your child doesn't get good grades?
6. Do your children usually get their way?
7. Do you focus on your children's shortcomings and limitations?
8. Does raising children and running the home take up all your energy so you have little time for yourself?
9. Are there things you would like to do yourself that you never seem to have time for?
10. Do you depend on your children for the meaning and fulfillment in your life?
11. Do you feel constantly overworked?
12. Are you a perfectionist when it comes to keeping house clean?
13. Do you resist asking your husband and children to help around the house?
14. Do you insist on making elaborate meals every night?
15. Do you secretly feel abused and neglected?
16. Do you feel you've lost part of your identity?
17. Do you feel others in your family take advantage of your good nature?

If you have said "yes" to eight or more of these questions, you may be a supermom! You have to learn to relax your standards if you want to make motherhood easier on yourself and more enjoyable.

10

Responsibility and the Alcoholic

LISA IS in her fifties and lives alone in a lovely suburban home. "I was born in the Midwest," Lisa begins. "I was shy and withdrawn as a child. But I was not unhappy. I loved to sing and I enjoyed nature. After high school, I got a job singing with a band in Chicago. It was a struggle to survive. But I was sure I was going to be special.

"For a while, I went to night school. I was an okay student, but I never studied. I was very good-looking by then so I always got lots of attention.

"I didn't have very much confidence in myself though. I needed someone to push me, I think. And I still thought men were the answer to my problems. Anyway, I met a man and I was married at twenty and had a son at twenty-one. I thought my life was over.

"Larry and I divorced. I did odd jobs—modeling, reception work. And I had long, serious, desperate relationships with men.

"I was also still shy. But when I drank, I wasn't shy. I was charming and funny and vital. I never had any trouble meeting men. I wasn't depressed then. Now I think my drinking and smoking were ways of covering up my depression and problems.

"As I say, when I was drinking, I was 'on.' I once got a public relations job. But I could only do the job when I'd had a few drinks and eventually I was fired. I was often trying to be someone I wasn't.

"I got an inheritance and lived off that money for a few years. But my drinking was causing me problems. It got me into some dangerous situations. Sometimes I'd wake up not knowing what had happened the night before. At the same time, I was so comfortable drinking!

"In 1962, I went to my first Alcoholics Anonymous meeting. But I was still drinking from time to time, up until 1969.

"In 1969, I met a man in AA who was recently separated from his wife. He was a doctor. He was one of the most attractive men I'd ever met in my life. Right away, I was getting presents, flowers, letters every day. However, after about five months, he told me we shouldn't be seeing each other so much. It turned out—and I hadn't known this—that his wife was upset that he'd become serious about another woman. She was hoping for a reconciliation. I really should have known that might happen.

"I've never been so desperate in my whole life. I called her up and we talked—which was a very good idea. I heard such a different side of the story from her. He was like many very attractive men—they can't be loyal. They are constantly proving themselves, constantly conquering other women.

"Right about that time, I started doing a lot of reading. It turned my head around. For instance, I realized that everything I got was basically through my looks —and I was terrified of getting older. I also realized I was overly dependent on men—and that this was cultural. However, I still feel at loose ends when I'm not involved with a man—like now.

"I was trying to keep going, however. I got up and talked in AA, something I'd never done before. Then I met another man, who was ten years younger than me, a marvelous man. He told me he was married, but had an open marriage. We became very close— then he cruelly broke off the relationship. I hate broken relationships. And I can't understand how men can be so cruel. I think they have to change reality in order to accept what they've done.

"I had a new job then and that really saved my life. It's still a struggle for me, however.

"Today, I haven't been involved with anyone for over a year and I'm depressed. I'm not drinking but I'm depressed. My son is thirty now, but I hardly ever see him. He is into his own life. I feel his withdrawal from me is society's fault. Once children grow up, mothers are expected to say, 'Okay, that's it.' Well, I don't feel that way: I want to meet his friends and be involved in his life." Lisa pauses. "I do have some good memories, however. You *have* to have some good memories."

Lisa selected a career, entertaining, which takes tremendous tenacity, stamina, and sense of purpose. Such a career demands qualities of strength and independence. Lisa did show some evidence of these qualities, but she was undone by thinking she could not really succeed without her beautiful face, men, and alcohol. In depending upon these, instead of her talent, intelligence, and consistent effort, she fulfilled her own implicit prophecy that she could not succeed on her own.

In doing this, she negated herself, wiped herself out as an autonomous person. She effaced herself as a thinking, goal-directed woman. She states that she "didn't have much confidence." But what young girl, ambitious to become a successful performer, can have such confidence? How can anyone *know* she will succeed?

How often we hear: You have to have confidence or you won't succeed. Well, confidence is not magically instilled in people. Very few people are confident at first, because they have nothing to be confident about. Confidence is developed slowly only as you grow and build steadily upon what has gone before.

Lisa seemed to be living out a script which allowed her few options. She needed "someone to push" her. "Men were the answer" to her problems. Her "life was over" at twenty-one. Because she had learned these clichés well, she was unable to question or disprove them. Thus, her approach to herself and her involvement was a shallow one.

Through such remarks she is saying in effect: "I am not a complete person. I have no strength by myself. Let me become attached to another person and, presto-chango, I can become what I want to be. But only through another person will that be possible." We can suppose that Lisa had no female role models to show her there was any other way to live.

In this way, Lisa confers responsibility for her success on someone else. She also, perhaps without being aware of it, confers responsibility for her failure on someone else. It has to work that way, and there is good reason for this. If someone else is responsible for your failure, then you are relieved of self-recrimination and self-hatred. "Oh, well," you can say, "if it hadn't been for my destructive relationship with Jack, things might have turned out differently. But I loved him. So what else could I do?"

Rationalizations for your behavior are not "bad." They are often necessary to relieve you of the onslaught of your self-hatred. But we see in Lisa, as a prototype of the love-addicted woman, the rationale for her self-effacing surrender. She believes that surrender to be an essential element in the achievement of her goal, love, for which she truly yearns. She will not relinquish her dependency because of her fear of change and of possible failure.

Between her sense of failure (for one can never be completely successful at externalizing the responsibility for failure) and her shyness, Lisa has to find some means of relief. Some women use depression as a relief and as a preoccupation—that is, a preoccupation which is less troublesome to them than ongoing anxiety.

While depression may, therefore, be an "out" (although a painful one to be sure) for some women, it may be intolerable to others, especially those who cannot rid themselves of their ambitious strivings. Lisa was one of these persons. This is why she was attracted only to ambitious, successful men. Depression made her nonfunctional. She had to find another means of relief from this depression and her muted feelings of failure. She also had to find a means to overcome her "shyness" and to elicit her "charming, funny, vital" self. Of course, we don't know how charming, funny, and vital she became after drinking. It is not too likely that there was a marked change in her; in all probability her charm and vitality were there all the time. But she may not have been able to acknowledge her vitality and charm before she took a drink, because she was too tense. Aware only of her fear and "tightness," she probably could not appreciate those qualities in her which might have been quite obvious to her friends.

Nevertheless, because Lisa felt better, more functional, by using alcohol, she became addicted to it, using it to overcome her depression and other personal problems. That this solution was failing miserably is revealed in her inability to maintain any ongoing work or relationship.

Lisa's constructive efforts became evident through her involvement in Alcoholics Anonymous, in her reading and new job, and through the accumulated wisdom of age. Clearly, however, this new struggle is just beginning. She feels she has overcome her addiction, but she is still "depressed." But today this depressed state is more tolerable to her, for she does not have to obscure it with alcohol.

By now Lisa has learned that alcohol actually has a depressant effect on the nervous system. That is actually one of its effects. By depressing those impulses which reach consciousness and make one feel tense, anxious and self-critical, alcohol serves to inhibit recognition of those feelings. By diminishing normal neurological integrity in that fashion, that is, by interfering with the messages that reach the mind, alcohol seems to offer relief from anxiety, shyness, and depression.

But quickly following upon that relief is another

wave of depression, this time physiologically induced because of the toxic effects of the drug. An attempt to overcome *that* wave of depression is made by taking more alcohol. A relative euphoria follows. Thus there are alternating stages of relief and depression and/or anxiety. The alcoholic's goal is always to deal with the greater depression or anxiety following the relief.

In time, the euphoric relief becomes minimal. But the depression and anxiety remain. So continual drinking then serves as a form of anesthesia in a futile attempt to deal with mounting anxiety and depression. It becomes hell to drink, but it is a greater hell not to.

The choice to drink or not to drink becomes irrelevant, however. Neither will actually bring relief. That is why the uncured alcoholic usually reverts to a drinking pattern. In that, there remains at least the promise, if not the fulfillment, of relief. No, the choice to be made by the alcoholic has to go beyond that of taking or not taking a drink. It has to include other choices—the choice to investigate oneself, the choice to be open to shifts in attitude, the choice to assume responsibility for one's sobriety.

It is the magnitude of this task that makes it almost mandatory for the alcoholic to have some kind of outside help. Yet "inside help" is also crucial. For everyone has a reservoir of resourcefulness. Sometimes that knowledge alone may help a person to go forth and discover what untapped sources of strength lie within.

Lisa has begun that journey. It is a journey without end—not because we are all so riddled with pathology, but because we are all so rich in unmined resources. You can spend a lifetime of digging. It takes persistent effort and some little optimism (not even too much) to find out what's there. But your very humanity insures that you have this ability to introspect. Your only task is to bring it out into the light of day, to free it from self-imposed, culturally imposed, retarding forces.

Interestingly enough, the woman who does not drink, but who is married to an alcoholic suffers many similar problems. Such a woman is Rona. She is in her early thirties and works in a travel agency.

"I don't think you ever get rid of depression," Rona begins. "It's part of your life, like anger, jealousy, love. But there's a way of coping with it.

"My first depression began when I was twelve—practically on the stroke of midnight! We had moved from an interesting university town where I went to a progressive school to a small town that was bleak and grim. I was stuck there until I went to college. I was angry at all times, depressed at all times, because I couldn't wait to leave.

"I went to college for a year. I do remember having some depressions during that year basically because, I think now, I thought I had to have them. They were so much a part of my adolescence.

"When I left school I did secretarial work. Then I went to Louisiana and met a man and married him. Everything grounded to a halt. There wasn't enough to do. I did try to kill myself. I didn't succeed and that depressed me.

"I went to Mexico and got a divorce. I felt a great deal of relief. I had a marvelous affair then with a man who left his wife for me. Then I met another man who was, well, you know, Mr. Right.

"I married him and I knew I had *not* made a mistake. However, ninety days after we were back from our honeymoon, I learned that my husband was an alcoholic. If that isn't the ultimate downer! In fact, we later went to a doctor who told me that he would probably die because alcoholism is a terminal disease.

"I was paralyzed for about three weeks. I didn't know what to do or where to turn. I got all kinds of books on the subject. They would tell you how to stop your husband from drinking. Of course nothing worked.

"Then I heard about Al-Anon, and I went. He joined Alcoholics Anonymous.

"I still had this terrible depression hanging over me

—and fits of anger. Through Al-Anon, I've learned so much. I remember looking around the room when I first went in and seeing these little slogans on the walls and thinking, this isn't for me. I'm a sophisticated girl! However, some of these chestnuts have enabled me to live my own life without depression and the terrible paralysis that follows it.

"Al-Anon simply taught me I do not have to take the depression trip. One way to get out of it is to put myself in action. And to make myself comfortable in any situation I am in, to take control. For example, I was at a meeting, and the only woman present. Someone said, 'Who will take the notes?' Well, you know traditionally the woman takes the notes. I turned to the agent next to me and said 'Al will take the notes.' I learned that I have the right to make myself comfortable.

"It's very selfish, but only if you're good to yourself can you reach out and help other people.

"The morning is a bad time for me. I'm not a morning person. So I get myself out on the street. Just go out with the dog and get on the street. It just breaks up your little world—because then there you are in somebody else's world.

"I also learned that if I carry a positive attitude, people will respond to me in a positive way. And, if you are a positive person, you will remove yourself immediately from a negative personality. That gives you a sense of power.

"Al-Anon says that you cannot make your husband or brother or friend stop drinking. But it says that your attitude can help to improve the home situation. You learn detachment with love. You don't clean up after them, for example.

"My husband hasn't worked for three years. He's been hospitalized. So I supported us. I must say I do extremely good work.

"A lot of depression, I think, is an excuse. It's saying, 'I am frustrated. I have no outlet. Poor me! If I feel that way now, honestly, polishing the silverware will get me out of it. Just simply putting myself in action so I can become rational again. If you're comfortable and taking care of yourself, then you're free to move on." Rona pauses. "My father is a perfectionist and I inherited that from him. He was a compulsive worker, and prone to depression. I'm very hard on myself. Now I'm learning to be happy with what I do accomplish rather than berate myself for what I didn't do! This is something I'm learning to do. . . . These changes that you have to make in yourself come slowly."

Rona's initial comment, that she feels depression is always "part of your life," is quite revealing. She equates it with anger, jealousy, and love. The only similarity here, however, would be to jealousy, for anger and love cannot be compared to depression. Feelings of anger and love are natural responses that every person experiences. Feelings of jealousy and depression are the outcome of some aspect of neurosis, and bear directly on one's sense of substance or, better still, lack of substance.

Rona's words leave the impression, however, that for her, depression is part of life. She certainly has had enough familiarity with it. First in her father, then in herself from the age of twelve on. While it is certainly possible that a youngster can be severely depressed, we must question Rona's statement. Children do not go from "interesting" lives to seriously depressed lives just because they move to another town. Rona may have been disappointed and angry over the move, but she may not have been depressed over it.

We make a point of this because many young people use the term "depression" indiscriminately. In so doing, they are misinforming themselves, as well as their parents, teachers, and others. Such young people refer to different feelings as depression. These feelings include frustration, disappointment, discouragement, or plain, ordinary feelings of dejection. Again, a feeling of dejection is something that every-

one probably experiences at one time or another—
and maybe quite a bit. But dejection is not depression and depression is not dejection.

Even the low-grade, chronic depression described
in earlier chapters, which may be extremely mild in
character, and not too obviously incapacitating or
troublesome, is a bona fide depression, and not classi-
fiable with dejection which has a short duration. Perhaps the most distinguishing characteristic of a true
depression, whether mild, moderate, or severe, is its
ongoingness. This form of depression is often unsus-
pected until after it subsides. Betty Friedan, in *The
Feminine Mystique,* was referring to this condition
when she described the house-bound woman who
seems unable to make any moves in her own behalf.

Rona uses the term "depression" as a catch-all for
unpleasant, negative, or troublesome feelings. Nowa-
days, depression makes fairly good copy, and young
people are aware that the topic can elicit sympathy
from peers, as well as be used as an "ice-breaker."
Used in this way, it becomes a handy "filler-upper," a
handy focus with which to experience and occupy
oneself. A woman once said in a warm friendly fashion, "I feel almost undressed without my depression."

There's a purpose in all this. Preoccupation with a
depression, even if in name only, may serve to bind
anxiety, or to obscure other troublesome feelings such
as self-hatred, loneliness, and anger. For Rona, the
very familiarity of her "depression" may have been a
most comforting feature. If any feeling stands out
to characterize her clearly, it seems to have been one
of anger. She seemed enraged by the move from a
progressive school to a small town, and she remained
angry until she attended college.

The first time Rona may have actually been depressed was when she married and realized she had
made a mistake. The second time was when she
learned of her second husband's alcoholism. Even
then, however, with all of her "paralysis," she got
books on the subject, went to Al-Anon, and showed
remarkable strength in her response to what she was

able to learn there. All the way through her story, one receives the impression of vitality, curiosity, and gradually growing awareness. In seeking a cure for her husband, she clearly benefited herself to a large degree.

Initially, she felt that the program was a simplistic one. But she tried it and learned that *activity, effort, and willingness to change* were crucial. She listened, really listened to all that was said, and applied these lessons effectively in her own life.

While she regrets her husband's inability to help himself, she seems to have accepted his disability. She is not allowing her anger and disappointment, nor any feeling of being abused, to interfere with her own development. She keeps plugging and is fortunate that, in her early thirties, she has come to believe that "A lot of depression is an excuse" and "If you're comfortable and taking care of yourself, then you're free to move on."

Perhaps the most liberating thing that both Lisa and Rona have learned is how slowly changes in oneself occur. Both women state this explicitly. Recognition and acceptance of that truth can relieve one of tremendous impatience and continued self-beratement, thus freeing one to "move on."

All addictions are the outcome of severe underlying compulsiveness in the personality. The specific addiction we see is a concrete, outer manifestation of that inner compulsiveness. That outer manifestation may be called a *compulsion* or a *compulsive act*. When it revolves about a specific substance, a form of drug, upon which a person is both physically and psychologically dependent, we refer to it as an addiction. Alcoholism, as other addictions, is characterized by a preoccupation with alcohol and loss of control over its use.

While alcoholism is seen as an addiction, it is not commonly labeled a compulsion. But that's what it is, a form of compulsion. The alcoholic is driven in the same way that any other compulsion-bound person (a food addict, for example) is driven. Alcoholism just as surely is the end product of the stress of your inner demands (your "shoulds"), unresolved conflicts, and the anxiety and/or depression that can result. It differs from certain compulsions in that it can harm a person's physical health in very tangible ways, and in almost every instance will interfere or destroy the ability to function and relate. Affecting the central nervous system, it can eventually impair learning ability, memory, and judgment. Even minor drinking can impair coordination and judgment. Tissue in the brain, liver, heart, and gastrointestinal tract can undergo change and destruction. It is some comfort to know that any damage is reversible if it does not go beyond a certain point. Compulsions that do not include addictiveness to a drug may not be so obvious in their destructive power. But in the long run, they are no less potent in generating pain and despair.

Alcoholics are frequently unaware of their inner worlds. Many of them do not tend to be very introspective. They may know little or nothing of unconscious conflicts, frustrated expectations, and self-hate. They are aware, however, of a gnawing generalized discontent, of a sadness, an apathy, irritability, restlessness, or anxiety. Early in their alcoholic careers, they find such feelings diminished when they take alcohol.

To put it another way, *alcoholism is a defense against uncomfortable feelings associated with the onset of anxiety and/or depression,* for whatever underlying reasons. Addiction to any drug serves as a similar defense. Any compulsion serves the same function. That alcohol is used, instead of something else, depends upon various environmental factors. Sometimes the use of alcohol can be almost accidental. If alcohol is available in the home, and there are explicit dependent attitudes toward it, a youngster may learn, early on, about its relieving characteristics and use it, not casually as many adults do, but compulsively, as the *sine qua non* to make him or her "feel better," get to sleep, or to "perform well" in a stressful situation. Alcohol use may be initiated through the urging of peers. An alcoholic parent may be responsible for a child's choice of alcohol as a relieving agent. Or some other purely accidental introduction to alcohol may be the initiating factor.

Jackie, for example, had begun taking some medication many years ago that had a high alcoholic content. She felt a slight increase in her well-being shortly after taking it the required three times a day. When her doctor told her she no longer needed it, she "forgot" not to take it. One day she told her doctor that she still took it because it made her feel relaxed. He remarked that it was probably the alcohol in it that relaxed her, and repeated that she no longer needed the medicine for her condition. Once she knew that, however, she went to the family liquor cabinet, and continued to "medicate" herself with small doses of wine and liqueur.

As her children became older, her life grew more empty, and those small doses became larger and larger, as if to fill in the void. Over a period of years, she had become a "closet drinker." No one knew about her "habit." She herself was hardly aware of her physical craving for alcohol and her loss of control over its use.

She never let herself miss one of her "doses," which eventually became half-tumbler shots, even if she had to carry a container in her purse.

In later years she denied keeping it a secret. She insisted that there was nothing to talk about. This secrecy is one of the cardinal signs of alcoholism.

Inattentiveness to her problem is not too surprising for two reasons. One, her addiction was such a gradual process that she never had the sense of loss of control. She also had little interest in keeping a high profile of awareness about behavior she knew on some level to be antithetical to her, behavior which could only cause her to feel deep shame.

Today we know that alcoholism is a disease. Nonetheless, some alcoholics themselves, as well as their families, still regard it as a "moral weakness," as something to be ashamed of and to hate themselves for. This attitude, together with the physical effects of the alcohol, can result in a monumental depression, the major element of which is a devastating self-hatred. In many people this is experienced as: "I am not worth saving, there is no redeeming feature in me, the faster I can fully destroy myself with alcohol the quicker I'll die and thus relieve everyone of my monstrousness." And we do know that this person often achieves the self-destruction he or she seeks.

For the alcoholic woman, then, and for the wife of an alcoholic man, the first step is to look to one's resources, to tap one's inner strengths. As both Lisa and Rona show us, alcoholism can be overcome, just as depression can be overcome. There is no "easy" way. But it is possible.

11

Suicide

"O river, I see drifting
Deep in your flux of silver
Those great goddesses of peace
Stone, Stone, ferry me
        down there."
—SYLVIA PLATH, *Lorelei*

PEARL IS A writer who had looked forward eagerly to working for a publishing house after many of years of freelance writing. After only a few months in her new job, she awakened one night with the "heaves." She thought she was going to vomit. These heaves seemed to be originating in her abdominal region, but they were not heaves of nausea. They were coming from her chest also and seemed to be huge air outbursts, constricted by her throat and mouth muscles. One outburst was followed by another, then another. Every muscle was straining from every part of her body, trying to push something out.

Pearl got out of bed and staggered into the bathroom, clutching her abdomen and chest, struggling for some kind of control. But she didn't know what she was trying to control. There seemed to be only a one-way breath, needed to push out the next great sob. In the bathroom her cries finally came out; they were more like barking sobs. She was crying as she had never cried before, or had seen or heard anyone else cry. On thinking about it later, she described it as a naked, ravaged soul crying out its monumental despair, and she wrote a small poem about it.

> Naked,
> a ravaged soul
> calls out
> its torrential despair.
> No sound,
> no help comes
> from out there,
> only from within.

While she was sobbing she thought of killing herself. That swift thought puzzled her even then. Nevertheless, it seemed like the only solution. There was no use living, she thought. Her life was a charade, a joke. She had done nothing with it and never would.

In different contexts, and perhaps not with such sudden drama, this episode is reenacted over and over by persons who attempt to kill themselves or who feel that they want to make the attempt. In Pearl's case, her unexpected outburst (probably following an unremembered dream) was a final recognition that whatever it was that she had been waiting for, hoping for, expecting, was not to be, had never been, had never had any possibility of being, and was therefore forever lost to her. She couldn't know at the time that what she was really entering into was the beginning phase of a new relationship to herself.

Fortunately, Pearl was able to keep from following her impulse to kill herself. She thought she was "going crazy," but later she said that maybe, for the first time, she was "going sane." She learned that her breakdown had been caused by a collision between her neurotic pride in her ability to sustain "freedom" (I *should* be free) and her self-loathing at succumbing to the security of a routine job.

Pearl had had it drummed into her by her father that a steady job was a prison, that one should remain free of such drudgery. His admonitions became Pearl's inner bible, her set of inner directives. Always working uncertainly as a nonsought-after freelance writer, she had nevertheless maintained the illusion of an idealized freedom. She had no office to go to, no time schedule, no boss. She took pride in that sense of freedom and the excitement that that uncertainty provided.

As she grew older, that brand of "freedom" palled and she sought the "freedom" of economic security. She regarded this as a mature decision. But the new job conflicted with her original fantasy of freedom. She felt coerced by the job's regularity and the need to keep to a schedule. She felt a mounting self-contempt for her wish to feel financially secure. This contempt threatened to overcome her pride in herself as a free spirit.

At the same time, Pearl was becoming aware that her former state of freedom had inflicted all kinds of inconveniences upon her. She had had little money, little recognition, and had often felt isolated and alone. She wondered if, during all these years, she had really chosen a productive way of living.

Perhaps the final blow came when it began to dawn upon her that the glamour and acclaim she had envisioned as part of her new job were figments of her imagination. She had expected to be able to come and go, to have two-hour lunches, to be sought after and catered to. When these things didn't occur, she couldn't forgive her "error in judgment." She was enraged at her "stupidity," the fact that she had been seduced by the promise of a steady income.

As Pearl's recognition of the "phoniness" of her past life grew, her self-hate also grew. The whole wretched system blew up—blew out of her—in that single night. Her subsequent depression persisted for months. She was grief-stricken. She kept repeating, "But it's been so long. How could I have been so wrong so long?" She could find no pity for herself.

Pearl felt cornered and her depression was primarily based on seeing no available options. The freedom she thought she had had was actually a kind of negative freedom. And the new job did not change her life as she had hoped. In despair over ever being able to attain the happiness she'd dreamed of, killing herself seemed the only choice she had left.

Pearl's heaves turned out to be the last gasps of a previously intractable pride, a pride that had held her in chains all her life. She had seen her Perfect Self as being totally "free," untainted by the wishes and demands of others. She had taken pride in being special, different from other ordinary mortals who had to "slave" at routine jobs for a living. The need to stick to a schedule went against this concept of herself as a free spirit. She had hung her pride, so to speak, on her self-sufficiency and independence. When she saw that she was not a unique free spirit, that her life had been a phony bid for safety—the safety of uninvolvement—she felt she had no "self" at all. It was an acute exacerbation of her self-hatred that caused her to think of killing herself at this particular time.

In Pearl's struggle toward health she discovered that personal freedom does not depend upon where you are or what you are doing. Freedom begins from your outer skin and travels inward. It is not something that can be grasped. It is not measurable or absolute. It exists only in one's inner self—or not at all. It has the substance of a thought. It is an inner sense of autonomy enabling one to be flexible about the opportunities that life presents.

Because she was compulsively driven to be "free," Pearl couldn't enjoy the good things her new job had to offer her. Because she felt she *should* remain free, she felt impossibly constricted by her new schedule. This *should* become a rigid restraint, making choicefulness—true freedom—impossible for her.

The classic story of a woman's suicide is Tolstoy's *Anna Karenina*. Anna is a charming and beautiful woman, the mother of a beloved son, who feels her life with her husband, a man she does not love, is suffocating her. When she meets handsome and charming Vronsky, she falls in love. She tells Vronsky, "Love. The reason I dislike that word is because it means too much . . . for me."

Passionately in love, Anna and Vronsky begin a clandestine affair. Anna is filled with both shame and exquisite happiness. She finally confesses her affair to her husband, who has nothing but disgust and disdain for her adultery. As head of the household he decides they must "keep face"; she must give up Vronsky and continue the marriage as before.

Anna becomes ill. Feeling she cannot live without Vronsky, she leaves her family to join him abroad. In the beginning, she is inexpressibly happy. The more she is with Vronsky the more she loves him, and he returns her love. Yet Anna becomes more and more jealous and unreasonable. Cut off from "respectable" society, she becomes more and more unhappy. "For me," she says, "everything centers in him."

Vronsky demands some time for himself, time to be with other companions. Feeling that she is a burden on him, that she needs him more than he needs her, believing she will never receive the total love she wants and needs, Anna throws herself in front of a train.

What happened was that Anna had found herself impotent in a sado-masochistic marriage. The sadism was inflicted through her husband's courteous coldness and constant criticism of her—explicit and implicit criticism. Through her own unconscious self-hatred, she unwittingly allied herself with her husband's disapproval. This further incapacitated her, and she accepted her helplessness as an inevitability. Without realizing it, the only way she could "win" was by doing the one thing that dishonored him as well as herself. She became an adulteress.

When she first met Vronsky, she recognized her weakness and lack of courage. That recognition vacillated with pride in her martyrdom, with her gracious resignation to a cold, loveless marriage and with her willingness to remain in it for the sake of her child, the only person she could love. It was an uneasy balance that she tried to sustain and the vibrant presence of Vronsky unsettled it. With him she came alive momentarily, for his passion diminished her self-hate and her pride was restored. It is this sequence of occurrences that accounts for so much of the neurotic love that passes for "undying" love. This love is desperately clung to because of the relief it brings from feelings of deadness.

When her husband ordered her to send Vronsky away, Anna became ill; she was depressed. Self-hate, guilt, rage, and hopelessness swept over her. Her previous martyrdom could not comfort her. She had tasted the fruit of aliveness and would no longer be satisfied without it.

However, in going away with her lover Anna merely substituted one dependency for another. She can live only *through* another person, a man, whether he is kind to her or not. If he is not kind, she is unhappy. But her happiness or unhappiness always depends upon someone else. Someone else has to be made responsible for her feelings and moods.

This depth of dependency is not only self-defeating in terms of autonomy, it is also a smothering burden for the other person. In this case it is Vronsky who is responsible for her happiness. Vronsky loses all his freedom of action in trying to fulfill Anna's needs. She, too, loses all freedom by placing herself completely at the mercy of Vronsky's view of her, which she needs to sustain a more prideful view of herself as a good, beautiful, and loving person. It is like the vine which feeds off the tree it encircles. Without Vronsky there is no meaningful life for Anna. Here is the essence of morbid dependency. She feels all of her life is her relationship with Vronsky.

In Anna we see a woman who took tremendous pride in the power of her beauty and charm. In a sense, she triumphs over and controls others through this charm. When Anna says at one point, "He [Vronsky] loves me, I know—he asks for tenderness, but some strange force in me will not let me surrender," that "strange force" is pride. Others will buckle under to her; she will not buckle under to them. But then we see her need to dominate conflicting with her need for love. A romantic image of herself "in love," together with the excitement she feels for Vronsky, decide the issue and she gambles on love. She makes more and more demands on Vronsky. When he cannot fulfill them, she feels mistreated and abused; somehow her charm isn't working. Feelings of despair well up in her.

Anna's tale reveals much to us about suicide. It is not enough to say that suicide is anger turned against the self. Suicide arises also out of a profound sense of hopelessness. *The purpose of the suicide is to destroy the hated self, to restore pride, and to end suffering.*

Since Anna lived in an oppressive, Victorian society, she had fewer options for a satisfying life than women do today. However, as we've seen, the element of morbid dependency is alive and well today in millions of modern women. The woman's movement has pierced the armor of this age-old model however. Only those women who recognize that their own freedom from dependency unchains their men as well will finally learn the meaning of a truly reciprocal relationship, in which both partners can maintain the dignity of an uncompromised integrity.

Poor Anna had no opportunity for consciousness raising discussions nor access to any of the other means which have helped and are helping modern women. She was stuck, both culturally and in her own neurotic battle between her Perfect Self and her Despised Self.

What does a loving woman do then if she cannot live without her love but also cannot live with him because she is smothering him? Since she cannot live without him, then she cannot live if she gives him up. This leaves her only one choice—to die.

Anna is reckoning with an even greater burden, however. She is reckoning with her inner opinion of herself. She feels a total and complete failure in all respects. She has failed to maintain the dignity of her socially appointed role of wife and mother. She has disgraced her husband and has failed to keep

Vronsky's "love" as she demands it. Rejected by him, she is irretrievably humiliated by that rejection. She is disgraced in her son's eyes. Only death will vindicate her. Only with death can she triumph over her husband and lover, win back her son's love through his pity, and possibly restore her honor.

But this is not all. Her hurt, rage, and guilt are such that she can see no possible atonement, no possible future for herself. There is no ray of light, no shred of hope. The only alternative remains death. And Anna is not devoid of courage, as she demonstrates when she goes away with Vronsky in the first place. Unfortunately, that same courage permits her to undertake the final step in her self-destruction. And so she submits to the final self-effacement, the final atonement, the final vindication.

In some instances the decision for suicide is an outcome of increasing tensions. Two general conditions prevail: Feelings of deadness or feelings of intense anxiety. The first is a feeling devoid of all hope, a deadness which becomes so agonizing that anything to reduce the agony of it is welcomed. The involvement in thinking about suicide, and in possibly planning its execution, becomes, paradoxically, more life-affirming than a previous retreat into a dead state. "Anything is better than nothing" is the theme.

Perhaps if we use the illustration of the totally paralyzed limb, we can clarify this point. In the case of complete motor and sensory loss a part of the body becomes flaccid, completely devoid of voluntary movement, as well as all sensation. Its existence can no longer be experienced by its owner, unless he looks at it. For all intents and purposes, it is gone. Yet, if the afflicted person tries to handle this limb, it is found to have substance, weight, and astonishing warmness. A more frustrating contradiction is hard to imagine. The feeling that there is nothing there is constantly confronted by a glaring contradiction. Not only is there something there, but it has to be dealt with. It has to be moved and lifted, kept clean, nourished.

We ask this afflicted person to learn all the ways of accommodating to that disability, to "learn to live with it." "How? How?" cry the afflicted. "How do I accommodate to that!" But they do.

Now let's move back to our original frame of reference. A woman who feels dead, who is devoid of any joy, still must carry herself about. But she, like the person with the paralyzed limb, is in anguish. It is not uncommon to see a previously depressed patient almost "overnight" become more animated. However, this dramatic "improvement" is shortly followed by a suicide attempt. For in making the decision for suicide, the patient experiences great relief—a relief so great that a depressed mood can be "miraculously" overcome.

A sense of deadness may be accompanied by a condition of severe anxiety. The presence of total unmitigated anxiety is incompatible with survival—physical or psychic. It is just too painful and places too great a burden on the body. It is this pain which drives a person to develop compulsions or to use anxiety-relieving measures which may include, as we've seen, the compulsive use of drugs, food, work, sex, or alcohol among other things. Whatever anxiety-relieving action is taken is justified on the basis of that need to survive.

If we search for the source of such intense anxiety, we will find it in the conflict between the Perfect Self and the Despised Self. The Perfect Self is constantly subjected to onslaughts of self-hatred which are powered by the system of inner "shoulds." (What you *should* or *should not* be doing, saying, or thinking.) This ongoing conflict between pride in the Perfect Self (I am great!) and the self-hate of the Despised Self (I am despicable!) generates the feeling of anxiety. The heat of the contest determines the level of the anxiety.

In the suicidal person, the attempt to become the Perfect Self has not been successful. It has not overcome the self-hate. In fact, self-hate has overcome. And the verdict is death for the hated one. Once that verdict is rendered, the conflict abates and anxiety subsides. This outcome may bring so much relief that the severely depressed mood is lifted.

In fact, the decision to commit suicide restores a certain amount of pride. The suicide is saying, "See, I have really outwitted everyone. I have now decided to call a halt to this suffering and I'm not going to tell anyone about it. This will be my secret. I will plan it carefully and execute it. My success will be my final coup. And f——— you."

One can begin to appreciate the pain that the poet Sylvia Plath must have experienced, pain she has described in her only novel, *The Bell Jar*. The story by now is well known. The nineteen-year-old protagonist goes to New York as a guest editor on a magazine. She sees women who have found success or who are more socially at ease than she. Unable to make any decisions about her life, she plunges into a world of fantasy in which she will triumph over others through her great artistic ability. When she fails to gain a place in a summer creative writing course, depression descends. "All in all, I felt upborn on a wave of creative, social and financial success. The six-month crash, however, was to come."

A hopeful pride in her fantasy of success (the successful Perfect Self) could not compete with her disgust at the person she actually was: a young, inexperienced, hypersensitive dreamer with talent, promise, enthusiasm. That was not enough.

That Plath was a perfectionist is well known. Her husband, poet Ted Hughes, has written: "Whatever teaching methods were used, Sylvia was the perfect pupil. She did every lesson double. Her whole tremendous will was bent on excelling. Finally, she emerged like the survivor of an evolutionary ordeal; at no point could she let herself be negligent or inadequate."*

In addition to her compulsive need to dominate, excel, and control, she had severely conflicting self-

---

Poetry Book Society Bulletin, 1966.

effacing needs. In her poem *Daddy* she writes "Every
woman adores a Fascist, the boot in the face." Here
she expresses the need of the dependent, love-addicted woman, who feels only weakness in herself
and is, therefore, vulnerable and needs the "strong"
partner to protect her. She can feel safe only through
this strength. If acquiring this protector and holding
him means "a boot in the face," so be it. The Fascist
behind the boot will be "adored," not for his boot, but
for the promise of perpetual safety.

When her marriage to Ted Hughes was ending,
Plath was bitter and hopeless and became deeply
depressed. ("A ring of gold with a sun in it. Lies. Lies
and a grief.") In despair, death, as it always had,
seemed the only alternative. Sylvia Plath recognized
some of the conflicts within her. In her poem *In
Plaster* she writes: "I shall never get out of this! There
are two of me now. This new absolutely white person
and the old yellow one."

There is a fight within her over which one shall
survive: the old yellow "ugly and hairy" hated self or
the "white person," the "saint," or Perfect Self.

As the battle between her pride and her self-hatred
rages, death is seen as the only escape.

> And I, stepping from this skin
> of old bandages,
> boredoms,
> old faces
>
> Step to you from the blackcar of
> Lethe,
> Pure as a baby.

> —from *Getting There*

The last throes preceding a successful suicide are
often prideful ones. Not that we feel Plath "enjoyed"
writing about suicide. It was more a matter of wanting to survive. Her writing was probably an alternative to suicide, something through which a lifeline
was maintained. That the lifeline ran out and was re-

placed by utter, abject hopelessness is a conjecture that we might make.

We can see the difference between Sylvia Plath and Pearl, whom we spoke of in the beginning of this chapter. The contemplation of suicide, as we saw in Pearl, strengthened her resolve to do something about her condition. It was from that point—from her awakening in the middle of the night and thinking that she *had* to kill herself—that she saw she *had* to grow in a different way. She was not a young woman, but for the first time she saw hopefulness for what it actually is—a direction rather than a goal, a process rather than an end.

PART III

12

Helping Yourself

By now you probably have a good idea of what "shoulds" are and how they control what you feel, think, and do. If you can appreciate how your "shoulds" restrict you and often compel you to respond in self-hurtful ways, you may be able to live in more peace and harmony with yourself. Without being hampered by interfering, disruptive "shoulds," you can be freer to develop yourself in any way you want.

Be forewarned that merely recognizing a disruptive "should" will not be the end of it. These forces are compulsive (that is, non-selective) and tenaciously rooted in the personality. The more you can see how they operate in different areas of your life, however, the better you may be able to cope with them. Our discussion about the following women illustrates some of the ways you can begin to do this.

Sally is in a car with her husband. He is driving, while she is reading him directions to her sister's home, directions which she had taken down that morning over the phone. As they continue driving, they both realize they don't see the signs they expect to see. Sally's husband suggests they may be lost. Sally begins to feel "panicked," although her husband is relaxed and sure they'll find their destination. But Sally can't stop feeling anxious. She tells herself that this is a perfectly legitimate way to feel since they may be lost.

In this example we see how nonselective Sally's "shoulds" are. She reacts with "panic" in response to a very ordinary and inconsequential event. While being late anywhere can be annoying, it hardly merits panic unless there is something important at stake and one absolutely cannot be late. But it is crucial for Sally to maintain her image of herself: "I *should* be on time always; I *shouldn't* take directions badly; my husband *should* feel the way I do." No matter which way she turns, she bumps into another "should."

However, if Sally were helping herself, she could ask: Do I think I am so perfect that the idea I may have made a mistake in copying down the directions is enough to upset me? Am I afraid that I will be late to my sister's? Do I feel I *have* to meet other people's expectations in being prompt? Am I afraid my sister will be annoyed with me? Do I feel I won't be able to defend myself is she is angry? Why am I getting so furious with my husband? Do I demand he should get us out of this? What difference does it really make if we have made a mistake and are late?

Once Sally asks herself these questions she might begin to see how demanding and self-critical she is. After all, what's so terrible about being lost? So what if you're late? In other words, by confronting her need to avoid making *any* mistake, she can begin to shake herself loose from the bind she is in.

Charlene is on the telephone with Margaret. Margaret states that Charlene's friend, Mary, is "blindly adoring" of Charlene, and that Charlene likes Mary only because of this blind adoration. Charlene doesn't say anything. When she gets off the phone, however, she feels anxious. She doesn't recognize the anxiety as such, or even that it derives from her sudden irritation with Margaret, irritation with Margaret's criticism of her. Charlene's sudden response is one of fear at feeling the way she thinks she *should not* be feeling. She makes herself a scotch and soda to "relax."

If Charlene allowed herself to go to the source of her uneasiness instead of running to make herself a drink, she might begin to ask herself these questions: Is what Margaret said true? Actually, she doesn't think it is. Mary is a dear friend. Perhaps Margaret is jealous of her close friendship with Mary? If so, why couldn't Charlene speak up and defend herself?

The answer would seem to be that Charlene has a taboo on disagreeing. (You *should* be nice. You *should not* disagree.) She likes to "get along." She doesn't like to make waves. If she spoke up, she would have to risk Margaret's anger. But she needs Margaret's approval to feel good about herself and to avoid feeling uneasy. (If people don't like me, then I must be awful.) She can't risk losing *anyone's* approval.

If Charlene were to go a step further, she might ask herself whether she really likes Margaret, who, every once in a while, is inclined to put her down. Actually, there are many things about Margaret which she can't stand—her selfishness, her materialism, her inconsiderateness for others. Yet she continues the friendship. Why? Perhaps she feels "sorry" for Margaret and her shortcomings? In this way, she may be able to feel she is better than Margaret. She may be afraid of losing a friend. She may feel guilty if she does what she wants to do (break off the friendship), rather than what Margaret wants to do (continue the friendship). This would again show a quality of submissiveness—submitting to Margaret in order to ensure her friend's approval. Charlene gets a further reward. She comes off as a "good" person who never hurts anyone.

All of these questions cannot be resolved right away. But by raising them, Charlene might feel more in control and less prone to run for a drink each time she feels tense. If she decides Margaret's friendship isn't worth the hassle, fine. If she finds she likes Margaret, but is unwilling to put up with her put-downs, fine.

She can tell Margaret this. Either way, by asserting herself when similar situations arise, she will gradually be less tense.

Kitty is a compulsive worker who has been raised to achieve, achieve, achieve. She is having trouble, however, because her immediate boss in her new job likes to work very closely with her. She finds herself becoming so angry that she can hardly talk. The question is: Why? Kitty could inquire: What is making me so hostile? Is it the fact that I take great pride in not needing anybody? Do I resent the help my boss wants to give? Do I need to feel I am accomplishing things by myself? Is this what makes me feel proud? Is this what I demand of myself? Is it that I feel I *should* not need anyone's help in anything I do?

If Kitty needs to work alone to be anxiety-free, her boss's closeness will cause her to feel nervous. If she doesn't understand her needs here, she will blame him and feel hostile toward him. If she can understand her needs, her hostility might lessen. That could enable her to make a more rational decision concerning whether or not she wants to keep this particular job.

Charyl, a secretary, is sitting home alone. It is Saturday night. Her married boyfriend, Mark, is, as usual, home with his family. Charyl sees him during the week; on the weekends, she "relaxes" and watches television. Charyl tells herself she is content. Yet she is a compulsive eater who is always talking about dieting. Eating calms her, she says.

Charyl's life seems to be at an impasse. She is an example of the uninvolved woman who has put a lid on many of her wishes and feelings. If she becomes sufficiently frustrated by this state of affairs, she can begin to inquire: Why am I so undemanding? So contented with so little? Why am I so willing to take second place? Why do I dread making demands on others?

Charyl is willing to put up with loneliness, second place, and no future in terms of a permanent relationship, because she remains more anxiety-free under these circumstances. Her arrangement is not a fulfilling one and may even anger her. But this solution is better than feeling conflict.

To make the efforts she has to make to find her own man would mean to risk rejection and hurt. These moves would make her feel so uncomfortable that she is loath to make them. Yet, as Charyl eats and sits watching television on Saturday night, she is beginning to feel the imprisonment of a primary "should": Leave things alone; don't rock the boat; let sleeping dogs lie, and so on. Yes, a certain level of comfort is maintained. But is it worth what she gets for it? This is a question she must address herself to, sooner or later.

Clara is a housewife who wants to do volunteer work. However, she is shy and will not speak up at meetings, even when she has something to say. Clara doesn't understand why this happens to her, and she would like to change.

Clara can ask: Do I take such pride in being perfect that I am afraid to say anything that might jeopardize that view? Do I think I can win respect from others by keeping quiet? Do I feel I have to always say the right thing and yet not arouse anyone's disapproval?

There are probably very few times that she could meet both of these latter injunctions, for if she does say the right thing, it is possible that she may arouse someone's hostility. So her shyness is actually a way of remaining safe. In order to change, Clara has to be willing to leave her little cave of safety and venture forth. She has to remember how she has involved herself in activities in the past, how she has taken chances, how she has not melted away when she spoke up, how she has been able to evaluate her experience and use it when it was needed. She has to be willing to regard fear and being afraid as facts of existence, facts which do not preclude the possibility of a full life.

Harriet works in fashion. She seems unassuming, sweet, and likable. Yet underneath a quiet facade she is frantically ambitious. Although she won't admit it to anyone, she wants to be a "star." She works very hard, but no matter what she achieves she is always self-critical. Nothing ever seems to be enough for her.

Harriet will never *completely* change. She will probably always remain a hard worker, which is an asset. But by relieving herself of even some of her drive, she will actually be better able to enjoy her work and the nice things her success will bring her. The frantic quality of her ambition can be lessened once she sees how her perfectionistic demands and her corrosive self-criticism keep her from ever being satisfied with what she has accomplished.

Marie had a party which she wanted to be a huge success. However, one friend ran into a problem and didn't come, three left early, and one arrived late. On top of that, although she'd invited many people she hadn't seen in a long time, she was so anxious she couldn't relax and have a good time. The next day she cried all day and then berated herself for not having a good time at her own party—after all the money she'd spent! She complained to some of her friends about their too-early departures and too-late arrivals, but they felt she was wrong. "I stayed until midnight," said one. "I'm sorry. I would have stayed longer, but I got a terrible headache." The fact that her friends thought she was overreacting made Marie stop and think. Perhaps *she* was the one who was distorting what had happened.

But why? She felt so *wronged*. So abused. She began going over the party again. Was feeling abused her way of projecting (or handling) her self-hatred? She thinks: "Nobody likes me. They all left early. I gave a terrible party and I'm despicable. No! I'm not so terrible. *They* are the awful ones. They let me down. I am the considerate one. They are the culprits.

I am not to blame; I am the victim of *their* thought-lessness."

She can also ask: And why was I so anxious? Do I need to be such a great hostess? Give a smash party that people will talk about for weeks? Do I need to impress others so much?

Once Marie has had this talk with herself, she has several choices. She can decide that, since entertaining does make her anxious, she will forget about giving parties. Or, she can try to give smaller parties, and perhaps not be so tense. She can explain to her friends that she is usually anxious about parties and would appreciate it if they would arrive on time and stay a little longer. She can tell herself that next time she will work to avoid feeling judged by an impossible set of standards. All these options are open to her. By recognizing that she has options, she can be more hopeful about enjoying her parties in the future. In this way she can also prevent herself from being overcome by the excruciating self-doubts that plague her.

Marguerite, a young saleswoman, is easily bored and marginally depressed. She has tried to overcome her boredom by taking courses, starting projects. However, her enthusiasm never seems to last. Somehow, her interest dissolves—whether it be in yoga, pottery, or sewing. If she were analyzing this lack of interest, she could ask: Do I have such high expectations of these projects that when they don't make me feel better very soon I abandon them? Does the fact that I don't quickly excel make me pull out and lose interest so that I don't have to confront my mediocrity?

Seeing herself as an ordinary student may run so counter to the kind of student she believes she *should* be that she cannot tolerate such a mundane view of herself. But by withdrawing, and being uninvolved, she doesn't really solve anything for herself. She senses that she is cheating herself, but she manages to obscure that, too, from herself, so that she doesn't have to deal with her withdrawal and the reasons for it.

At first it may be difficult for Marguerite to tolerate her irritation when she does something she feels is "ordinary." But if she learns to stand it instead of withdrawing or becoming depressed, she will be more able to pursue the activities she likes and to accept her level of proficiency, whatever it is.

Anxiety is always with us and it is not possible to escape it entirely. The attempt to do so is what leads to extreme uninvolvement. However, there are means by which anxiety can be tempered and made less painful. We have made suggestions throughout about ways you can do this—i.e., trying to identify your "shoulds," asking yourself questions, taking part in physical activity. These can help you to accept more challenges and eventually to feel stronger.

Diane gets headaches easily. The last time she had a headache was at her mother-in-law's. In fact she often gets headaches when she goes to her mother-in-law's, perhaps because she goes there every Sunday.

Diane might feel that she is just one of those people who get headaches easily. However, if she were analyzing her condition, she would ask: Am I angry that I go to my mother-in-law's every Sunday? Do I want to go or do I feel *obliged* to go? Am I unable to take my own needs as seriously as those of my mother-in-law? Am I too compliant? Am I afraid of being the source of my mother-in-law's resentment and anger? Do I too easily let other people walk over me? Am I afraid to stand up for my wishes? Do I take great pride in being the dutiful and obedient daughter-in-law? But am I also angry at feeling that I have to do this?

Diane certainly has room to maneuver, but she has to decide how *she* wants to deal with the situation. Does she want to continue going every Sunday? Does she prefer going once a month? If so, how can she make the transition? Will she just start skipping Sundays? Can she tell her mother-in-law she cannot make it every week and gradually work it up to once a month? What will she do when her mother-in-law complains? When her husband complains? Will she keep trying regardless? Will she discuss the matter privately with her husband and see if he feels the same way? Can she take months or more to accomplish this change, remembering that she has future years and years of relationship with this woman?

We are trying to set down a model here for proceeding in similar situations, whether they involve inlaws, spouses, children, or other relatives. The matter of accommodating to relatives is a very common and needlessly troublesome one. There is a significant transition made when a person marries. From living and having to accommodate only to your primary family, you are suddenly thrust into having to accommodate to three families—your primary family, your spouse's primary family, and the new family you have created through your marriage. Surprisingly, this change is given little attention. While the marriage can offer you a treasure in affection and companionship, it can also create the ongoing, tension-provoking position that Diane found herself in because she had not taken the time to think through how *she* wanted to conduct herself. Thinking through her position is her first step.

There are many things that disturb Carrie about her relationship with John. He's made several dates and broken them at the last minute. If she complains he becomes irritated, telling her he has "good reason" for the last-minute cancellation, and that she is too dependent on him. Why can't she make other arrangements? Surely she has a girlfriend she can call or a movie she wants to see? This makes her feel guilty. ("Why am I such a nag?")

In addition, he often makes dates at the last minute and is annoyed if she is unable to cancel her plans. Actually, she usually does change her plans, or keeps her plans "open" in case he calls. She justifies this to herself by saying there is really nothing she would rather do than see him. ("I can always find a book to read or some work to do if he doesn't call.") However, when she is pressed, she reveals she resents his high-handed behavior.

Carrie could inquire: Why am I so "in love" with John? Suppose she answers: Because he's like a rock. Nothing can upset him. He is successful, and confident. She feels safe, cared for, and protected with him.

She should ask: Why do I need to feel protected? What is at the root of this dependency? Is it my inability to feel capable of taking care of myself? I *do* know that I dread his leaving me. When he is withdrawn or noncommittal, or when he doesn't call for several days, I become depressed. (Carrie can see that when he is around, she is happy if he is happy. Her moods always depend on his moods.)

She can further ask: Do I have to cling to anyone I admire? Do I feel I become worthwhile and admirable if he loves me? That seems to be the rationale for Carrie's behavior. But this "transfer" of qualities doesn't work, and Carrie remains anxious, angry, and often depressed.

In order to resolve her dilemma, she would have to make her wishes and needs known, in as direct a manner as possible. It is not useful to cry or complain, "You don't treat me right." It is more useful to state: "I am not comfortable with waiting for you to call me. In order for me to feel more comfortable with this relationship, I need to know in advance what days we are going to see each other. That will give me a chance to make other plans."

At this point, John may protest that she is trying to "manipulate" or "control" him. Yet her behavior is exactly the opposite of being manipulative or controlling. She is being honest and direct. She is aboveboard. (Actually, she is being manipulative by feeling abused because that can make him feel guilty.) Of course John may refuse her request. Then she has two options: either to end the relationship or to continue an unsatisfying relationship. Hopefully, if John senses she means what she says, he will be able to respond to her needs in a more constructive way.

Although men like John want to maintain the upper hand by keeping a woman in a quandary (as was Carrie), they do not actually like themselves for it. It is a continuance of compulsive, neurotic patterns of behavior which they have set up and which repeatedly destroy their relationships with women. What Carrie can offer by a direct, firm, but not unkind, confrontation is a shift from the neurotic to the healthy. She can say, in effect: Let's stop being babies about this. Let's be fair. Let's be considerate of each other. We don't have to be irrevocably caught in this old pattern. We can change something that causes me pain and probably causes you pain too, because of your guilt. So why don't we do it another way?

Thus she opens the door to a more optimistic future relationship. Can John enter? If he insists upon persisting with his neurotic pattern, he cannot, and will be the loser for it. But Carrie will never know if she doesn't take the chance. For the most part, such a man will welcome the opportunity to leave his den of self-imposed iniquity. It may not work initially, but it is worth many, many tries.

13

Awakening Through Dreams

"Nothing is more yours than your own dreams.
Nothing is more your own creation."

—NIETZSCHE

YOUR DREAMS release tension and so help you to continue to sleep. When your anxiety and tension become too great, however, you can have a "bad dream" and wake up.

Beulah would not describe herself as depressed: she sees herself as simply restless. (Remember that restlessness is one sign of depression.) Yet one night she had a dream that life had lost all its value. She was wandering around alone and lost. This dream gave her a clue to what she was feeling following a break-up with her boyfriend.

Your dreams are often some of the best indicators you have of your inner conflicts. Carla dreamed of a slim, pretty woman happily holding the hand of a little boy. Carla was not slim, not did she have a little boy. Yet this was Carla's perfect image of herself (you *should* be thin, you *should* have a child), although it differed greatly from who Carla was in "real life." Her neglect to follow these dictates was the reason for the guilt she complained of. Her dream helped her to see why she had such overwhelming feelings of guilt: She wasn't living up to her unconscious image of herself.

Marlene dreamed a tiger was pulling apart a lamb. The tiger and lamb personified conflicting aspects of her personality; two opposing "shoulds." One "should" was represented by the lamb who was her self-effacing, love-addicted self, ready to be sacrificed to the more powerful one; the tiger was her domineering self who fought against the puny little lamb in her. How each one must have despised the other! This dream helped Marlene become aware of her stringent and mutually exclusive "shoulds" (i.e., You *should* be sacrificing and sweet. You are despicable because you are self-effacing and you *should* be strong and domineering). Anger at herself, symbolized by the tiger's rage, was strongly motivated by her need and wish to dominate. Each element of the conflict rails at its opposition.

Susan, who is becoming aware of her deep inferiority feelings, dreamed she was the Queen of England. While her dream obviously is a wish fulfillment dream, it also tells us that the only way Susan feels she can "solve" her feelings of inferiority is through great power over things, through being superior, through being admired. (i.e., You *should* be superior. You *should* be great.)

The people, objects, and animals in your dreams often represent different aspects of yourself. The woman who dreams of a tornado can be the tornado, with its bottled-up power and energy. The woman who dreams she is a tourist in the ruins of a foreign city evidences her feelings that she is an onlooker of life with no deep connections (that is, the uninvolved woman). She sees her life as bare as the ruins in her dreams. On the other hand, the dream could represent a turning point in that it identifies her feeling of being an onlooker. This can lead to a readiness to explore ways of changing, of becoming more of a participant in life.

Dreams, too, often reveal to us repressed feelings we have about others. Joan began dating a confident and outgoing man who appeared to be everything she wanted. But she dreamed he was a criminal and that a sheriff was chasing both of them. After her dream she realized she had real misgivings about his business dealings. She had been repressing this knowledge because she needed him so much and wanted the relationship to work out.

Most dreams are personal. They are not about politics, war, or art. Most of the time they have to do with our relationships—to ourselves and to other people. They usually concern the present, not traumas about the past. Dreams are not necessarily good indicators of reality, but of how we feel about things.

Claire remembers a dream in which she was sitting in a cafeteria with her mother. They were both eating tuna fish. A policeman walked by and threatened to throw them in jail if they didn't eat *all* the tuna fish. Claire felt that the policeman was really her mother, but she also felt she had internalized the policeman in herself. If she didn't obey the policeman's wishes (You *should* eat. You *should* be a good girl), she would be a criminal, a bad girl. Her own self-hatred and self-rejection are apparent in the dream.

Christine told of a dream in which she was being chased by a man who wanted to rape and destroy her. At the time she was beginning an extramarital affair which was causing her great anxiety. The dream revealed her fear that she was going to be destroyed by her behavior.

Marsha dreamed that a person she was talking to disregarded her and walked away. She saw how her *own* feelings of self-rejection were projected onto other people, in this case the stranger in her dream.

Sometimes the people in our dreams are stand-ins for other people. Marta dreamed her brother and his wife were having their marriage annulled. At first she couldn't understand the dream since her brother had a warm, loving marriage. She began to wonder if she wanted her own marriage annulled. A few nights later she dreamed she was kissing a girlfriend's husband. In the dream, he was suffering from a nervous disorder. Again she wondered if her girlfriend's husband represented her own husband whom she felt was weak. But in kissing him did she feel she was trying to make an effort to accept him as he was? Another possible interpretation might be that she was trying to acknowledge her own weaknesses and to accept them.

Jung has suggested one tool for dream interpretation called "interior dialogue" in which, after you wake up, you talk with one of the people in your dream. He theorized that by doing this you would learn more about the character in your dream who might represent some part of your repressed self.

Another way you might be able to get some idea of what your dream is telling you is by first writing it down in your journal. It isn't necessary to record all details or all segments of your dream, just what you remember. Later, when you have at least fifteen minutes of uninterrupted time, and you can be quietly alone, sit or lie down comfortably, and slowly read what you've written. Put the paper down, close your eyes, and just keep the dream in mind. Don't try to do anything. Various thoughts will come and go. Let them drift through. One of them may suddenly give you the feeling of: Of course, *that's* what I want. Or, *that's* what I think. Or, *that's* how I feel.

Any tiny discovery you make will probably occur as you make the effort to *stay* with the dream, although this may not happen every time. In any event, spending a quiet fifteen minutes with yourself is pure gold.

Here are some further examples of how some women saw their dreams. A woman alcoholic dreamed she was walking down the street and met an intoxicated woman. She felt that this was a *positive* dream because it was telling her that a break was possible between her healthy and alcoholic selves.

Another woman dreamed she was humiliating an enemy and elevating herself to his position of power. She took this dream to be a neurotic need for triumph and self-glorification.

Wanda dreamed she had killed Tom the elevator operator. From her dream analysis she recognized that Tom represented certain things that she hated about herself. She hated his subservient attitude, his refusal to take a stand for himself, his refusal to get ahead in life. Her dream indicated a wish to work with those aspects of herself that were blocking her growth.

A few days later she dreamed President John Kennedy was holding her hand as they walked down a garden path. She believed this dream indicated her wish for a charismatic and powerful man to rescue her from her mundane life. Her dream also pointed to the quality of her expectations. (Nothing but the best for me.)

Our dreams tell us the way we feel about ourselves, and how we can change and grow. Doris dreamed she was a patient on an operating table—passive and helpless. (*Most women who are depressed, by the way, see themselves as losers and victims in their dreams.*) This dream showed how helpless she felt in everyday life. As she began to take steps in her own behalf, her dreams about herself changed. Two years later she was able to see herself at a table arguing with some people. There she was, standing up for her own point of view.

How different this was from Lydia's dream, in which she had an argument and retreated to a cave. This dream pointed up Lydia's uninvolvement and indicated that withdrawal was her method of coping with stress.

As you relate to your dreams, remember that *dream symbols are not fixed and universal*. A cat in a dream will mean one hundred things to one hundred different people. You are responsible for your own dream symbols. Schopenhauer, a German philosopher, said that everybody acts in his dreams in agreement with some aspect of his character. These aspects come from deep within you, very often beyond consciousness. This doesn't mean that you are going to do what you *do* in the dream. The dream may only relate to some small bit of your intrapsychic or interpersonal life.

Nellie, a woman in psychoanalytic treatment, was

relating a dream. "I was in some far-off, isolated country. There were fortifications like the Maginot line in France. I was in one of them, and to protect myself from the dangers outside I was to secure a metal plate over the only opening. No one could possibly get in." As she talked about her dream, she exclaimed, "Is that what I've done? Surrounded myself with concrete and cut myself off from humanity?" This was, in fact, her main defense—an iron-clad withdrawal, or uninvolvement. She was troubled by the dream and returned to it again and again. The image remained the same. One day, sometime later, she said, "I don't have to stay in there. I put myself in there and I can get myself out." She burst out crying. "But I'm afraid to come out. Anyway, I can't get out of that covered window. It's permanently sealed." She raged back and forth, wanting to come out and not wanting to come out. She complained that treatment wasn't "so hot" because she had not felt in such conflict before starting it.

As she talked more quietly about her dream, she was asked, "Can you imagine yourself climbing out of the fort?" She was silent for some time and then smiled. "I was looking around for a way to get out when you said that. And then I noticed the floor was made of very hard earth. I suddenly realized that if I dug down deep enough, I could *dig* under the wall. Because that hatch was closed—but good." Nellie had begun to sense that perhaps the way to health was not the way she had come, but another way. Using her dream material, she thought that if she dug down deep enough, she would find a solution to get out of her "tomb."

Aggie, a woman in her late fifties, had not been feeling well for some time. As was her custom, however, she disregarded her health, feeling that her first loyalty was to her family, not to herself. She had suffered from chronic depression through most of her adult life, but the feeling she had now was "different." Yet no one could persuade her to see a physician.

She had the following dream: "I was in a long, low

house with many rooms. They were empty and kind of dark. But there was a naked bulb in the middle of the ceiling of each room, bulbs of very low wattage. I was walking through the rooms, turning off the light in each one. I felt I was ending something—like moving out—and I wouldn't come back."

Aggie went on to speak of her feeling of discouragement. "I feel, what's the use? It wouldn't make much difference where I went now." This session was followed by a break during a vacation period. When she returned, she announced that she had been to see her doctor and that she had been found to have a minor heart condition. She was taking medication for it and the "new tired feeling" had left her. Much later she revealed that she thought her self-neglect had been a form of slow suicide. Her dream, she said, had sparked a new feeling in her that if she didn't take care of herself she might very well die. (Remember, the light bulbs were of very low wattage.) Something in her wanted to struggle against that. She saw the turning off of the lights, one by one, as the gradual extinguishing of her own life. "They weren't giving very much light anyway," she said ruefully. "And those rooms were all empty. Why does an empty room need a light?"

Very often such dreams serve as turning points in one's journey through life. In an analysis of many years, there may be three or four such dreams among hundreds of others. Women often work with such dreams as if their very lives depended upon the work, as indeed their lives do, in some sense. These dreams are returned to again and again, sometimes with the repeating of old insights, sometimes with the awareness of new ones.

Many women have a cozy, proprietary attitude toward their dreams. They feel, "This is my creation. I made it. It's all my very own. It's my baby. No one else can have it for me, or tell me how to dream." The dream may, in fact, be the only facet of their lives in which they feel they have any autonomy.

Some women are frightened by their dreams. But

the dream is only expressing some inner thought, wish, or conflict. Having a dream is like having a conversation with yourself—a conversation that is impossible in your waking hours because there are so many distractions, sometimes so many inhibitions, and so much anxiety toward the idea of communicating with one's own depths. But how can you "furnish" an empty room that troubles and depresses you if you don't know it's there? Once you are aware of it, it is possible to make it into an area of beauty, comfort, and delight, if you choose. We all have empty, dully lit rooms within us. But we can all explore and alter them as we desire.

14

Help from Your Body

"Since for such a long time woman's only attainable fulfillments—whether they are involved in love, sex, home or children—were obtained through men, it necessarily became of paramount important to please men. The cult of beauty and charm resulted from this necessity. . . ."

—KAREN HORNEY

STUDIES SHOW that in some women, feelings of depression and irritability are insignificantly higher at menstruation. Dr. Natalie Shainess has found that feelings of helplessness, hostility, anxiety, and yearning for love characterize the premenstrual phase. Katherine Dalton found that half of the women who commit suicide do so in the four premenstrual or first four menstrual days of their cycles. Dr. Judith Bardwick found that self-confidence and esteem were high at ovulation time, but that the premenstrual period was a time of anxiety. All this points to an assumption that the endocrine cycle does affect mood. Dr. Bardwick theorizes that estrogen and progesterone probably influence the central nervous system because they alter the monoamine oxidase levels, and high levels of this substance are associated with high levels of depression. Dr. Bardwick says that when women are in the high estrogen phase of their cycle, depression levels are low.

If you feel your feelings of depression might be related to your menstrual cycle, keep a chart of your moods for several months. See if they follow your cycle. If you can predict your feelings and moods, you will be better able to deal with them. They may also relieve your guilt over your seeming instability!

This was stressed by Andrea Eagan who teaches a "Know Your Body Course." Ms. Eagan has found that most women she sees report that depression, anxiety, and irritability accompany the premenstrual cycle, and she finds that this is understandable since Katherine Dalton has reported that a drop in hormonal levels coincides with these symptoms. It is a myth, she says, that only neurotic women who have "not accepted their womanliness" get cramps.

She stresses, too, how important glandular factors are. She tells of a woman who, just past her midcycle, became depressed. Her face broke out and she developed a rash on her body. When she called her gynecologist, she learned that her corpus luteum hadn't broken down and that she had too much progesterone in her system.

Ms. Eagan warns her students that they may find themselves depressed several days after an abortion. This, she says, is from a readjustment of the hormones which drop when a state of pregnancy no longer exists. She stresses that it's important for women to know this. Otherwise, a woman who finds herself crying on the third day after an abortion may feel she is having a psychological problem. Ms. Eagan also believes that breast feeding gives women some protection against postpartum depression.

Pregnancy

The changes taking place in your body during pregnancy can affect your moods. Elaine says, "I was supposed to be happy about being pregnant, but I was scared. All these strange things were happening to my body. I feel as if I were being invaded —I didn't like the feeling. I also felt ugly—as if I were big and clumsy. People would come to me and say horrible things, like, 'Oh, now you're in for it,' or they would even come up to me and poke at my stomach. I felt so conspicuous—and I wanted my privacy.

"Toward the end I got terribly frightened. I thought, what if I'm like my mother who was always bitching about having kids. Then I began to be afraid the baby would be deformed.

"I also didn't like the way my doctor treated me— as if I were silly. If I asked a question, he'd say, 'I'll worry about that.' Now I see that I felt I had no control over my pregnancy. I felt at the mercy of doctors and that made me feel terribly vulnerable—a feeling I don't like ever!

"Boy, with my second pregnancy, this was different. By this time, I had gotten involved in the woman's health movement. I was interested in learning about midwifery and nursing—all that stuff. For my second baby, I insisted that I be delivered at home. I did the breathing exercises and I also read about my body and the fetus—and the changes that were taking place in both of us. I felt as if I knew what was happening to me, and I wasn't nearly as depressed. I would recommend that knowledge to all women.

"One last thing: I practiced the Lamaze method, but don't let anybody tell you that there's no pain. They tell women that and then women feel guilty when they start screaming. Again, they feel they're not doing something right. Again, it's their fault. Well, it hurts, Lamaze or not. The breathing just helps you feel more in control and more capable of going through with the birth experience without being drugged or gassed, but it's still painful."

Elaine has good advice for some of you. Learn everything you can and find other women to talk to. Compare your experiences. Discuss your feelings and fears. Find a doctor who will treat you in a noncondescending manner. Try to get together with other women to force changes, if need be, in hospitals. Up until women demanded it, husbands were not allowed in the delivery room, for example. Now women are demanding that they be allowed, if they wish, to have their babies sleep in their rooms, to have their husbands or other key people with them, to be treated not as ill patients but as competent women who are going through a natural process.

Above all, don't feel guilty if you feel depressed or listless. Instead, make sure you are not trying to live up to some idealized image of the always happy pregnant woman, who is calm, relaxed, assured. This just isn't realistic. Even lawyers have stage fright. Actors and actresses have stage fright. And pregnant women have their kind of stage fright.

Body Image

Even if you aren't pregnant, however, it is a good idea to get acquainted with your body. After all, your body is not a thing apart from you. It is you. You are it. The body–mind are one unit, and when you feel depression you feel it in your body, so that eyes tear, legs feel listless, and other processes slow down.

Unfortunately many more women are more alienated from their bodies than are men, for a number of reasons. Women are not usually encouraged to be athletic, and after they pass the age of thirteen, and indeed even before, they may be discouraged from roughhousing, from being "tomboys." Little boys are usually brought up with more of a sense of their bodies.

Not using their bodies, but merely prettying up their bodies, can be one contributing factor in women's alienation. Few women with whom we spoke had positive body images. Jeanne said, "I was very awkward as a child and very ashamed of the way I looked. I was flat-chested until I was in high school—and I felt this was worse than having leprosy. I was ridiculed, and I felt my parents were ashamed of me. My father would have loved to have had a busty daughter!

"I had a very bad posture which I think was related to not feeling good and proud about the way I looked. I really wanted to hide.

"I got better-looking as I became older. But I have always felt self-conscious about my body. I've always had this feeling that other women had much better bodies than I did—*always*."

Celeste, the mother of one son, says, "Pregnancy changes your body. You get stretch marks in the oddest places! They're like scars to me. I'm ashamed of them. I see all these young girls on the beach and I die inside.

"I don't like to admit this, but the way I feel has so much to do with the way I look, and yet I tell myself that it's the real me that counts, not the plastic image. Still, that's where it's at.

"I think what women have done is internalized the male fantasy of what beauty in women is. I remember this funny conversation I had one day with a friend. I was telling her that another friend of ours had gotten together with some women friends and they all had taken off their clothes, showed each other their bodies, and talked about what they liked and didn't like about themselves. This woman had found this a very supportive experience. She said at the end, 'I like my body more now.' To which my other friend replied, 'Yeah, and just let one man tell her she's less than she should be and she'll start hating herself again.'" We hope not.

Feelings about our bodies are the products of a culture which has not blessed women with varying positive images of themselves. Skinny young girls are the cultural ideal. That look became internalized as one feature of an ideal image, which most of us can never realize. This can be one of the many sources of self-hatred that contributes to depression.

Some women's magazines are attempting to change this unhealthy situation by putting older women on their covers. "Ordinary"-looking women are being shown demonstrating home products. Yet women still receive information telling them they must dye their hair, have face lifts, wear "in" clothes. This "information" can be negative in that it carries subtle and repeated put-downs, i.e., You don't really look so good but can look better if you do these things.

Alienation from one's body can also be traced to a deeper cause. An unconscious body image which develops in a child is often related to the body image the parent has of the child. If you were raised by a mother who did not feel positively about her own body (who felt sex was dirty or something women were obliged to give to men, who felt she was too fat or too thin, too flat or too hairy), her attitudes might have influenced the way you feel about yourself.

As Martha says, "My whole body image was always my mother's. She would buy underpants and then divide them up with me—even though I was so much younger than her. I would think they were too big, but she would say they fit.

"I recently lost thirty-five pounds. I'm very proud of losing it. I feel now that I am myself—and not my mother. But she hates the fact that I've lost the weight; she keeps telling me that I'm too skinny.

"I think I lost weight because I am changing—emotionally and sexually. My pattern has always been to give up, and this extended to dieting and exercise. But now I feel as if I can do things, and that includes exercising. I do yoga now and I can do a headstand. But you know, it's funny. I had a dream that I was showing the headstand to my mother and she was trying to push my legs down. Which tells me what I know already—my mother doesn't want my body to change."

Learning to Like Your Body

What solutions are there to this alienation so many women feel? These women made the following discoveries for themselves.

Lorraine says, "I always disliked my body until I joined a health club. There was a women's dressing room with a sauna and steamroom, and I saw women standing and sitting around naked—and luxuriating in their bodies for the first time. It made me realize that my body was pretty good, not so bad—and that there was an infinite variety of bodies. I got more comfortable about walking around naked, and I began to feel more comfortable about myself too."

Aphrodite says, "I was very depressed after my divorce and I joined a judo course. It helped me enormously in many ways. For one thing, my lethargy went away as I was forced to do strenuous exercise.

"For another, once after about six months, I was able to see that if I were attacked I had a chance of fighting back. I still had a long way to go—but it was a beginning. This was great for my ego. I would walk out on the street feeling strong and powerful. I didn't feel as vulnerable as I always had and that was important, because I was frightened to be alone, without a man. I had always been used to having a man around to protect me. The idea that perhaps I could protect myself was positive.

"Another very important thing for me was to learn how to express anger and judo helped me with that —enormously. For example, in the beginning we had to learn to make a fist. I couldn't do it. That kind of assertive behavior had been alien to me, and I felt so unfeminine and so ridiculed by making a fist—it made me feel like a man and I didn't like feeling that way at all. But I struggled against this feeling because I felt I should. And, *voilà!* Finally, I was able to make a fist. And to punch. And not only that, but to give a yell when I did it!

"I saw myself for the first time as a forceful person. All of that self-effacing behavior I had, always smiling even when I wanted to yell or scream—well, I could feel something changing in my body. You must understand I had to fight against this tooth and nail. I was confronted with enormous self-hatred because I felt so ugly and masculine and everything. I was fighting against a terrible conditioning. But I put up the good fight and eventually I didn't feel so funny any-more when I yelled as I punched the air with my fist.

"In my bedroom, alone, I'd punch as I said No, No, No! You'd be amazed at the good this did me. If you don't believe me, try it in front of your own mirror, saying No, No, No. You may find you have a little girl voice which isn't at all effective. I think most women have this problem. I remember reading an ar-ticle that said women couldn't yell when attacked because they were embarrassed to disturb anyone— or they were afraid to call attention to themselves. That is masochistic. It's important to feel that you can express anger when you must, when you want to."

Marty, another woman in Aphrodite's class, says, "I had never realized how much self-hatred I had toward my body until I was in a judo class. In the beginning I felt like this wasn't even me in there—I learned that I had seen my body as something apart from me.

"When I was doing these exercises and running around in a sweat suit, I remember feeling and think-ing: *How weak you are. How ugly you are. You can't do anything. You'll never be good at this. You're just a woman. A helpless, vulnerable, feminine woman.* In the beginning I would cry with rage. But the other women in my class encouraged me to stick it out. Now I feel more in touch—with my tissue, my muscles. It's not just a question of not getting backaches any-more. Anyway, in the beginning, you are sore as hell. . . . No, the thing is that you feel strong, and I be-lieve that when you feel strong in body you are pre-disposed to feel strong in spirit. There's a connection there, a connection that women have overlooked in their search to become stronger."

Claire says, "When I'm feeling good I exercise. When I am depressed, it's hard for me to get on a bicycle. It's like: Where am I going to go? Who am I going to see? I can't, I'm stuck here!

"Then I have to talk to myself. I say, 'Look, you're not going to be like your mother, sitting and waiting for something to happen. You can't just sit here. Get up off your ass and do something!' That usually helps."

Getting in touch with your body can involve much more than simple physical exercise. Samantha, for example, was in her forties when she found herself going through a terrible depression. "Life is full of disappointment," she says. "Mine is that I've never married and never had children. When I became forty, I felt as if I were falling apart. And insights alone didn't seem to help.

"One day I said to myself, if I stand up and take a deep breath, it will be all right. I think I'll take singing lessons. I wouldn't wait—I started at once. It was just what I needed, a way to use my body. I developed a lyric soprano voice—and this was after I'd turned forty.

"I know how to use my total energy now. And I've learned that when you're depressed, if you can pull out a new aspect of creativity in yourself, you'll be all right."

Jamie says, "For years, I hated myself because I never measured up to what the girl on the *Seventeen* magazine cover looked like. It was only in recent years that I learned not to be angry with myself, but to be angry at magazines for oppressing me with their images of what I was supposed to look like."

It is a big step to overcome this cultural conditioning. Women who have had mastectomies have to fight terrible feelings of anger, embarrassment, and shame. Clarissa said, "After I had my right breast removed, I did not feel that I was the same woman. I used to be confident and pretty and easy-going. But I felt that people were talking about me, ridiculing me. It was the most terrible time of my life. I had to reevaluate the way I felt about myself."

Perhaps one of the most important questions for a woman in this position is the one Betty asked herself when she continued to feel anguished over the loss of a breast. That is, "Is there nothing more to me than a breast?" Betty realized that even two years after the operation, although she was in excellent health with no evidence of a recurrence, she still felt depressed and even guilty that she had "done this" to her family!

But when she finally asked herself "Is there nothing more to me than a breast?" she realized she was feeling like an incapacitated person when, with few exceptions, she could do everything she had ever done. As she thought about the question, she grew more and more indignant. And one day, as she was driving to the shopping center, she exclaimed out loud, "Of course there is!" As soon as she said that, she saw that she had grieved too long over the loss of her breast.

Her mood began to improve slowly following this incident. When her family remarked that she looked better, she had to share her new discovery with them. "I realized I was more than a breast." They answered that they always knew that, but were worried that she would never realize it herself.

Her question "Is there nothing more to me than a breast?" could be translated dynamically: Is perfect the only possible way to be? Her answer to that helped her to make a breakthrough. She could then begin to think in terms of the many alternatives she had. Her cure from her depression began.

The Body and Depression

We know that certain drugs can relieve a severe depression, just as certain drugs can have a tranquillizing effect on anxiety. However, the questions of how and why remain.

Dr. Nathan Kline, the author of *From Sad to Glad,* believes that depression "is probably triggered by some disarray in the biochemical tides." He believes that depression is fundamentally a "biochemical disorder" and believes there is a biochemical predisposition to depression.

The biochemical causes or effects of depression continue to be studied just as there are continuing studies of other psychological disorders. Whether the issue of a biochemical predisposition to depression can ever be decided one way or another is debatable, for it may not be a matter of either/or. It is highly possible however, that constitutional factors—that is, biochemical factors—have an influence in some cases of depression.

Just as some children are born with a greater or lesser sensitivity to sound (e.g., noise, music) or to visual stimuli (e.g., nature, art), just as they respond differently depending upon the physical structure of their bodies, just as they may be more or less susceptible to physical illness and trauma, so may they be more or less susceptible to psychological trauma. It seems that we would have to accept this premise if we believe at all in the principle of wide-ranging individual differences. We want to make clear, then, that we are not negating the premise of a biological predisposition to depression. We are only saying that it is necessary to secure incontroversial research data to that effect.

In the 1950s there was an impressive clinical study reported on depression in preschool children. These were children in families of naval personnel who lived at a naval station. Some young children were admitted to the hospital with vague complaints. Signs and symptoms included paleness, poor muscle tone, poor appetite, sleep disturbances, irritability, fatigue, disinterest, lethargy, and low-grade fever. Without any special treatment the children improved in the hospital and were sent home, without a medical diagnosis. But it was clear that they had had symptoms compatible with depression. Within a few weeks or months some children were readmitted into the hospital and again returned home with a spontaneous improvement.

Some detective work was done. It was found that these children were permitted to watch television for six to ten hours a day. In watching so long the children were not being as active as young children ordinarily are. It is not known if they began to produce any substance that may be associated with depression because they were not tested for anything like that.

But when the children were hospitalized (where there were no television sets) and had the opportunity to move about and play with other children, their symptoms would quickly subside.

In the author's clinical work with depressed college students, a frequent finding coincides with that found above. Without the required physical education classes, without the encouragement of participation in physical activities, without even having to get up in the morning to attend classes regularly, many students seemed not to be fulfilling basic personal requirements for physical movement that their bodies needed. One can conjecture that they may have been accumulating a toxic substance in their bodies as a result (effect) of such inactivity and that their depression was precipitated partially by that accumulation. Whenever possible, along with psychotherapy and/or medication, a regular program of some form of physical activity was recommended. While this area has yet to be further researched, the results with such a program were encouraging.

The body normally depends upon the movement of its various parts to maintain itself in good order. As muscles move, they assist the circulation of blood throughout the body. That movement might be understood as a massaging effect, encouraging the proper flow of blood through the tissues of the body, where the exchange of substances (nourishment and waste) takes place.

Suppose we regard the body as a finely honed machine which requires a particular level of lubrication and fuel to maintain the best balance for functioning. We provide it with the foods it needs to conduct the business of keeping us alive and feeling well. That food travels along the digestive tract and some of it is expelled as waste. When the rest of it is reduced sufficiently in size and composition, it enters the systems which eventually convey nourishment to each cell in the body. Each cell uses (anabolizes) that nourishment for its maintenance. Simultaneously, it is forming the waste products (catabolizing) which must be eventually returned to the blood stream to be eliminated through the kidneys, lungs, or skin.

Each body has its own rhythm, or pace, at which this process takes place. If the process becomes sluggish for any reason, toxic waste products may accumulate and cause symptoms of illness and eventual breakdown of tissue. Anything that interferes with the particular pace of any one individual might interfere with a sense of physical well-being.

One question remains, however: Why were the college students so inactive? In each case the student's history included neurotic factors which could have been responsible for the development of depression, as well as for the very low-profile physical involvements. But why didn't all inactive young people succumb to depression? Some of the reasons are that many of them had other strengths, a greater sense of purpose, deeper interests, and a stronger sense of self. We might say, therefore, that depression is only one form of illness pointing to a failure in neurotic defenses.

Some other factors that cause depression include: toxic reactions induced by drugs, physical illnesses, and hypoglycemia. Hypoglycemia, or low blood sugar, is a problem easily corrected by proper diet. That's why it's a good idea to have a complete medical checkup regularly and to be checked for hypoglycemia.

To Do

The best formula for liking your body is to be involved with it. Play tennis, jog, golf, swim, do yoga, go bicycling. Get acquainted with how your body functions. Take a martial arts course or singing lessons if you think either might help you. And do fight the cultural and internalized "shoulds" of the standards of beauty which can cause you needless pain.

Some people feel that ordinary activity suffices for keeping the body fit (i.e., exercising thirty minutes a week). However, this is not sufficient for the depressed person. If you can put your body to work in the ways we have suggested, you will find that your depressed state can be significantly altered. Very brief periods of exercise are of course better than nothing but they will not do the work we are talking about.

A somewhat vigorous activity regime is helpful even for the nondepressed or most mildly depressed person. You should not make the mistake of thinking that quiet, limited activity will do more than merely maintain your present state.

Without exaggerating or spending much time on it, moving the body vigorously usually results in a sense of well-being that cannot be attained in any other way.

Last of all, remember that you have to express your feelings in order to overcome depression and inertia. How better to express yourself than through the use of your body? Try it!

15

Stages of Growth

CAMILLE, a woman of seventy, described "stages" in her life this way. "Up to the age of twelve I was a child, with a child's concerns, pleasures, and occupations. By the time I was fourteen, I was a worker and remained one for ten years. Concerns specific at that time were fun, money, family, money, boys, money, and getting married. When I finally did get married, I kind of skipped the phase of *being* married because I so quickly became a mother that the marital relationship seemed to exist only as a minor adjunct to parenthood. We took our marriage very much for granted, didn't talk about it, or ourselves. We emphasized children's needs, children's educations, working and having enough money for everything. It wasn't an unhappy time, but a very busy one, and the years went by so quickly that it seemed almost suddenly I didn't have mouths to feed, laundry to do, and all the hundreds of other things there are to do with a family.

"The pace changed dramatically then. It was as if I became a completely different person. And I really was. The two largest factors in making this such a different stage was the availability of time and money. That's when I became a student again. It was such a satisfying time because I could savor so many things I had heard of but had only sampled in tiny amounts. I think it was the time, too, when my husband and I began to have a marriage just for the two of us. This student/marriage state merged into a belated career stage. Here, again, the marriage gradually assumed second place. But it was quite different from the first time. We remained attentive to the marriage, but we didn't give it a great deal of time. Both of our careers were so important to our well-being.

"Now with my husband dead two years, I'm in another stage, still active in my career, but more of a grandmother and family person. It suits me very well now. The amazing thing is that I couldn't have predicted the way any of it happened, the time spans, the reasons for the changes, when they occurred. Each stage seemed so permanent while I was there, and so different from the one before."

One woman's stages cannot be another's. But there are certain generalized stages which most of you can identify in one way or another. Each stage has its different feelings, expectations, rewards, and pitfalls.

The Terrific Teens

Is there anyone more in conflict than an adolescent girl? She wants to be independent, but can't give up her dependency. She wants to be a person *apart* from the family, and her mother may be insisting upon closeness. While she feels she needs some room to grow as this new person, her mother feels left out.

We call these years "terrific" because things are either "terrifically great" or "terrifically terrible." Adolescence is a time of extremes, and one is either deliriously joyous or in the sloughs of despondency.

Because of all the changes the adolescent girl is going through, she may be happy as a lark one minute and "depressed" the next. This depression is not quite the same as the depression we've been talking about. Adolescents and young adults often describe a potpouri of feelings—feelings of discouragement, anger, pessimism, humiliation, frustration, or guilt—by saying "I'm depressed." This "depression" can last an hour or two, a day or two.

If an adolescent has learned, however, that drugs are useful to treat "down" feelings, she may easily conclude she needs to pop a pill when experiencing her brand of depression. This may account for some of the drug abuse we have seen among young people who feel compelled to "treat" a condition that might well have come to a natural conclusion with the setting of the sun.

We do not mean that adolescents do not become clinically depressed. They do indeed, and severely. Depression among adolescents may lead to suicide, the fourth highest cause of death among their age group. But the kind of depression that is actually a temporary dejection and precipitated by a minor disappointment doesn't require treatment. However, if a young girl has an ongoing sense of worthlessness and emptiness, and if her relationship with her parents is very troubled, these sudden "lows" will point more specifically to an underlying, ongoing, low-grade depression. On the other hand, depression may be masked by such behavior as drug taking, drinking, destructive sexual behavior, indiscriminate rebelliousness, or periodic running away from home.

The cultural "shoulds" that operate in an adolescent girl are horrendous. She *should* look like the models on the cover of *Seventeen* magazine. She *should* not imitate anyone's looks. She *should* have a boyfriend. She *shouldn't* be boy crazy. She *should* call boys. She *should not* call boys. She *should* be popular. She *should not* be interested in others' opinions. She *should* be independent. She *should not* be too independent. She *should* get good grades. She *shouldn't* be a bookworm. We could go on and on. No wonder adolescents suffer so!

Adolescent girls can keep several things in mind. They can accept their needs for privacy and apartness as legitimate. They need not feel guilty about them. They can try understanding that becoming independent is a gradual process. They can discuss their feelings about their bodies, their looks, their social problems with teachers, parents, and friends.

Most important is the parent-child relationship. Although most parents believe that their adolescent children don't want them around, don't like them, and reject them in every way, this is not entirely so. It is true that adolescents are straining away from those parents who find it difficult to "let the reins hang loose." These are the parents against whom adolescents must battle. At the same time, these youngsters want and need their parents, perhaps more than at any other time in their lives. Parents need to be told this and must remember it. *No child is ever too old to want or need a parent's love.*

The Trembling Twenties

Here again, we find a whole set of parental and cultural "shoulds" which can make a young woman feel totally inadequate. She *should* be independent. She *should* get married. She *should* have children. She *should* be self-supporting. Need we go on?

For some women the early twenties are often quite similar to the adolescent years. These women are still in school, still very hazy about their lifework, still financially dependent, still inexperienced in many areas. By the end of the decade, however, these young women can have become financially and emotionally independent of their families, can be well on their way regarding their lifework, can have established their own particular patterns for living and have evolved autonomously in many respects.

Maureen is a twenty-six-year-old woman who is beginning to come to terms with her life. Her biggest problem has been trying to break away from her parents and make a satisfactory life for herself. She tells her story as she sits in her apartment, which is a small and sunny studio.

"I didn't feel accepted by my parents—well, by my father. I remember that anything I ever did for myself or them it was never enough. If I came home with a B, it was, Why didn't you get an A.

"My mother always accepted me but I didn't care

about my mother. I just wanted acceptance by my father. They always wanted me to be a good daughter, which meant getting married, having children, and keeping a good home, and going to visit them on holidays, and calling them.

"My mother stayed home. She was depressed all the time. She was always walking around whining. My father got out of it by working all the time. When he was home, he slept. I was necessary for my mother's survival—I had to be there all the time. She would say to me, 'I'd divorce your father if it weren't for you.' Guilt!

"He also had affairs—which he was not discreet about. I know she felt almost totally impotent—she would have hysterical fits on what seemed like almost every Saturday. She would cry, he would break something and she would run into the bedroom. I'd have to talk to him, then run into the bedroom and talk to her, then back to him. This gave me a terrific sense of power. I'm the only person who can do something for these two people An eight-year-old kid walking around with a lot of control.

"I learned from them not to get angry. *If you get angry something would get broken or someone would cry.* I had my group of friends in high school, but I wasn't competitive as I remember. I was a cheerleader —which, now that I think of it, is a socially acceptable area for women to compete in.

"My looks . . . everything was awful. My hair— which was curly and frizzy—was awful. I used to spend hours ironing my hair. I tried a lot of products to improve my skin.

"I remember always wanting a dog. They always said, 'When we have a house.' I wanted to have friends over and they said, 'When we have a house.' But we continued to rent.

"My parents didn't think clothes were important. My mother would take me shopping, but always to expensive stores. We'd see all these gorgeous dresses and then she'd say, 'But we can't afford to buy them!'

"I met Joe while I was in college. He was the first

young man I had gone out with who my parents really liked. And his parents really liked me. And he
was attractive physically—and seemed like he'd be a
good catch. You know, he'd make money, work hard.
We got married. I think there was a lot of adoration
on my part. That continued for a long time until I
started wanting more.

"I had been pushing for us to go to marital therapy.
He said he didn't see any need for it. I was afraid
too, for what I would find out about myself. But he
finally agreed to go because I was carrying on in
different ways—mostly I wouldn't talk. I was feeling
very ridiculed a lot of the time. We had gone for a
joint consultation session and then I was waiting to
go into therapy alone. I'm sure I was depressed during
this time but it was a very quiet time—no talking, no
feeling.

"He was very emotionless. I had said I wanted to
return to school for a while and he didn't want me
to. He said he never wanted me making more money
than he was. The question of children also came up.
He said, 'Let's have a child.' I didn't want a child. I
had seen my mother confined by having me—I was
the only child. I thought that if I had a child, this
was going to be it. I'd be in the house and everything
else would be cut off.

"After a while, he said to me, 'Look, you have to
make a choice, it's either me or school.' I said I was
going to school. I can remember the scene of me sitting in the living room writing my biography sketch
and Joe sitting in the bedroom watching television,
not talking to me about it.

"I was doing social work, but I needed a master's
to get further. So while in the beginning I liked the
job, after a while I felt stuck, which also made me
feel depressed.

"I also began having an affair. It made me feel
good, but I felt guilty. My husband and I had a lot of
difficulty about sex. He often told me I was frigid.
That my body wasn't developed the way he'd like it

to be developed. I had terrible feelings, in which I incorporated a lot of what he said.

"This relationship began about five months before I had made the definite decision to get a divorce. It was good for me, because it made me feel that I had a pretty good body and that I wasn't frigid. That I could give someone else pleasure. It was also like a game I was playing. Joe would say, 'Why don't we go to bed?' and I could say to myself, 'Well, I'm doing it elsewhere, I don't need you.' There was a joke in my head: 'I'm getting it at the office.' That did push me to making a decision about a divorce.

"I remember I called him at work and he came up. I was sewing buttons on my coat. He said, 'Hi.' I said, 'Joe, I want a divorce.' He said, 'You don't really mean that.' I said, 'Yes, I mean it.' And then we started talking about telling our parents. I was totally flat. He started getting very emotional. I was very quietly depressed—almost as if I moved myself out of the situation.

"I moved back to my mother's. Joe said he would try to change, but I felt as if my mind was made up at that point. I was very cold.

"I started therapy soon after, and continued working. Then I found my own apartment. I was glad to get out of my parents' home because they were urging me to try once again with Joe, to give up ideas of school, and to have a baby.

"I got a job, but there were layoffs and I was laid off and I was depressed over that. I had to learn not to blame myself, that it wasn't my fault.

"I was also depressed because I wasn't able to get into a relationship that I liked. I was talking with a woman friend, and I was telling her that I was feeling better about myself, and saying I was learning that I could have not only female but male friends who could be platonic. I was also learning to be more comfortable with women. She said, 'Have you ever thought about why you've never been able to get it together with a man?' That night I was so depressed.

I remember crying. That was the night I started smoking again. I tried to write some of my feelings down.

"Sex has always been a criterion with my friends. If you're not sleeping with anyone, how can you feel fulfilled?

"I joined a women's group. I had a very negative view of my mother, therefore of me and other women. Now my feelings about women are much more positive.

"I did meet a man at a church group, but he was bordering on schizophrenia. He was a hustler, a scalper. He drank. He was attractive, different. I knew it wasn't going anywhere and I knew it was destructive. He was into sado-masochism . . . and I knew that I wasn't *that* sick! I knew afterward why I had gotten myself into that relationship—because I would be an object—and it wouldn't be a relationship. There would be sex, but no commitment.

"I think because I had to be accepted and liked, no matter who the person was, I didn't tell him that he frightened me. But eventually, I was able to tell him that I didn't want to see him anymore.

"I would smoke grass to escape, but it never worked if I was depressed, although occasionally it helped me sleep, so I could fall asleep and not think. I have taken acid, and smoked hash, and taken coke, but that was just experimentation. I've never been part of the drug scene. I think, luckily for me, I couldn't afford it. I do like grass when I'm with people, and I'm feeling fine and it's a social thing—to relax, to feel better.

"Now I can express anger to my father and he's learning to accept it. He's accepted, too, that he doesn't have to be the idealized, all-perfect father who never makes a mistake.

"Therapy has shown me again and again that my mother is who she is, and I'm me and we're not the same people. Because my mother is sitting in the house and not doing anything doesn't mean that I'm going to do the same thing. That's been a very big thing.

"Therapy has also taught me that I'm not responsible for my mother's life. I'm not responsible for my father's life. I don't have the power or control. And I don't have to sacrifice my life for them because that is not going to accomplish anything.

"Before, my mother would call and I'd think, 'Oh, she's going to make me feel guilty again,' and I'd take it. Now I tell her firmly, 'Look, I don't want to talk about this. I can't listen. I'll talk with you another time.'

"I would like to run something eventually, to have control over an agency. I'd also like people to know who I am. I've felt that I've not been recognized and I want to be recognized. I am ambitious and I am a hard worker. I don't know how much of that I'd like to retain. . . . I'd like to travel and see what's going on out there. I'd also like to take a lot of courses, to see if I like painting, sketching. I felt that my parents didn't give me enough of that when I was young, so now I feel that I'll try to give some of it to myself. I have a list!

"Next week I'm taking a macrame course—and I'm taking Spanish, which is good for my work, too.

"The more I do, the better I feel. Absolutely.

"I think I got into social work as a way to help people. I feel I will do what I can, but I am not going to bang my head against a wall. Yes, I am also going to ask other people for help.

"Today I will do things on my own. Before I wouldn't do anything unless somebody were doing it with me—preferably a man.

"I know my depressions are less frequent and are of lesser intensity. Now that I'm getting more independent, I like myself more. I don't cry much, but I sometimes get these blanking-out periods when I'm at parties and I feel as if I'm being ignored. People then will occasionally say to me, 'You don't look like you're here.'"

There is a repetitious theme running through so much of what Maureen says and does. Her initial contact with the world, through her parents, was a sadly distorted one: Men are uninvolved with family and untrustworthy; women are impotent and whining. While it was burdensome that a little girl had to be peace-maker, arbitrator, and the only reason for the family's remaining together, that position did afford her a sense of importance, of strength. She was forced not to be disinterested as her father was, and not to be weak as her mother. Her position in the family provided her with strength. At the same time, it robbed her of a carefree childhood.

In marrying, Maureen felt that she could be with someone who accepted her and upon whom she could depend. She could also get away from her role as family caretaker. She was ready to use her strengths. But her husband seemed unable to let her expand academically and in her career. He unconsciously tried to immobilize her by ridiculing her and casting doubts in her mind about herself.

Having learned "not to get angry" early in life, she could not—would not—respond with the resentment and rage she felt. She remained silent: "I wouldn't talk." She felt guilty about wanting so much. She felt ashamed for not being a "good wife." Her solution was to repress everything—"no talking, no feeling." It was during this time that she thought she was depressed and sought treatment.

Joe wanted to solve the dilemma by having a baby. But Maureen was wise enough to know what her feelings were about that. A child hadn't cemented her family together, and she wasn't about to place her own child in that position.

This belief has frequently provided a common motivation for having children. A baby is supposed to make a poor marriage "work better." Sometimes a second and third baby is supposed to make it work. But the partners in a shaky marriage can rarely stand the added restrictiveness and burdens of parenthood. The marriage may then go further downhill, while satisfaction in living together revolves solely around the children. These are probably the most hollow of poor marriages, for when the children no longer provide a mutual central concern, the partners have nothing left to say, to do, to share, or to enjoy together.

Even though Maureen's husband pressured her a good deal and threatened "Either it's me or school," she held to her position. But she paid dearly for it in keeping her feelings deep inside. She felt no right to her anger or her wishes and could only feel guilty that she harbored them.

While the divorce seemed inevitable, it did not solve Maureen's dilemma. She did not suddenly lose the signs of depression. She still had to go through a growing, developing process. So many areas of her life —relationship to peers, to men, to parents, to her own growth—had been stunted. A divorce could not automatically change all that.

She had to work to establish all kinds of relationships. She had to learn to deal with her parents' demands without rejecting them as parents. She had to consult her own feelings to find out what opinions she held, what attitudes she espoused. She had to become entangled in a destructive relationship to discover that it was destructive and that she wanted none of it. She had to learn where her responsibilities began and where they ended. She had to say: This is what I want for myself and I don't have to feel ashamed of it, or unworthy, or undeserving. She's learned much of her limitations as well as her strengths. She learned to be alone and depend on herself.

These have been painful lessons. They've been learned with many failures, with some successes. Perhaps most important, Maureen has learned that even a failure may point the direction to hope, for failure is not the end of the road. It can be a beginning, can motivate a new effort, can add to wisdom, can lead to satisfaction in the recognition of failure as an element in living and not as an indictment of one's humanity. These experiences in growth are what the trembling twenties are all about.

The Threatening Thirties

One of two things seems to happen to most women during their thirties. One, they begin to feel their "cheerios" and sense their intrinsic power. Or, they may resign themselves to a predictable, but flat, existence.

Women who do well in this decade often find it an extremely busy one. They may be raising their children, which helps keep them on the move and feeling young. They may have stable friendships by this time which are very strengthening. If they have worked at having a career, they may have learned how to fend well for themselves in the work world.

Of course there are conflicts and struggles to overcome. Reaching thirty is not easy for many women. "I'm not young anymore," is a common and frightening feeling. Or, "I haven't done what I expected to do yet." There may be a restlessness, a need to fashion a new self.

Melame says, "When I had my thirtieth birthday, I panicked. When I was in my twenties, I felt that *anything* was possible. But now I feel that my life is closing in on me. I have to ask myself: What am I doing with my life?

"Also, I'm terrified of not being as pretty as I used to be. I've become very jealous of young women. Their bodies are nicer. They don't have lines in their faces. I worry about whether men will still find me attractive."

Aretha, a thirty-one-year-old waitress, says, "I find that I've become preoccupied with sex. I was never that interested, but now, it's gangbusters. I love my husband, but I want to sleep with other men. I feel very restless—and I want more experiences. I guess in a way I want to break out of the rut I'm finding myself in."

Sonia says, "I am in a difficult period now because I feel as if I want more. I'm questioning myself. And my husband can't stand that. He keeps making ridiculous comments like, 'You're not the woman I married.' I keep telling him that people change and grow. I just wish he would accept me for what I am rather than for what he wants me to be."

This theme—this plea for acceptance—was voiced by many of the women interviewed. Yet Joan, who had been a housewife in her early twenties and had gone back to work at thirty-two in a large bank, says, "I have never felt more in control of my life than I do now. I feel that I'm not a young girl anymore, and I'm treated with more respect. I enjoy sex more. Since I'm more self-confident, I enjoy people more too."

For women in their thirties, there are two important things to remember. The first is to avoid becoming an uninvolved onlooker and resigning yourself to sameness. Even if you haven't done the things you want to do yet, or even if you find your life not as satisfactory as you had hoped, don't spend energy looking back on the past and criticizing yourself for not having done something you can do now. Every year is a time for growth. You *can* begin to throw off some of the cultural "shoulds" that have helped to stagnate your life.

Second, remember that in your thirties, *staying power* is being tested. Can you tolerate the vicissitudes of staying with it—continuing to care for home and family without feeling overwhelmed, continuing to work at your career without the bright promise that the-best-is-still-to-come? Are you disappointed? Is it hardly what you expected? Maybe not. Yet here you are, at your busiest, at your peak. Yet it doesn't seem like a peak. It doesn't appear as "great" as you had anticipated ten years earlier. However, the task remains, and has to be done regardless of your disillusionments. Right now you need everyday staying power. You are building your life each day, not with fireworks or acclaim, but with hard work, one step after another. You are *living* every day. The sparkle may be gone, but the steady glow can persist. In that living, you can find your satisfactions. They are there, but perhaps not those you expected. However, keep in mind that your disappointments, no matter what they are, are probably not with life, but with your fantasies of what life *should* have been. Can you build something more solid, something more real? Second, third, and fourth beginnings are possible in your thirties.

The Friendly Forties

The forties can be a good time for a woman. For perhaps the first time in twenty years she has time of her own. She can make good use of the time, reading, learning, working, enjoying her freedom and solitude.

A children's-book writer says, "When I turned forty I remember telling myself it's now or never. I *had* to do the things I'd always wanted to do before time ran out. One was to take a trip to the Yucatan in Mexico. The other was to work on a nature book for adults.

"At the time, by my forties, I felt comfortable with myself. I had lived with myself a long time and I pretty much knew who I was. That's a nice feeling."

It is perhaps in this decade that marital partners have to be the friendliest with each other. While certain pressures are gone, there are others that can be devastating. Visible aging is one that many women and men find overwhelming. But a greater one for some couples is living with their teenage or young adult children. Comfortable traditions may have been thrown to the winds, and some middle-aged parents find that intolerable. Women in this decade have to be friendly to themselves, to their partners, and certainly to their children. Friendliness here can preclude bitterness and pave a smoother path to the next decade.

Perhaps the major accomplishment of your journey to the threshold of the forties is the acquiring of wisdom. With rare exceptions, this takes a long time. Undamaged children are often wiser than most adults. In general, however, wisdom is not a common commodity in human beings. But hopefully by this time some romantic fantasies of the twenties have been laid to rest. The thirties' sense of overwhelming commitment and responsibility is tempered by experience and greater depth of understanding. The sharp sense of the loss of impossible dreams mellows. In the friendly forties you are beginning to understand that life is not what you thought it would be, nor indeed, what you insisted that it *should* be.

Toby is forty-five. She has experienced what she calls two "very down" periods in her life. However, today she says, "I've never felt more together in my life.

"I was brought up very conventionally, and I married early and had a child. I really enjoyed being home with my baby. But my husband's business wasn't doing well, and I went back to work as a secretary and administrative assistant. I really resented going back to work. Now I see how foolish I was. I made my husband feel very guilty. I was the great martyr.

"The second bad period came when my mother died. I had been very close to her. I really couldn't bear the fact that she wasn't around anymore.

"But those two periods are behind me. About a year after my mother died, I realized what a nice friend I had in my husband. He really had been very sweet to me. His business was also getting a little better, and he told me I didn't have to work anymore. But by that time my daughter was a teenager, and I couldn't sit home and brood about her all day. So I went to my hometown library and spent a week just walking around. Just picking up books and looking at them. I thought some book had to give me an idea of what I wanted to do with myself. It was really fun. And I settled on three projects. The first was to learn pottery. I'd forgotten, but it was something I wanted to do in my childhood. That was just my fun project.

And the other thing is that I'm going back to school to become a nurse. At my age! But I feel I would be very good at it. And the third thing is that I'm volunteering at a hospital one night a week, so that I can really learn more about what it's actually like on the job."

Toby has many years of studying and hard work ahead of her. But because she is doing what *she* wants to do, she is hopeful, optimistic, and feels alive. Her depressions do seem to be behind her. Her energy is not being sapped by the heavy worries found in depressions. It is, rather, available for the work before her.

American literature has not given us many strong women characters over forty. *The Summer Before the Dark*, however, by Doris Lessing, takes on precisely this theme. The heroine has devoted her life to her husband and family. As her children grow older they do not need her as much and, indeed, resent her intrusions. Through a friend of her husband's she acquires a job as a translator. However, it is her administrative skills, the skills which she has perfected while running her home, which turn out to be invaluable.

When her work comes to an end, she goes on vacation with a young man she's met. They do not have much in common and soon separate. Not too long after, the heroine becomes ill, but it is an illness of the spirit, as if she is suddenly sick of her old self. Living alone in a hotel, she goes through a profound identity crisis. Later she lives with a younger woman who is also searching for the new ways to be, to live.

In the end she returns home to her family, but she feels different about herself. She is less intent on pleasing others and more intent on pleasing herself. Symbolic of this, she refuses to dye her hair red anymore and lets the gray show through. Knowing she is able to survive on her own, she feels validated as a person. The book has a "happy ending" in the sense that here is an "older woman" who feels good about herself and her relationship to the world.

The Fabulous—or Frightening—Fifties

During the late forties and early fifties women experience menopause. Menopause is a natural condition which occurs in all woman sooner or later. It is caused by a decline in the level of hormones in the body, specifically the hormone estrogen. While there is a gradual decline in estrogen over a number of years, it is only when the level reaches a certain low point that menopause symptoms are experienced.

Estrogen levels influence various physiological functions. One of them is the heat-regulating center in the brain. Instead of sending out gradual and appropriate signals to the cardiovascular system for making temperature adjustments, this center seems to lose its thermostatic sensitivity, and it sends out gross signals which result in sudden vasodilatation. It is this sudden dilatation that causes a rushing of blood to the skin surface. Sudden flushing is seen, profuse sweating takes place, surface temperature increases, and there is a subjective sensation of intense and sometimes unbearable heat.

Reactions to this phenomenon vary widely. Some women will throw off their clothing to cool themselves immediately. Some sit quietly and wait until it subsides. Some become frightened and upset. Some get very angry. Initially, these "hot flashes" are irregular and infrequent, lasting from a few seconds to a minute or two. Later on they usually become quite regular, from cycles of every forty-five minutes to every two or three hours. Some flashes may be more intense than others.

These episodes are usually associated with increased irritability, fatigue, and sleeplessness. Phlegmatic women have reported that they feel these symptoms occur only because the sudden temperature changes awaken them all through the night. It is the repeated loss of rest that accounts for the irritability and fatigue, they feel. If their hormone level can be readjusted, these women report that they immediately sleep better and therefore feel generally less "dragged out."

Hormone levels also control the level of fluids in the tissues. When hormone levels drop, the skin is more subject to dryness as a natural adjunct to the aging process. This dryness may produce itchiness which may, in turn, also contribute to restlessness and irritability. The menopause, then, refers to the time during which irregularities in the menstrual cycle occur, and to the associated symptoms. It usually occupies a period of several years, with symptoms becoming less and less severe with the passage of time.

Subjective reactions to this process cause much concern for physicians and psychotherapists. Women who have depended inordinately for a sense of well-being upon their physical vigor and attractiveness are sometimes devastated by these very concrete signs of aging, signs which cannot be ignored. Because treatment is now available, however, no woman has to subject herself to this suffering.

A woman who tends toward depression as a solution for her problems may find herself more easily depressed during this period and for more prolonged periods of time. Extremes of depression associated with the menopausal period have long been called *involutional melancholia*. It is a severe, prolonged depression which may not respond to psychotherapy but only to carefully planned medication, administered by a person experienced in the field.

This extreme form of depression is not common. More common are the anxiety reactions many women have in response to such obvious changes in their bodies. Besides the flashes, women report palpitations, shortness of breath, vertigo, faintness. These symptoms may very well be caused primarily by physiological changes, but they may also be due to the fear and apprehension of being in such a vulnerable position. In either case, *no woman should feel guilty about having these symptoms*. Her obligation is to seek medical advice and to ensure her greatest possible comfort.

We mention guilt because the woman who has a need to be in control of herself at all times may suffer greatly when she finds her physical and emotional dependability threatened. Polly had been a "superwoman" all her life. She enjoyed her reputation and had been able to reaffirm it year after year. The menopause was the only period in her life when she could not dictate the terms because she tired more easily. She became furious with herself, feeling she had let herself and others down for the first time in her life. She found she could not push herself beyond certain limits. And when she actually dozed at a meeting, she became agitated. Later on she began to develop signs of depression. Her feeling of guilt at the time was enormous. She would not even see a physician because she felt that no one could help her.

Fortunately, her friends and family did not allow her to sink further into a depressed state. She responded well to medication, but resisted the notion that she might have to make some changes in the way she planned her activities. It was only after some years that she was able to relinquish, just a bit, her demanding "super" standard.

It is worth repeating, however, that many, many women react minimally to the symptoms of menopause. It is not inevitable that all women will feel terrible during this time. Moreover, whether or not a woman has to deal with the menopause, she would still be faced with her own aging process, with the changes in her family composition, and with changes in interests and occupations. Inevitably, these matters have to be confronted. When the menopause seems to be an insurmountable hurdle, it is more likely that a physiological condition is being made to "take the rap" for the fear of a confrontation with issues that bear no relation to physical fitness, except that it's more difficult to arrive at solutions of emotional problems if you don't feel well.

Today, the "empty nest syndrome" often occurs simultaneously with menopause. Pauline Bart did a study of 535 depressed women in Los Angeles and concluded that they were suffering from role loss. Many of them, she says, were Jewish mothers who had sacrificed for their children and had felt that the needs of their families always came first. Bart talked to one woman who had the same personal characteristics as many others: ". . . a history of martyrdom with no payoff . . . inability to handle aggressive feelings, rigidity, a need to be useful in order to feel worthwhile, obsessive compulsive supermother, superhousewife behavior and generally conventional attitudes."

Because she is rigid, this woman cannot give up the mothering role, nor can she help but resent her flown-off children for whom she feels she has sacrificed her life. Depression, Bart says, may also be a way for a woman to regain "the attention, sympathy, and control over her children she had before they left."

Bart found that Jewish women had a higher rate of depression than gentile women and she attributed this to the superwoman role many Jewish women play. However, she also says you don't have to be Jewish to be a "Jewish mother!" Bart concludes, "If one's sense of worth comes from other people rather than from one's own accomplishment, it follows that when such people depart one is left with an empty shell in place of a self."

If these self-effacing women have not had occasion to or need to find interests other than their families and homes, this is a time when many can seek to explore new opportunities for involvement. One woman found herself working for the Board of Elections as a result of a series of coincidences. "But I was really ready for it," she said. "And when the opportunity presented itself, I was smart enough not to let it pass me by."

Another woman had a friend who had tried to persuade her to work in an antique shop one day a week. She had always refused, feeling she didn't have time, was too old, and wasn't interested. However, one day she felt, "Why not? What else do I have to do that's so important?" Within a few years she had become quite involved in the business, had learned a great deal, and had been able to use her new knowledge as the focal point for many interesting trips.

Very few women approaching fifty think of having another twenty or thirty years at their disposal to do with whatever they will. There may be a tremendous freedom in these years for many women. For the most part, the daily nitty-gritties of ongoing family care are at an end. Things that seemed crucially important in earlier years assume a less critical position on your list of priorities.

Just think of what a twenty- or thirty-year-old woman would conjure up for herself if she were asked: What are you going to do with the next twenty-five years? Is a forty- or fifty-year-old woman less imaginative? She is twenty or thirty years richer in experience, in wisdom. She's twenty or thirty years more resistant to illusions and impossible expectations.

If a woman in this age group wanted to do it, she could educate herself in a completely new field, and have enough time to succeed in it. We're not talking about careers in the performing arts, or even as presidents of companies, but jobs and activities that millions of women work at when they are twenty, thirty, forty or any age. That a woman hasn't started a new interest by the time she's thirty, forty, or fifty is not evidence against her starting one when she's in her fifties. Believe it or not!

Sometimes it's not even necessary to start from scratch. A grandmother of fifty-five had worked briefly in a legal office before she was married. She had almost completely forgotten that she had had a particular knack for putting her finger on the right research material in the law library. When she decided to start a "new life," she asked for work as a research assistant in law. Her "knack" became known and she was soon in demand. Someone suggested that she attend law school, but she did not want to do that. Instead, she entered into a paralegal training program and is today a respected member in the law office where she works.

She brought to her employer and co-workers so very much more than any twenty-year-old could possibly bring. There is no substitute for the years that one lives. Yet women often do not value their accumulation of years. Instead they fear them, despise them. The value of their experience in many areas is something that women will have to discover and learn how to use to remain fit and involved in living.

The Significant Sixties

How a woman has handled her forties and fifties will probably determine how she feels in her sixties. If she has replaced family interests with interests of her own, if she has her own goals, she can find these years a rich time in her life. Much, too, will depend upon her health and upon whether or not she has good personal relationships with friends and family.

Women in their forties, fifties, and sixties inevitably encounter the notion of "ageism" in our society. Some men are thought to become more attractive as they mature; rarely is this thought of a woman. In order for a woman to cope with this prejudice, she will have to first fight ageism in herself. Marjory Collins puts out a monthly newsletter called *Prime Time* which is specifically geared to the older woman. *Prime Time* calls for older women getting together to prepare for new careers and better health care. It urges women to form menopausal rap groups, to share "our knowledge and fears," and to build positive images of aging.

Here are the stories of two women in their early sixties, both of whom have suffered from depression and who now feel optimistic about the possibilities still opening up to them in life.

Thelma is sixty-one. She has a sharp eager face and short blond curly hair. She lives with her husband, a doctor. They have a daughter, who is presently living in England.

"I had an ideal childhood," Thelma says, "but my

father died when I was very young and my mother had a breakdown and went to a sanitarium. I had to live with relatives and go to a different school. During that time I had a seizure—doctors were not sure if it was epilepsy or not, but was probably related to stress. Whenever I was happy, I didn't have seizures. It was some kind of a hysterical manifestation, I think.

"When my mother came out of the sanitarium, she and I lived together and I went to college in New York. I was very active in the theater. During college I was put on phenobarbital to prevent any further seizure.

"In the 1930s I took a teacher training exam and was able to teach French for $4 a day. I was also active working in radio, going to political committee meetings. I joined the American Theatre Wing, which Helen Hayes founded, in order to do radio work.

"At the time, I also went on dilantin, which you don't get any side effects from. Dilantin was a marvelous control. I'd only have a 'seizure' maybe once in two years.

"I married in my thirties. I don't remember wanting to marry—I just did. After, I badly wanted a baby. However, the first time I tried, I had an ectopic pregnancy. I was very depressed. The only two things I remember wanting to do were to learn to drive a car and to have a baby. This from a woman who loved Russian literature, political meetings, acting, teaching! I see now that my goals were to do what society had taught me women should do.

"I went to doctor after doctor to try to have a normal pregnancy and eventually I did find a woman doctor with whom I became great friends. My daughter was born in the early fifties.

"I was terribly protective of my daughter. She was born in an incubator and I worried if she were going to live. One night I came home from the theater to find she had a high temperature. I was tired to begin with and I had a seizure. That frightened me and I began my long trek to doctors again—and I went to 'the best and the brightest' doctors.

"My experience with some of these doctors was horrendous. One told me to go home and have another baby. Another told me that my depressions, worries, and seizures were nothing to worry about. 'You're carrying a five-pound pack on your back and you act like it's one hundred pounds,' he said. Another pointed his finger at me and said, 'What do you expect me to do, make a new package out of you!'

"I was doing a lot of volunteer work, but I was still depressed, although I wore a social mask with people. When I was in my late forties I went to see a doctor about depression. He gave me a pill combination of tofranil and elavil. I told him I was still on dilantin and he said that was okay. On my daughter's sweet sixteen, I had a battery of eight seizures—which I believe was caused by the combination of the drugs.

"I felt the doctors didn't take me seriously. Two years later I was going through a terrible period with my daughter—she was in her teens—and we were always fighting. One night I didn't know where she was and I got hysterical and I was taken to a hospital and given electric shock treatments. This was in 1969. When I came out of there I said, 'Never again.'

"In the meantime, my daughter was getting involved in the women's liberation movement. And I began reading about it too and all of a sudden everything fell into place. I realized that I had hardly ever done things for myself. I began to change my life then. I told my husband I wouldn't entertain people I didn't like anymore. I also took a long trip with my daughter and there we were able to talk to each other and renew our friendship. I am still wondering what place there is for me in the world. What should I do? I am looking for answers. But at the same time, I am going to be me."

In contrast to Thelma's upbringing, Gerri was brought up in a house with too many children, and she had to go to work when she was fifteen. Gerri has white hair and a ruddy complexion, and what one would call a sweet face. She is sixty-two.

"All I can say about my mother is that she was a good cook. She wasn't a wife, a mother, or a house-keeper.

"She was a very domineering woman—she had six children, but she should have stopped at one. She loved the first one, my brother. Then there were four of us in the middle and she couldn't have cared less about any of us. The youngest, a daughter, was the one my father loved.

"When I stopped fearing her, I hated her. She had a cat-o'-nine-tails that she would beat us with—and when I got older I'd hide it from her, so she had to keep buying more. Even my father was afraid of her.

"She used to curse us so bitterly. And I had to do all the housework. Even after I got married and had children, when I visited her I had to clean the windows and floors.

"She had been a servant in her own home and she made her children the same.

"When I was fifteen I wanted to continue school but she had such a fit I went to work. When I was nineteen she tried to squelch a romance of mine—and she succeeded. I was so angry and miserable I drank a bottle of iodine. When I came to at the hospital, my father was there. I told him I wouldn't go home and that I wasn't going to spend the rest of my life in a crazy house.

"I went to live with relatives, but my mother resented that. And in those days you weren't to live alone. You weren't a 'good girl.' So my father introduced me to a boy and three months later, at twenty-five, I married him.

"Once I married I realized he wasn't normal. I mean he knew how to act—and he usually had his friends around him and they protected him. I think he must have been brain damaged—he just wasn't right. I felt betrayed that he had lied to me, and I couldn't stand living in that atmosphere of mistrust.

"I had two children, but for seven years I lived in a vacuum. I had to pretend it was a normal life . . . I even had to make myself believe it until I could go back to work.

"From the minute he went to work, I was me. I had friends, worked with the PTA and the Girl Scouts, and I had a part-time job. I knew what to do.

"My sister came to live with me for a time, but she was too jealous of the children. At thirty she committed suicide. We all did without a childhood, but I think she still wanted one.

"One day I turned on the gas. I was in despair over the marriage. But my father walked in unexpectedly and so I said to myself, 'Okay, you're going to live.'

"As soon as my daughter was seven, I told my husband to leave. He went back to live with his mother. I moved into a ten-room apartment and took in five boarders. I only had two hands—if I were an octopus I'd have done more!

"I had various jobs—I was a receptionist for a doctor, did bookkeeping, worked as a cashier in a theater.

"I was so busy then, but nobody was sitting on my head and I was not depressed. I tried to give my kids what I could. My mother had always bought us clothes too big so that we would 'grow' into them. Well, first they looked lousy because they were too big and when they fit right, they were old. So I tried to dress my kids nicely.

"My daughter married a man who turned out to be an alcoholic—I think she copied me in marrying a weak man. She finally filed for a divorce, but she has two young children and it is tough for her. I want to see her more than she wants to see me. I think she thinks her friends are more important. I keep saying Sunday should be family day, but she doesn't agree.

"My son is doing fine—we always got along well.

"When I became fifty I was sick a lot with respiratory problems, but in spite of that I enjoyed life. Both of my kids had moved out but there were holidays and birthdays and we went to the park with the grandchildren. I had many friends then too.

"I retired at sixty, but I found that I wasn't used to sitting alone all day not talking to anyone. I was bothering my daughter too much, wanting too much of her time. Also, three friends died. So I had to take stock. I asked myself, 'What do you really want?'

"I knew I didn't want to play bridge and see the same friends for dinner every week. I didn't want nothing to replace nothing. So one night, I was watching television, and I heard about The College of 60. It's for people who are sixty years old and over. I knew then that that was what I wanted to do.

"I am now enrolled and I am taking a science course. I'm rusty, but I like it. I am also involved in helping get more funds for the college, and I've met many nice people my age. I like to study and read. I've always learned a lot from reading biographies.

"Now, I've found what I wanted—mental stimulation. I've always liked a good mind. Now, just by listening I learn something. It's recycling!"

Both Thelma and Gerri have been fortunate in the sense that they have made efforts all through their lives to make changes. So many women and men give up when the going becomes a little rough or when they get older. They then live their lives out almost as automatons. They set up "safe" barriers within which they do what they feel is expected of them. Their main purpose in life is not to "rock the boat." In this way they avoid anxiety and encourage predictability. This system is fairly effective but it renders one so limited, so restricted and constricted that it is a life only partially lived, filled with fear that anxiety will strike if the "rules" are not followed to the letter.

Thelma and Gerri do not seem to have "given up." No doubt they have suffered considerably, but they have also lived full lives. It is interesting to note that Gerri, coming out of tremendous adversity, actually seems much stronger. Her life was a more vital one, lived more vigorously. While adversity can break a child, in her case, it seemed to strengthen her. Managing to grow through a childhood of such trauma, she acquired a resiliency and hopefulness that kept her generally optimistic and forward-looking.

Thelma, on the other hand, had an "ideal childhood." It was probably a very protected one. Perhaps her mother's illness, following her father's death, provided Thelma with an opportunity to strengthen herself. Yet she never achieved the toughness, the self-confidence that Gerri had. Thelma tended to use dependency as her main solution. Yet she vacillates between that and autonomy, for we see her repeated successful efforts to move into a different position.

Both stories illustrate the regular proximity of neurosis and health in the same person. This point is a crucial one for us to keep in mind. No one is ever all sick, or, in fact, all well. Even the most neurotic woman harbors "islands of health" within herself. Even the healthiest woman harbors "islands of illness." The majority of people always harbor a combination of characteristics, some of which could only be described as self-destructive and retarding, and some as growth-promoting. This is the principal reason mental health practitioners can feel that even a discouraging condition may have a good prognosis. For we know that all human beings harbor large reservoirs, sometimes almost completely untapped, of stamina, of vitality, of energy, of resourcefulness which they can use to cure themselves, if they can only find the incentive to do so. *This is the substance of any hopefulness inherent in all depressions.*

The tenaciousness of hopelessness is directly related to the standards, or expectations, or "shoulds," that we have referred to throughout this book. It is sometimes difficult to distinguish between standards for living that are established to provide a sense of direction and order to one's existence, and those which can produce the rigid, flagellating demands that undermine self-trust. But even if some standards are appropriate to one's goals, initially, they ought to be discarded should they later be shown to be inappropriate and nonconducive to well-being.

To the extent that you can recognize the restricting and retarding character of rigid expectations, to the extent that you can ferret out your relentless insistences, to the extent that you can accept the absurdity of your strangling "shoulds," you can live with less tension and rage at your inevitable "failures." The changes and plateaux can then be better relished and always serve as enhancements in an ongoing stream of living.

16

Loneliness, Shyness, and Other
Special Problems

KNOWLEDGE AND INSIGHTS are not enough to solve your problems, but they certainly become part of your solutions. Change comes by taking the time and having the will to work at your problems, while realizing that the need to work on yourself never ends. Once you see how harmful the "shoulds" you harbor are, you will have to decide whether or not you are going to try to change them.

At first change may seem too threatening or too painful. Often, an "I can't" is an "I won't." But as you find your pain and anxiety diminishing, as you begin to see how constricted your life has been, you will become more hopeful, stronger, and more resilient. You can feel more alive, and feeling alive, you will take possession of your true heritage, your right to be yourself.

The next section will discuss some of the specifics that have led to your constricted way of living. They include: inability to relax; shyness; lack of assertiveness; problems in expressing anger; loneliness; difficulty in making decisions; psychosomatic illness.

Inability to Relax

Some women yearn for the weekend, then find they can't enjoy it. They may be uneasy about not working. They often say, "I don't deserve to be idle. I feel guilty when I'm not working on some chore.

267

I feel so lazy." These are the same women who think of leisure time as empty time, and this is frightening to them.

A simple definition of leisure, however, is *to have time:* time to watch a child jump rope in the park; time to wonder if that noisy bird is really a blue jay; time to walk aimlessly; time to clean out the attic; time to watch a bird in a tree; time to paste pictures in a scrapbook; time to talk casually to anyone; time to wander into three shops to match some thread; time to find the right shade of lipstick; time to brouse in a bookstore; time to read a book twice if you want to; time to look at the funnies; time to doze on a quiet afternoon; time to let thoughts wander; time to write a silly verse; time for just about anything you might decide to do or not to do, but which *need* never be done at all. Leisure time is *now* time. Leisure time needs to have no past or future; it may or may not have a plan; it may or may not entail work. For example, you may like to write in your diary in your leisure time, or you may want to help paint a boat in that time. Use of your muscles and your mind do not contradict the notion of leisure.

Another simple definition of leisure might be the use of time which fulfills a sense of timelessness. To be pleasurably and willingly occupied, or daydreaming, even for a short time, but without any sense of beginning, middle, or end, would seem to be the very essence of leisure time.

An almost goal-less purposeless period of time devoted to anything that pleases or relaxes can be an anathema to goal-oriented women. They know themselves only in one way, and can accept themselves only in one way. Thus a leisurely, open-ended day is regarded by them with suspicion, with feelings of unfamiliarity and strangeness, and even with anxiety. "What is this strange monster of leisure? What am I to do with it? How do I cope with it? I wish it would go away and leave me in peace!"

If this is your problem, experiment with experiencing small snatches of leisure—five minutes here, ten minutes there—until the feel of *unmarked time* becomes familiar. You might start with something easy, like star gazing for example. You can build up to longer periods then, if you like. You may have to be active for some part of the time, but try to give yourself these little breaks.

When you start to feel edgy, force yourself to sit another five minutes. Breathe deeply. Let your mind go blank. Then, get up and do what it is you want to do. Practice this several times a week. Tell yourself: I am allowed to relax. I have the right to make myself as comfortable as I can. There are also publications available that describe, in great detail, methods for physical relaxation. They can be helpful in relieving tension, and ought to be tried if you think they might be useful.

Carla said, "I used to hate vacation time. We'd go off on camping trips and I'd hate it. I was so busy keeping the tent clean, washing up pots and pans, washing out the kids' clothes, that I never had time to enjoy the trip. I was always so relieved when I got home. But then I realized that I felt guilty about not doing anything. The next year we divided up the chores among all of us. Each person was responsible for keeping his own clothes clean. I brought some books and some knitting and my husband *made* me relax. After a while, I really started to enjoy myself."

Shyness

If you are shy you may be concerned about one or all of the following: How do I look? How do I sound? How will I impress others? How will I compare? Persons who are shy often have exorbitantly high standards or "shoulds" that they have established for themselves. But because these self-imposed demands are so extreme, they feel they are unattainable. And so the only alternative these people have is not to participate at all in a situation in which, in their view, they might appear less than "the best." They cannot subject themselves to the possibility of exposure, which perhaps will reveal them as ordinary rather than "the best," "the smartest," or "the wittiest." This makes them shy away from rendering an opinion, going to a party, or talking to a person they don't know well.

The fact is that shy people contain within themselves a perpetual self-judgmental mechanism against which they measure the things they do and say. Although they may experience the judging as external, it is usually *they* who are doing the judging.

Most domineering persons do not suffer from extreme shyness. But when they do, it is usually for the same reason, because of their need to be "on top," the "best." A woman who had attended an important business conference says, "I was not afraid of not knowing something, but I was afraid I would not say what I wanted to in the very best way possible. I could not be satisfied with just the right answer or comment. It had to be the best answer anyone could ever make. I wasn't out to satisfy a requirement, I was out to 'knock them dead.' If I had any doubt about achieving that goal, and yet wanted to say my piece, my heart would begin to pound and I'd perspire. I was so afraid I wouldn't say it right and end up by making a fool of myself."

This woman's "fool" was not really a fool in the common way we use the term. Her "fool" was a person who was less than great. She couldn't just say what she thought and what needed to be said in the context of a discussion. Her comments had to "floor" everyone.

A large number of shy persons are predominantly self-effacing. They feel their opinions and experiences aren't worth very much. (He's somebody. I'm nobody.) They believe they will please others by agreeing, smiling listening; and they *can* please up to a point. But their companions are often contemptuous of this fading-into-the-woodwork behavior. They feel, "If she thinks she's so uninteresting, why should *I* be interested in talking to her?"

There are ways, however, to overcome shyness. Here are some things you can do to help yourself. Be aware of your inner "shoulds" and "should nots." For example: I *should* not give my opinion for I am nobody. I *should* not state my point of view because it might be wrong. I *should* not compete with what Marge is saying, because Marge is brilliant and I am not.

When you are in a group, if you can speak up very early in the conversation you can frequently break the barrier of your inhibitions and feel more comfortable. If you delay, it becomes more and more difficult to say anything. A good tactic then would be to plunge in immediately, before other opinions have been expressed. That way, you establish a certain level of competence with the group. Once you've made the plunge, other remarks will be much easier to make; even if you don't make any other remarks, at least you've said something, and you won't go away feeling that you were a washout.

Have some chitchat ready for ice-breaking. How about, "Gee, I just came from an antique store." Or, "I've been gardening all day, but I feel great. I got my tomato plants in."

These are both good openers because (1) they reveal something about you to the listener, but not too much; (2) they convey you feel good, which is always nice to hear; (3) they give the listener a chance to give his or her point of view on antique stores or gardening; and (4) they are not "heavy" topics and therefore can be discussed for as short or long a time as you prefer.

For longer conversations you might prepare about three topics. These could be: "I'm reading this interesting book . . ."; or, "I had the most interesting problem occur in my office this week. I wonder how you would have handled it. Here's what I did . . ."; or, "I'm taking a pottery course at this new place in town. . . ."

Avoid bringing up topics or joining discussions that

make you angry or tense. Remember that you have the right to make yourself comfortable in a social situation.

When you talk, try to be physically relaxed. Sit back in your chair. *Listen* to what is being said. Try not to look grim. Don't worry about the sound of your voice. Look at the person you're talking to. Notice the color of hair, eyes, skin. This can help to distract you from too much concern about yourself. Comment, if you like, on something the person is wearing. Try to react to other people as they talk. Try responses like: "That's a fascinating story. What happened then?" Avoid yawning. If you're that tired, go home.

Search out new things to talk about. Says Laura, "I used to depend upon my husband to carry the conversation when we went out. But I felt inferior. I began to ask myself, 'What makes *me* interesting?' Well, to tell the truth, I found a few things, but I wanted to be something special. So I went to the library and took out some biographies. I found people are always interested in discussing other people—their motives, their problems. You might laugh, but it was the best thing I ever did."

Reading your local newspaper for about twenty minutes a day will also provide you with enough material to raise questions and converse all evening. Try to avoid preaching about the moral decline of youth, the sad state of the economy. People go out to enjoy themselves, not to nod as you preach about the woes of the world.

When you leave a group, don't just walk away. Many shy people who don't want to call attention to themselves feel the best thing to do is leave when they feel uncomfortable without having anyone notice. But people do notice and will feel reassured if you say, "Excuse me, I want to freshen my drink," or "I want to speak to Slim a minute."

If you enjoy people they're more likely to enjoy you. If you continually act hostile to them, you'll probably get critical or hostile feedback.

When someone tells you something, for example, "I have just read this interesting statistic which says that the Aborigines each have 1.1 children," try not to say "Oh" or "Oh, really" or simply smile. Someone has thrown you the ball and you're expected to receive it. If you can't think of anything to say, why not ask a question. You might say, "Why does that interest you?" or "Why do you think it's so low?" or "Does that statistic pertain to those people who have gone to live in the cities?"

Remember that while others may not be as shy as you are, they might also be casting about for topics of conversation. Anything you can offer to keep a conversation alive is probably appreciated more than you think.

This may be especially appreciated by the predominantly uninvolved person. She may not be suffering as you are, but she too might enjoy having a conversation. Because of her need to keep apart she will usually not initiate one, but will often respond warmly and gratefully to your overtures of interest and friendliness.

Lack of Assertiveness

Many women have problems being assertive. Some women feel that assertiveness implies aggressiveness, and that it is unfeminine. Taught that their charm resides in being submissive, "social," helpful, and understanding, they are unable to speak up in their own behalf. Yet at the same time, they feel helpless and vulnerable, unable to say "no," to state what they want, or why they want it.

This lack of assertiveness has been learned through traditional pathways—the family, the school system, the media—and can therefore be unlearned.

The two cornerstones of assertiveness are: awareness of what you feel and think, and the ability to state your position. While assertiveness implies speaking up firmly, you don't have to be abrasive, shrill, hostile, attacking, or offensive in any way. This point has to be emphasized for there is great confusion between being assertive and being offensively aggressive, and perhaps self-destructive. Some people are also confused in that they think assertiveness means leaping from awareness of what you think and feel to immediate expression of it. That can be counterproductive, however, and may spoil a personal relationship that you are not ready to terminate.

True assertiveness can be practiced with gentility, courtesy, and kindness. Any woman (or man) can be assertive without losing a modicum of charm or likable qualities.

In the dictionary, to assert is defined: to affirm or declare; *to state as true*.

That's all you have to do to assert yourself—state your true position, as much as you choose to state.

As already indicated, that requires no attacking of the other person, it requires no rudeness or show of hostility which will cause your listener to react defensively. In order to state your true position *you must be aware of what it is*, the first cornerstone of assertiveness. This is even more important, perhaps, than cornerstone two. For there is absolutely no way you can affirm or state anything unless you understand what it is that you are trying to state, a point that has been little understood in the problem of non-assertiveness. People malign themselves for not asserting themselves, little realizing that you have to know what you feel and think before you can assert anything.

By now you can understand something about the blocks to assertiveness. The principal block has to do with your image of yourself as a kind, understanding, non-demanding, always loving and accepting woman who equates agreement with all that is good and wonderful in a woman. We all recognize how spurious such thinking is. But we have emphasized over and over how much in the grip of this kind of thinking some women are. Their first impulse is to think they have to behave according to the way this image says they *should* behave. So when they are being nonassertive they are actually trying to live up to their "shoulds," and you know already from reading this book and from your own experiences what a drag that can be!

In addition to becoming aware of what you think and feel, there are two *intermediate steps* between recognition of your position and the asserting of it. These intermediate steps have to do with *evaluation* and *selection*.

To know you feel that Jack is a rude boor when he greets friends and stands talking to them without introducing you doesn't mean you are obliged to state, "You are a rude boor, Jack." That would probably bring the relationship to an end (which is good or bad depending upon your wish), and it also makes you something of a rude boor as well.

The intermediate steps require a screening on your part and an evaluation after you know what the issue is. Then, *select* what you feel is the *appropriate* thing you want to say, and how and when you want to say it. For example, sometime after the date, maybe, on the telephone some other day, you might say, "I want you to know, Jack, that I feel very uncomfortable when you are standing and talking with friends I have not been introduced to. Do you think you could remember to do so?" If Jack says, "Why don't you introduce yourself?," don't feel stupid and guilty that you are being demanding. Just say, "That's a good idea, but I find it difficult to do. Will you try to remember to introduce me?" And that's all.

You don't have to argue your point, try to convince, or anything else. You will probably lose anyway, because people like Jack can undoubtedly out-argue you anytime. So don't engage on that level. All you really want is to let Jack know how you feel. If he cannot hear and accept a simple request of yours, he will probably be even less disposed to comply after an argument. Remember, you have to do it your way. You cannot use the "weapons" he is so adept at using, unless you feel comfortable with them. You can rely on the truth of your position and your statement of it.

It is so important to find your own way, that is, your own method for asserting yourself when you are ready. You cannot pattern yourself on anyone else. Even the suggestions we make have to be sifted through your own screening and evaluating system to see how they suit you. You have to change the words to ones that are compatible with your personality and your way of expressing yourself.

Here is a general suggestion that has been found to be useful when you are afraid of engaging with someone you think can overpower you. The premise here is that if such a person feels attacked in any way, he or she will counterattack viciously. Since this person is so sensitive to the slightest suggestion of attack and even reads one into a completely innocuous phrase, it is important to keep this person from feeling attacked in order to make your point.

Hal automatically reacts defensively when you say "I wish you could have let me know you were going to be so late. I really rushed to get here." This type of defensive person will give you six good reasons why he was late. Furthermore, he will feel attacked, maligned, scolded, and ordered about by your words. That is because he is caught among the tenacious strands of his own "shoulds" which tell him that he *should never* let himself be in a position to be criticized. Therefore, he is driven to defend himself in order to restore his sense of inner unity. Beating you down is the only way he can do this without being overcome with his own self-contempt.

Your comment was a common one, but the use of the word "you" really offends Hal and sets him off on a defensive tirade—which will get neither of you anywhere. If you want to make your point without an argument, a shift from the second person pronoun "you" to the first person pronoun "I" very often prevents an ugly confrontation. For example, "I wish I had known I didn't have to get here so early. I could have gotten some pantyhose before taking the bus."

Nothing more needs to be said. You have informed Hal that you feel you've wasted your time, without accusing him of anything. Although he may still feel accused, he doesn't need to defend himself as strongly as he might with the original statement.

To repeat the four steps:

1. Awareness of what you think and feel.
2. Evaluation of what you think and feel.
3. Selection of *what* you want to say and *how* and *when* you want to say it.
4. Statement of your position when you are ready to state it.

$$\left.\begin{array}{l}\text{Awareness}\\\text{Evaluation}\\\text{Selection}\\\text{Statement}\end{array}\right\} \longrightarrow \text{ASSERTIVENESS}$$

In addition, you need to avoid sounding as if you expect to be rejected. Don't say, "It's probably too much trouble, but I was wondering if you could give me some change?" Say instead, "Can you make change for me?"

Say what you want to say without putting yourself down. If you are asked, "What do you do?," avoid saying, "I'm just a housewife," or "I haven't gotten my act together yet." You can say, "I work at home," or "I'm active in raising money for the library."

When you feel you have been put down, speak up. You have a few seconds to react, so try. As we've said earlier, you can always say, "Was that a put-down?" Or, you can follow the four-step outline above.

If you are being unfairly criticized you may be able to handle this with a little humor. Suppose you and Tim are going over a budget report. You disagree with a point he makes, and he says condescendingly, and *perhaps* unwittingly, "You don't understand this point." You can smile and say, "No, I don't usually understand much of anything." This is so patently untrue (for you wouldn't be doing what you're doing if it were true) that the absurdity of the remark can hardly be lost. It's a kind of left-handed put down of him, but the humor softens it and hopefully helps to instruct Tim as to his patronizing attitude. (Some women, of course, may prefer to say directly to Tim, "That was a patronizing remark you just made.") Don't, however, be surprised if your remark goes over his head. Just enjoy it yourself and go right back to the discussion. You'll feel better having said it. Who knows, perhaps Tim will register your absurd statement later on and get the message.

When you feel uncomfortable, or feel someone is trying to manipulate you, don't ignore the feeling. Listen carefully. If you feel anxious, take a deep breath. You don't have to make an immediate response. If asked, "Why are you so quiet?," you can say, "I'm considering what you've just said." Then, when you are ready, you can state what you feel about the situation. "I don't feel comfortable with the plan as it now stands. I feel that too much of the work is on my shoulders." You don't have to apologize for your feelings. Simply state them.

Nonassertive people often avoid any situation with which they are uncomfortable. If you can't bear to return items to stores you will sometimes keep the lampshade you bought, even if it's the wrong size. You'll avoid talking to a friend rather than confront her with something she's done that annoys you. This type of behavior often leaves you feeling unable to cope.

The best way to change is to practice what you are going to say beforehand. Role-play with a friend if that will help you. For example, "Listen, Mary, I have to talk to my boss tomorrow and this is what I'm going to say. What do you think?"

Give yourself a small assignment in which you can be more assertive than you ordinarily might be. For example, ask for change, return a dress, make a point in a discussion. Remember, one step leads to another.

Here are twelve common situations in which women have major assertiveness problems. Think how you would handle each one.

Situation: Betty has worked at a major department store for the last two years. She feels it's certainly time for a raise.

Unassertive Betty: Mr. Stone, I'd . . . uh . . . like a raise. I haven't had a raise in two years and I feel I deserve one. Besides, prices are going up and I just barely make it through the week.

Mr. Stone: Well, you've done great work, Betty, but money is tight these days. But I'll keep it in mind. (He picks up the phone and prepares to make a phone call.)

Betty: Thank you very much.

Assertive Betty: Mr. Stone, when you have a few uninterrupted minutes, I'd like to speak with you. (She knows she should be sitting comfortably with him, without interruptions, for this discussion.)

Mr. Stone: Let's do it now.

Betty: During the past two years that I have been working here, I have noticed that our sales have gone up by 15 percent. That seems directly related to the suggestion I made about the new promotion material. I also had the idea for that cute jingle that we use on the radio to advertise. There are many other things I could mention, but I do think I deserve a raise.

Mr. Stone: Well, you've done great work, Betty, but money is tight these days.

Betty: I know money is tight, and I've considered that carefully. However, my stretched paycheck is getting pretty tight too, and I feel not only that I deserve a raise but that I need it very badly.

Mr. Stone: Well, I have to think about it. (Picks up the phone.)

Betty: May I discuss it again with you in a week's time?

Situation: Mary is at a party. She is talking to two people when the man who's been sitting next to her turns and says, "I've been listening to what you've been talking about and it's all a bunch of nonsense."

Unassertive Mary: Oh, why do you think that?

Assertive Mary: You sound as if you're in an encounter group. If you're looking for one, you can probably find one downtown.

Situation: Harriet is standing in line at a movie. The woman in back of her keeps pushing her.

Unassertive Harriet keeps quiet but is annoyed.

Assertive Harriet: (turning around and looking at the woman) Could you give me a little more room? It's pretty crowded here.

(We suggest this mild approach because people who push in line are usually difficult people and will engage you in an irrational, defensive argument at the drop of a hat. If you want to fight, however, you can say, "Stop pushing me!")

Situation: Gloria notices she hasn't gotten the right change from the parking lot attendant.

Unassertive Gloria: Did you give me the right change?

Assertive Gloria: I don't have the right change.

Situation: Matty is having lunch with Bill who is telling her in minute detail about his love affair with Kate. Matty is feeling edgy and realizes Bill always talks about what he wants to talk about.

Unassertive Matty continues to smile and nod, smile and nod.

Assertive Matty: This is really interesting, Bill, but there's something I've been wanting to talk to you about. Can we change the subject?

Situation: Jane is having lunch with two business colleagues, Dick and Tom. There is a strike for better wages and promotions going on by the women employees at a firm across the street. They are discussing it.

Tom: I just think these women take things a little too far. Do you know that in Florida they want to put a bill through calling manhole covers people covers!

Unassertive Jane: Isn't that silly.

Assertive Jane: Yes, that is amusing, but I think we have to look at the larger issue involved here. What we are talking about are women who are being underpaid and exploited.

Situation: Joan is in a travel agency getting her trip to Europe organized.

Travel agent: What countries would you like to visit and for how long?

Unassertive Joan: What do you think?

Assertive Joan: I haven't decided yet. I'd like to hear what you suggest and then I'll make up my mind.

Situation: Judy is at a party. She is discussing a friend with Hal.

Hal: Ann is just a ball-buster, that's all.

Unassertive Judy smiles sweetly, not wanting to be called a ball-buster herself.

Assertive Judy: Well, once we start putting labels on people, we make any discussion impossible. How do you have trouble relating to her?

Situation: Laurel is at a committee meeting to pick a slate for the school board. Ben disagrees with her suggestion and says to her, "You're just trying to ram your friend down our throats. I won't have it. That woman knows nothing about budgets. She is impossible. I won't work with her. You know nothing about school boards either. How long have you been involved anyway?"

Unassertive Laurel: Why, I've been involved for the past three years.

Assertive Laurel: I'd like to tell you more about her qualifications before we make any decision. Joan happens to be an outstanding candidate. Look at her record. . . .

Situation: Corinne is going on a job interview. She has not worked in seven years. She had worked in radio before she had children. This job is as an assistant to a program director.

Interviewer: You haven't worked in seven years.

Unassertive Corinne: Yes, I know. But I'd really like to work.

Assertive Corinne: I haven't worked in a radio station, but I've been working steadily. Last year I organized a program for our school which raised over $2,000. I had to think of a program that would appeal to a wide audience. I know many people in this community and I know what they are interested in. I could be very valuable to you.

Situation: Sally and Sam are planning a date.

Sam: What would you like to do tonight?

Unassertive Sally: I don't know. Whatever you say is fine with me.

Assertive Sally: I've really been interested in seeing the movie that's at the Bijou. Or, we could go visit my friend Terry. She's having a few people over this evening.

Situation: Fern is telling Jody what she needs done this week.

Unassertive Fern: Would you mind washing the kitchen floor? I'm sorry it's such a mess but we had company last night. Okay?

Assertive Fern: I'd like you to wash the kitchen floor today.

Expressing Anger

In order to express anger, you have to believe that anger is natural. You have to believe that it is as much a part of you as your sudden feelings of gaiety when you hear a joke, as your regret at unintentionally inflicting hurt, as your sorrow at a loss, as your joy in greeting a friend, as your disgust at smelling a bad odor. You have to accept anger as a human emotion.

It's not a feeling to be ashamed of, to deny, rationalize, or hide. For no matter what you try to do, if your anger is aroused, it is there whether or not you express it, and it will have certain effects on your psychic and physical being.

In order to avoid expressing anger and running the risks that that expression may entail, some women suppress or even repress their anger. They then believe that they never get angry. It is difficult for them to express anger because they fear that they will lose the admiration they desire, or because they will incur retaliatory anger, or because they want to maintain a self-image (a Perfect Self) of sweetness and light, a picture that is not compatible with angry feelings. If this sort of woman becomes aware of her anger, whether or not it is expressed, she will feel ashamed of it, and can hate herself for daring to harbor even one little angry feeling. One young woman's favorite self-characterization was: "Oh, nothing bothers me; I don't let anyone get under my skin." Yet if a stranger even bumped into her accidentally on the bus she directed murderous thoughts at him. No anger indeed!

There is little that can be done to avoid having at least some angry feelings. If we can trust ourselves and others to withstand our anger, our next task, which is within the scope of our control, is to decide how to express it.

You can modulate your expression of anger without denying or suppressing it, or harming yourself. You can be abusive, or you can do what Phineas Fogg did in *Around the World in 80 Days*. Having been followed and annoyed and finally unjustly imprisoned by an obnoxious detective who had trailed him halfway around the world, super-courteous Fogg finally expresses his anger toward the man when he politely says, "I have to say that I have never liked you. And what's more, you play an abominable game of whist!"

Another way of handling your irritation or anger is in a very straightforward manner. "You know, I cannot continue to pick you up here if you are going to be late every morning. It makes me late at the office." That can be dealt with by most listeners, who then have the choice of "shaping up" or losing something they want.

When you are expressing anger, you will be much more effective if you keep to the issue that angers you. You do not have to put down the other person, or criticize, or judge. Here are three situations that illustrate this point.

Situation: Your husband has been watching the television set for six hours, although he promised to take your son to buy a pair of shoes. You have been stewing all afternoon. It would be far wiser to speak up much sooner, say after two hours. Do so in a direct manner. "It doesn't seem that you'll be able to get the shoes. We'll have to let it go until next week, but Bobby will be quite unhappy that he will not have the shoes. He needs them this week." Again, your exchange deals with the issue and is not attacking in a personal way.

Situation: Your friend says, "That dress makes you look fat." Your become angry.

Consider first how you feel. If you think that the comment was made unkindly, you might say, "That was not a kind thing to say," and let it drop. This kind of a remark can be quite eloquent. You may also say to a friend, "That comment hurt me. I spent all that money on this dress and I feel terrible now that you say I look fat." This at least leaves you with a measure of satisfaction. You have at least let your friend know how you feel.

Situation: Your boss says, "I told you I needed those reports by two o'clock. Why aren't they ready?" He gave you the fifty pages to type only one hour ago.

If you feel angry you can say, "Do you really want to know? It's because I'm only a human being and I can't type more than one hundred words a minute."

Loneliness

If you're lonely, you've probably heard, or been told, that the solution to your problem lies in "going out and meeting people." That's sound advice, but it's also simplistic. For there are many different kinds of loneliness and different reasons for it. Before you read any further, answer the following questions. They will help you to pinpoint the kind of loneliness problem you have. Later, at the end of this section, we will answer each of these questions with specific suggestions.

1. Are you lonely only on the weekends?
2. Are you usually lonely and miserable on holidays?
3. Are you continually lonely?
4. Do you have no one person to whom you are close and to whom you can talk?
5. Do you need someone with you in order to enjoy something?
6. Do you feel like an outsider?
7. Do you feel you are an overly critical person?
8. Do you often feel bored or restless?
9. Have you recently lost or been separated from a close companion?
10. Do you feel people don't want you around?
11. Do you have trouble making a contribution when you are with other people?

Feeling lonely is a fact of existence, just as are feelings of joy, sorrow, interest, and disinterest. We all have feelings of loneliness now and again.

Any woman can feel lonely when she has been alone for a time. She may then want to seek companionship. We call this an ordinary feeling of loneliness. In a natural, unneurotic state, people will gravitate toward people after they have not been with them for a while. It is also a natural thing to want to be alone for a while. This is easily observed in healthy children who, without any fanfare, seem to want to spend small amounts of time away from others. The young child who wakes from her sleep or nap often enjoys her own company before she attempts to join her family.

Sometimes, however, the problem lies in the lack of stimulation we provide for ourselves. This lack can be overcome by making some effort. Clara, for example, persuaded her church to run classes and workshops for people in the community. Men and women were encouraged to teach crafts, music, writing, and singing.

Another woman began a woman's art gallery. She found many women who had been painting at home and storing their paintings in their attics. The gallery became a place for these women to show their work, and also a meeting place to exchange ideas and enjoy talking with each other.

Flora had never felt comfortable with traditional political organizations, although she was interested in politics. However, when the Women's Political Caucus was organized, she began to work as a member.

Terri had a husband whose job caused them to move frequently. She wasn't prepared to change that lifestyle, for the moving did give her a chance to see parts of the country she ordinarily wouldn't see. But she was lonely. Finally, she put an ad in the local paper stating, "New woman in town would like to meet others in the same boat." Now she always makes a few friends this way.

It seems impossible for some to make these efforts. Unfortunately, children view themselves as their parents do. If a parent regards a child as incapable of caring for herself, then the child will not care for herself because she believes that Mommy or Daddy know better than she. And then she may feel frightened when she is alone and will go to any lengths to have someone with her all the time.

Joan was raised by parents who kept her very dependent on them, and so she developed little autonomy. As an adult, she thought her loneliness would consume her. She really needed someone around all the time. Joan wanted to help herself. What could she do? A first step would be doing small things alone—going to the park alone, going to a movie alone. Just because her parents saw her one way does not mean she has to acquiesce to their view.

The person who is domineering and who is isolated from others because of a continual need to compete, control, or criticize has a different problem. This person has to learn to listen to people more carefully, to permit others to keep their positions, and to learn to back off when appropriate. Hortense "knew what was best" for other people, and usually told them. She couldn't understand why they didn't always appreciate her advice. She complained of being lonely, but it was only when she began to take responsibility for her own part in this loneliness that she was able to begin to get close to other people. In trying to live up to her "shoulds" (You *should* always be bright; you *should* always correct others), she was instantly, and unwittingly, alienating others. Hortense had many strengths and she is a good, strong, intelligent, and helpful friend. She simply had to relax her demands on herself that made it imperative that she dictate, rather than exchange, ideas.

The withdrawn woman has another problem. Marge had striven all her life to avoid "rocking the boat" so that she would feel safe. She had neither time (because of her job) nor the resources (i.e., interest and energy) to grow and develop those aspects of herself that could lead to a sense of fullness, richness, and satisfaction. All of this could have given her a sense of occupation and solace when she had to be alone. But she didn't enjoy playing a musical instrument, gardening, reading, or much of anything else. Consequently, she was driven to find companionship, not because she preferred it at that moment, but because she couldn't stand the void she felt in herself. Because she had not developed herself, she had little to bring to other people. Her first step in overcoming her loneliness would be to become *involved* in some interest, to break the shallow living habits she had practiced. In her childhood, for example, she had been interested in building knickknacks with her father who was a carpenter. There are many ways she could build on this interest, taking a course to sharpen her skills, building things for her own apartment and perhaps for her co-workers, perhaps eventually teaching other women her craft.

Women have been too isolated from each other. Some women live in their homes, care for their children, and rarely get out, even though they want to feel part of a larger community. Many have even denied themselves the beauty and value of friendship. They perhaps have forgotten that friendship can help you survive the worst disappointments and ordeals. Friendship can be creative, supportive, life-affirming.

Here are some suggestions based upon our original questions to help you overcome your loneliness problems.

1. If you are lonely on the weekends, you'll have to ask yourself some further questions. First, what would you *like* to do? Are you interested in painting, handicrafts, music, literature, helping others, sports, exercise?

Where can you go to become involved in the area of interest you've pinpointed? If you're interested in tennis, where is an indoor tennis court? If you're interested in music, where ia a music school which might know of an amateur music group? Could you invite friends to begin a singing group? Is there a church which has a choir you can join? Do you know what keeps you from following one of your leads? Is it inertia?

2. Holiday depression or holiday loneliness before and during holidays is a special problem that many people struggle with for years. The principal contributing factor to this particular despair is the absence of or estrangement from family and close friends. It is not very satisfying to celebrate a special holiday by yourself. You probably carry with you an image of previous happier celebrations, or you have

an image of what you think your holiday *should* be like. If you tend to be unrealistic in your expectations, a holiday may always be somewhat disappointing.

What can you do to combat this problem? First you have to consider the ingredients that make for a happy holiday—or at least a less lonely one. These usually are: family, food, fun. Starting with the most difficult, family, you can raise these questions: Do you have any family members, near or distant, whom you can contact? Or are you someone who decided a long time ago that family members cause you more grief than anything else?

If there are no family members available, can you find a *substitute family?* This substitute family doesn't have to be composed of your peers. It could be an old man or woman in a nursing home, or an elderly couple living in your building. It could be a large family with many young children who would welcome a friendly person in their midst at this time. It might be adolescent orphans or neglected younger children. It might be visiting college students from a far-off country who aren't able to go home for the holidays. It might be a storekeeper you happen to know. These suggestions may seem wild to you, but until you've had the completely unexpected pleasure of welcoming or being welcomed in such a situation, you cannot know what fun it can be. However you do it, the point is to find someone, anyone, who might want to share your holiday. Keep in mind that there are many other lonely people yearning for someone's company on a holiday. That company might be *your* company. But they might be either too shy or too proud to approach you. Can you set aside your pride and your shyness and approach them?

Once you find the people, arranging for food is fairly simple. You do not have to spend your last dime on this; just a little fussing over one of the items can make your party festive. Having your guests prepare something with you can be great fun—and be a good ice-breaker too. It doesn't matter how the food item turns out; the important thing will be the process of sharing the work together. If your guests want to bring something, accept the offer graciously.

Plan to have a punch, or some candy, and a fruit and nut platter. If you go visiting, take some fresh fruit or some nuts along. Holidays are not for dieting. Enjoy yourself.

Have some music: if you play a musical instrument, you might plan to entertain—or invite a guest who plays. You might have a deck of cards or some other game available.

Holiday loneliness is a special problem. But there *are* things you can do for yourself.

3. If you are continually lonely, you probably are also depressed. In your case, you need to find someone, someplace, you can exchange words with. You must ask yourself: What arrangements can I make so that I can have more time to get involved with others? And what would I like to do that I feel I could contribute to and enjoy? Would I like a job? Would I like to learn more about politics, art, fund-raising, mechanics? Where could I go to learn about this? Would I enjoy starting a day care group with other women? Would I enjoy teaching cooking to a few women? Would I enjoy giving two afternoons a week to working with handicapped children? Would I enjoy learning about photography?

You must ask yourself all these questions, and then carefully think through your position. If you teach handicapped children, for example, you will not necessarily be with other adults. Is this what you want? Will you get satisfaction from working with children? Or do you really want adult company? And what kind of company? If you are taking a course, whether it be mechanics or photography, you may not necessarily mingle with the other students. At the end of class, people may expect to go their separate ways. Is this all right with you? Will you be disappointed if you don't make friends here? If so, where can you go where you will make friends? Most likely, groups that do something together—as opposed to learning something—provide greater opportunity for friendship. A woman's political group, a church group, or a community organization might be more what you are looking for.

4. How could you find someone with whom you could share your feelings? What about starting a book discussion group in your neighborhood? Or you could organize a woman's center where women could meet to exchange ideas. You'd need help to do this, but if you put an ad in the paper you might be surprised at the response. What about starting a women's consciousness-raising group? The National Organization for Women will help you and send you guidelines.

Think of five women you know whom you might like to know better? What could you do to get to know them better? Could you invite one to lunch? To an afternoon of shopping? Can you buy tickets to a show and invite someone you'd like to know better to go with you? People are usually delighted to be invited anywhere.

5. As we've said throughout this book, if you begin to rely more on yourself you won't be so lonely when you have to be alone. So perhaps you can try to do some things alone and establish new habits. And what about the rest of the time? Can you plan your activities so that you have a standing date with a friend for a movie on Tuesday or a dinner together on Friday so that you have things to look forward to to make your week seem less dull?

6. The most significant question you can ask yourself is: Am I where I want to be? Probably not. If you're a musician, you'll probably feel like an outsider 'if you're among people who only talk about politics. If you want to get involved in politics you may feel like an outsider because of the traditional male hostility to women in politics. If you're elderly, you may feel discriminated against because of your age. We could go on and on. Certainly, there are many reasons to feel like an outsider. If you are a black

woman in a white neighborhood you may feel like an outsider. If you are new to a town where there seem to be cliques you may feel like an outsider.

Therefore, your question is: Am I where I want to be? Am I interested in being here? If your answer is no, your next question is: How do I find people with whom I can relate? What places and facilities can help me?

Again, if you love literature, and the people you know read only newspapers, why not put an ad in the local paper to start a book discussion group. Or join your local library association. Or take classes at a university where you'll meet others who are interested in what you're interested in. Or find out about local adult education courses.

If you're a musician you could do the same thing. Keep making phone calls until you have exhausted all the possibilities. Chances are there are a lot of people around who feel the way you do. One suburban woman found people with interests like hers when she got a job at an advertising agency in a nearby city. Another found she had finally found a "home" at a group called "Overeaters Anonymous" in which people talk about the problems which led them to overeating. A third woman found she had always felt "out of place" until she joined a feminist discussion group. A fourth woman found that her charm, warmth, and gaiety were finally fully appreciated in her position as director of a hospital gift shop.

7. Is there any way you can temper your critical facilities so that others won't feel so put down? You tend to put down others when you feel that they are not performing as you expect them to. You are not aware of your expectation of them. You only feel that they *should* know better. In other words, you take your own "should" and use it as the only measuring rod for another's behavior. Since neither you nor the other person could possibly live up to the expectation (the should), you are left feeling annoyed and frustrated. This kind of ongoing frustration is the basis of the *cold anger* we mentioned earlier, and anger which

needs to be relieved every once in a while. That relief is easily found through anger directed at someone else. And that is, most often, the basis for this kind of overcritical response.

8. Where can you put your creative energies that are now locked inside of you? What would you really like to do? What lost dream can you realize? Sculpting? Learning about astrology? Astronomy? Learning French? Cooking Chinese food? Getting a job you like? Learning about a country, you'd like to visit? Beginning a correspondence course?

9. Your problem of loneliness is a unique one. If you are in a period of mourning, you are probably intensely lonely. This is to be expected. Eventually, you will feel better able to cope with this loss. It is not going to be easy for you to find someone with whom you can be as close.

In the meantime, you are going to have to look to yourself for stimulation. What can you do when you're alone that will help you feel less lonely? Can you sew? Embroider? Start a vegetable garden? Go out for a walk? Bicycle around the park? Write in your journal? Reorganize your closets? Is there some project you've been putting off that you can work on now? What can you find solace in? Poetry? Music? Paintings? Perhaps talking with some clergyman? What kind of a person would you like to meet? Do you know anybody with whom you could develop a friendship? What places could you find to help you meet new people?

You must find your own way. And more often than not, when you least expect it, you will find that you feel strong enough to begin going out to meet others, to begin to enjoy yourself again, and to find other people who will respond to your grace and your strength.

10. Why do you feel this way? Is it because of the dispised self-image you carry around in your head? Are you always putting yourself down before giving yourself a chance? Do you expect others to immediately welcome you with open arms? Do you have

trouble communicating, and then blame others for not
understanding you? Do you really like other people?

What can you do to make you feel better about
yourself? What can you do to make yourself feel
more at home in your environment? Can you take a
course? Go back to school? Teach something you
know? Help other people? Who would you like to be
around? What kind of people do you feel most comfortable with?

11. Are you shy? If you are, read our sections on shyness and assertiveness. Try some of the suggestions
and see how they work. Ask yourself: Where could
I make the biggest contribution? What skill could I
bring to others? Do you like to sew? Perhaps a local
drama group needs someone to make costumes. Are
you a good organizer? Perhaps a local charity could
use you to help raise money by organizing a fair. Do
you know a lot about flowers? Perhaps you could
join, or start, a garden club. Are you concerned about
ecology? What could you do to help save the environment?

Once you know what options you have, you can begin to investigate. This can be fun. You may not strike
gold every time. You may find you don't like taking
courses in pottery, but you do love the League of
Women Voters meetings. You don't have to stick to
one and only choice. Keep experimenting until you
find a friendship or a lifestyle that suits you. It will
take time. Nobody finds instant friends or "fits in"
anywhere immediately. You must have patience and
courage. You must *plan*. But what you must always remember is that you must take the next step and the
next.

Making Decisions

If you are too compliant or self-effacing, you may
find you cannot make a decision that satisfies you
because of your compulsive need to always please
others. You fear their criticism, and since your self-

esteem rests on the regard you receive from others, you feel paralyzed.

If you have a domineering personality, you may not be free to make a decision which might be wrong. Your decisions must be the right ones in order to insure the recognition of your position of mastery.

If you tend to be uninvolved or detached, you may be afraid of becoming too involved by committing yourself to a definite position or opinion. You prefer to remain aloof. That way, you feel more secure.

If you feel that your inability to make decisions is a real impediment, there are ways to overcome it. The more severe your problem is the more help you will probably need. Psychoanalysis, psychotherapy, behavior therapy, in fact, any form of therapy conducted by a well-trained professional worker can be helpful. But here are two self-help procedures that can be used any time you choose.

Prepare yourself to make an *immediate decision*. This method cannot be used for major decisions at first. You may never be able to use it on such decisions. But it can be used for minor, unimportant decisions such as: Which movie shall I see; which restaurant shall we go to; which outfit shall I wear; which present shall I buy.

Say out loud: "Which color skirt do I want—the blue one or the green one?" Then continue talking and say, "I want the ———— one." Try not to be deciding or even thinking at this point. Just be listening to your words: "Which color skirt do I want—the blue one or the green one? I want the green one." Just listen to what comes from your mouth.

If the word you utter—in this example, "green"—causes you to go "Ugh!," *immediately* select the other choice and stand by it. Don't waver at this point. Remember, these are small decisions, and it really matters very little, if at all, which decision you make.

Keep using this method until you feel comfortable with it and can trust yourself to immediately accept either one decision or the other. You will have only two choices here. The first choice that you express can be discounted, but then you must take the remaining choice—immediately. You *cannot* go back to the first choice. You can see that this method is useful for only certain decisions. But when it is indicated, it can be very useful.

When you come to more important decisions, you can use this method *only* to make those decisions which have only two choices, both of which you can accept. The method cannot be used if the two choices are not *equally acceptable*. This method is not for the purpose of deciding the merits of the choices. It is only an aid in the making of a decision. For example, you have two job offers. Job #1 offers certain advantages, and Job #2 offers other advantages. Both are attractive to you. Both are in your field, and will advance you but in different ways. You have a few days in which to make the decision.

Now use the method: Which job do I want? I want the ——— one. Fill in the blank. Remember, you must say the two sentences all together, one immediately after the other, with no pauses. Then, if you are horrified at your decision, *immediately* select the other choice. You will probably feel relieved at this point. Try to follow up immediately. Pick up the phone and state your decision. If it's a Sunday night, write a note and mail it. And now on to the next decision.

The second method is based on two premises. The first premise is that you are unable to make a decision because you are afraid of offending or hurting someone. You may even know that this is not actually the case, but you still are worried. The second premise is that you don't like either of your choices, but you are not clear about what you do want.

With this second method, the questions are more sophisticated, but must be asked rapidly and answered immediately. Question #1: If I had *absolutely* no one but myself to consider, which choice would I make? I would ———. Fill in the blank. If you arrive at an answer, accept it. If you should come up with "I wouldn't do either" then your decision is also made. Question #2: If I didn't have these choices before me, what would I want to do in this situation? Be alert to the first thing that comes into your thoughts and say it out loud. This is a fascinating question, because it opens up completely new possibilities. Elaine was trying to decide whether she wanted to go to England or Greece on a summer holiday with one or another group of friends and couldn't make up her mind. She finally asked herself, "If I had no decision to make, what would I want to do in this situation?" Her answer came like a shot. "I want to go to Aunt Bessie's farm in Maine for a quiet, relaxing summer, and see all the things I used to play with as a child, and swim in the ice-cold stream." So she did.

Psychosomatic Illness

Your body will function optimally if you do not load it down with impediments. Optimal functioning depends upon the basic essentials of physical care, but it also depends upon the basic essentials of intellectual, spiritual, and emotional well-being. Then peak well-being can be experienced and maintained.

Psychic stress is often expressed through physical illness. Jolene, who was in excellent health, would have severe abdominal cramps whenever she didn't get what she wanted. The cramps were caused by an abnormal tensing of the musculature of her gastrointestinal tract. That tensing was caused by impulses arriving through those branches of her autonomic nervous system which causes the smooth muscle of the digestive system to contract. Those impulses originated in higher nervous system organs (e.g., hypothalamus and cortex) which are influenced by psychological stimuli.

To put it another way, the emotional response this young woman had to interpersonal interactions, or to reactions within herself, produced an impact on certain higher centers in the brain. These centers, through particular electrochemical changes, influence the autonomic nervous system and the circulatory system. These, in turn, produce a specific response (tensing) in the muscles of the walls of the gastrointestinal system. That tensing causes pain by temporarily cutting off the blood flow to a specific area.

Such a series of events can easily be tolerated by the body. But if they occur frequently, that is, beyond the point at which natural recuperative powers can repair any minor damage, then the muscle wall will eventually weaken because it is deprived of nutrients. In this case, the deprived tissue is subject to any number of diseases, including gastritis, ulcers, colitis, diverticulitis, and others. Tissue weakening and breakdown is partially caused by impairment of blood supply. And blood supply is impaired because a tensed muscle will squeeze out the circulating blood that it needs in order to survive *in top condition*.

Muscles tense because of stimuli (messages) that are coming from various nervous centers. These are influenced by the nature of emotional responses the individual has. The emotional responses provide the *psycho* part, and the physical weakening provides the *somato* part of psychosomatic illness. That is to say, psychosomatic illnesses are *real* and *treatable* diseases.

When Jolene didn't get her way, she couldn't confront the situation directly and deal with it. She couldn't *say* how she felt because she had a need to see herself (her Perfect Self) as always open to suggestion, always agreeable, and at the same time always winning. Therefore, she is perpetually caught in a conflict. She can't say to herself: Look, honey, you don't like what's going on. You're angry. Come on now, speak up and defend your position. Nor can she say: There is no way you can win in this situation; why don't you just back off and accept that. All she can feel is her insistence on what she feels she is entitled to, what she *should* be getting—that is, complete acquiescence to her wishes.

Jolene's anger (her reaction to an external stimulus) sets a train of events into motion. Those events lead to the cramping of her gut. All she is conscious of is the pain of her cramped intestine which is trying to give her the message: Look here, you are in trouble. You feel attacked and you are trying to defend yourself by placing me in a defensive position. I don't mind that and I will give you the message again and again, but I may wear myself out in doing so. Help!

This is only one example of many illnesses which can be caused by underlying emotional conflicts. These illnesses include those gastrointestinal diseases previously mentioned, as well as respiratory diseases, notably asthma; cardiovascular diseases, notably hypertension and migraine headaches; genito-urinary problems, notably sexual dysfunctions.

It is not necessary, however, to live a life of physical misery because of your inner conflicts. Certainly medical and psychiatric care are indicated in psychosomatic diseases, but you may be more interested in what you can do to help yourself.

We can offer some possible clues for you to work with. The main emotional ingredient of these illnesses is anger. Although you cannot treat the diseased organ yourself, you are the only one who can "treat" your own anger, in trying to identify it, understand it, explore it, and devise ways to deal with it.

In order to keep anger from hurting you, it has to somehow be dissipated. This can be done by expressing it as we have previously suggested: in releasing it by means of physical activity; in raising questions as to what makes you angry; in trying to be more aware of your feelings in general; in trying to understand what your own "shoulds" and conflicts are.

You may feel that you need a psychotherapist to do this work. And we cannot deny that one could well be used. But the fact is that a very small percentage of people enter into treatment for their emotional problems. So we are trying to offer you some alternatives that you might be able to put to use. Every suggestion that we have offered carries with it an obligation on your part that you make your own effort to be helped. In other words, each person has to put in something to get something out. Remember—nothing for nothing!

17

Roots of Strength

As WE MENTIONED in our introduction, we interviewed over one hundred women, women from all walks of life: rich, middle class, and poor, black and white, young and old. We have used many of their stories throughout. The following five stories, however, speak eloquently about the struggles women have to go through, the conflicts they have to resolve, the limits they have to learn to respect, and the ways women have learned to trust themselves, their resources, their strengths.

Ruth is in her middle twenties. She has long, light brown hair and a pleasant face and is wearing jeans and a poncho top. She works as a guide at an art gallery.

"When I was growing up," Ruth says, "I did get down in the dumps, but I didn't realize how miserable I was. My first big depression came after I'd dropped out of school. One summer I was just a zombie. I was working, but when I'd get off work, and on the weekends, I'd just sleep. Looking back on it now, I see that there were a lot of contributing factors—the guy I was seeing had left the city, my family had just moved away.

"Eventually I went back to school and I would have depressions off and on. It's only in the last six months that I'm beginning to understand the process, to see the pieces fit together. I used to think that my moods were just my personal psyche or my genes, because my mother would get depressed too, and I think that I saw her behavior and learned how to be depressed from her. Anyway, now I think that there are societal reasons for being depressed."

Her father, Ruth says, was "severe and successful." He rarely spent time at home with his family. "He even had an ulcer," she comments ruefully. Ruth's mother was loving and cheery, depressed only when she was alone. She had a master's degree, but never worked after she married. Ruth has one brother. She says, "He's just like my father, smart in business but totally unaware of how to relate to people on a human level."

Ruth continues. "My family expected me to wear a suit of clothes that didn't fit. My mother put a lot of pressure on me to be happy—to be popular and date. Well, I hated the whole dating game. I hated the idea that I had to be grateful for some boy paying for me to go to the movies.

"I also think I was getting double messages all the time I was growing up. I was supposed to be a super-achiever, but I was also supposed to become a happy housewife. I was supposed to be good at sports, but I wasn't supposed to beat men. I was supposed to be attractive and happy, but not sexy.

"I think, at the time, I always felt kind of embarrassed about being a woman. I felt trapped. I couldn't think of one woman I knew—we come from a midwestern town—who led an interesting life. For example, my mother had two good friends when I was a teenager, both of them were creative and bright. One of them cracked up and had to be institutionalized. The other was a painter who was married to a man who had very old-fashioned ideas about women's roles. She got no support from him or anyone. She developed cancer after her children left home, and she was dead within six months. I got the message loud and clear: if you are a woman and do what your society says you should do, you'll go crazy or end up dead!

"Today I'm used to not having a lot of societal support for whatever I do. But when I was younger I wasn't clear about that. I felt like a complete failure because I wasn't a California blonde.

"I think families perform society's dirty work. They make it impossible for women to be free spirits. For instance, in our family, *anything* was more important than what you wanted to do, if you were a woman. We were supposed to be the nurturing ones. I remember once riding in a car with my mother and we got a flat tire. I knew how to change it, and I wanted to, but my mother wouldn't let me because she thought that I would hurt the feelings of the men passing by!

"Now when I tell her I want to be a doctor she says, 'The day you become a doctor is the day I've lost my daughter.' I think she is seeking validation for what her life has been."

Ruth would not accept the stereotype she felt her parents wanted for her, a "suit of clothes that didn't fit." She seemed quite certain about this intellectually. But emotionally she wanted what every daughter wants—to be loved and approved of by her parents. To rebel was to run the risk of disapproval.

On a conscious level, she could say she didn't care whether they approved or not. Unconsciously, she clung to the dream of being "daddy's little good girl," and would not risk losing that. So she was faithful to her principles of independence and self-sufficiency on the one hand, and faithful to her image of good-girlness on the other. Being faithful to two clearly contradictory positions will not work, especially when they are simultaneously held.

In its simplest terms, this is the substance of conflict. But Ruth was not aware of the existence of conflict. All she knew was that she was striving to break away.

The double messages Ruth received from her parents didn't help her. As she describes it, it is clear that her mother was in considerable conflict herself. She said: Be a superachiever, but don't be one. Be good at sports, but don't be too good at them. And over everything was running the theme of the implicit inferiority of women.

It should be emphasized, though, that once Mother's groundwork was done, in terms of providing the matrix for conflicted attitudes, needs, behavior, and feelings, Ruth, in her own right, contributed to and kept the system alive. What Ruth did with her life, after she decided that she disagreed with and rejected many societal and familial principles, was, and is, her own doing and her own responsibility.

This point must be emphasized. This acceptance of responsibility has to be reached before any woman can claim autonomy. If a woman can assume final responsibility for the elaboration of conflict and for the neurotic defenses against it, then she can also one day assume responsibility for undoing the conflict, and for relinquishing the defenses that will no longer be essential to her.

This is not to negate the impact of parents and society. That impact is formidable. Yet one must try to move from dependency on parental and cultural imperatives to making one's own decisions about needs, goals, and lifestyles.

This is what Ruth is beginning to do. She became depressed when she was alone the summer her parents and boyfriends went away, just as her mother became depressed when *she* was alone. When Ruth was "achieving," according to her father's standards, she felt fine. But when she dropped out of school in order to examine what she wanted to do with her life, she felt guilty. She wasn't doing what was expected of her. All of her anger at her parents, at herself, and the culture she was raised in were masked, hidden under the cloak of depression.

Ruth identified with her mother's behavior. She says, "I learned how to be depressed from her." And why not? Don't all children learn some of their parents' behavior, sometimes to exasperatingly detailed degrees? Parents' voices, expressions, body movements, attitudes, ways of thinking are frequently and minutely duplicated. Why not, then, depression?

While no "bug" has been isolated for depression, does it seem too far-fetched to say that Ruth "caught" her mother's way of being depressed? It may be helpful for all of us to be better aware of how our parents influence us and how we influence our children—for better and for worse!

Today Ruth is able to see her conflicts more clearly. She is not depressed because she is learning to make her own choices. She is, in other words, moving away from dependence upon what she believes others want of her, to dependence upon her own resolutions.

Stephanie is the mother of two children. She is tiny and has short black hair. "I was the oldest girl of seven children," Stephanie says. "My mother and father were gypsies, but they were trying to become middle class. They traveled around the country, doing night-club acts, telling fortunes.

"My mother didn't care about us. I spent most of my childhood in various childrens' institutions and foster homes. When I was thirteen I tried to kill myself.

"The biggest depressing factor in my life was class differences. I was lower class and living in middle-class neighborhoods. I was totally alienated from middle-class culture. No one would be friends with me because of the way I dressed and the family of 'vagabonds' I came from. My mother and my teachers expected me to become a whore.

"At the same time, I couldn't get along with the few kids who were the same as me. They were into comic books and I was into poetry. I was desperate because I didn't see how I was ever going to fit in anywhere.

"I quit high school and got a job singing in a night-club when I was sixteen. I was called an emancipated minor. I couldn't take all the sleaziness of that life, however, and eventually I got myself accepted as a nonmatriculating student at college. If I got good grades the first year, they said, I could matriculate.

"I worked hard, supporting myself as a secretary

and waitress, and then in my second year I married an upper-class boy who was a graduate student. I never knew *why* I married him.

"I had a child, and he went on to finish his Ph.D. I was under tremendous pressure, going to school, working, raising my child. It was a rotten marriage, and he left us right after he finished school.

"A year after he left us I finished school and got a job in a hospital doing social work. Six months later I had a breakdown and was hospitalized for six months. What were my symptoms? I couldn't get out of bed. I'd cry all the time. I couldn't even decide what clothes to put on my baby so she could go to the baby-sitter.

"One of the doctors I worked with got me into a private hospital. My child was put with a temporary foster family. I saw a psychiatrist once a week, and we had groups and occupational therapy every day.

"I think I broke down because I was so sure things were going to be different once I finally got that degree. Then I'd be an accepted part of the middle class! When I found that my feelings about myself didn't change after graduation—well, then I cracked up.

"While in the psychiatric ward—this happened to be an excellent one, one of the best in the country— I worked through my feelings about myself and my family. I realized that even though I'd gotten an education, I still felt like a fraud—education was really for *other* people. I was terrified people were going to find out who I was. I had always lied and said I was an orphan. I was terribly ashamed of coming out of the working class, although, today, I see that as one of my great strengths. I know I can endure hardship and work hard.

"When I left the hospital I wasn't able to get my job back, although they'd promised it to me. I moved into a commune and eventually married one of the men there and had another baby. This was in the late sixties. I was very involved in the antiwar movement.

"I was very dependent then; I couldn't stand being alone. The time in the hospital had been the happiest time of my life up until then.

"At the commune we planted our own vegetables and took care of goats and chickens. I was really into babies, too. It was the whole Earth Mother trip.

"At this time I was lecturing about the war and about poverty, and I was getting stronger. *The more independent I got, the more hostile my husband got, and the more depressed I got.* I was going to a woman therapist at the time, and she said there was some need on my husband's part to keep me childlike and subordinate.

"Anyway, my husband got a new job and we had to move. I didn't want to go. I felt the commune was my home. But he made me feel guilty and said I owed it to him. I said I'd come and stay with him a year, and if our relationship didn't improve by then, we'd have to end it.

"It didn't work out and I was still very depressed. I felt so guilty! But finally we split up. Once we did, the depression lifted. We're still friendly now. Today I'm doing what I want to do. I'm working and raising my children. I'm hoping to live one day on a farm with other women like me. Today, for the first time in my life, I feel good."

Stephanie believed that her degree would provide her with a be-all and end-all, a piece of paper that would catapult her into the middle class. When she found that her feelings about herself remained the same after she received her degree, she could not bear that final great disappointment, that lost dream. She slipped quickly from great expectations to complete hopelessness, and that's when she "cracked up." She felt she was "only a fraud"—her despised self.

What a tragic rejection this was of what she actually was! But she eventually saw her background, her experience of hard work, of looking after herself, as "one of my great strengths." She had finally come to the realization that the roots of anyone's strength lie within. Her hospitalization seems to have served as the beginning of a new phase in her life. But she still needed to be dependent on her husband. Each of her moves toward independence aroused hostility in him. That, in turn, aroused guilt in her and sent her scuttling back to her depression where she could mask her hurt and anger, where she had to be taken care of, and where she could not offend anyone because of her immobilization.

But Stephanie persisted in her own behalf and finally could acknowledge that the relationship was a destructive one for her. Having made that decision, she was better able to attend to her own needs and finally have some experience with "feeling good."

Rachel is a secretary in her early thirties. She lives in a small town.

"I was depressed for some time about a year ago," she says. "I had been going out with a man who was so withholding. The relationship made me angry. I got sick to my stomach. I feel better now since I broke it off. He was a businessman. He came on strong in a sexual way which I liked. But he wasn't emotional. The relationship existed more in my fantasies. But I was high over him.

"My mother and father and I all got on well. My mother is like a sister to me, warm and permissive. She's very pretty. I think my parents expected me to grow up extremely attractive. But when I was twelve I got fat. I was fat for ten years—and a bookworm.

"My father was much older than my mother and is a doctor. He is very attractive and well liked. I think my father is withholding also. And I think he's intolerant of my mother's ups and downs, her depressions. They get along all right but he treats her in this paternal way. She has a lot of anger toward him.

"I tell my mother everything like I would a friend. I remember in high school I had to write a paper. I took a topic that was beyond me. I was trying to impress my advisor by doing it. I expected the paper to be totally brilliant. But then I 'crashed' and believed I was not only fat but stupid. I developed insomnia.

Whenever I had to write a paper I had trouble sleeping. I did the paper at the last minute, and cried for hours after I handed it in.

"I used to have a recurrent dream. I had to perform in a play and I couldn't do it. I'd forget my lines. I think this has to do with wanting to do something with my life, but not knowing what it was.

"I see that I have a critical parent inside me which specializes in self-criticism. I sometimes still get foggy in groups. A shell builds up and I can't relate, especially when I think people are judging me. Then I feel like a piece of nothing with a shell around it!

"But finally I'm beginning to like my independence. I went to Weight Watchers recently and lost thirty pounds. I am starting to go to church socials. I can now go to the ballet and to the movies alone. And I have more friends. I'm not as aloof as I used to be. When I'm 'up,' I have energy and optimism. Then I feel as if I'm functioning like an adult."

Rachel too was and to a lesser extent still is, a victim of her "shoulds." She *should* have written a brilliant high school paper. Where she lost faith in being brilliant, she couldn't bear her feelings of shame and humiliation and became depressed.

Later she became involved in a morbidly dependent relationship with a man who "came on strong," but who was emotionally withholding as her father was. She was "high" when she was with this man, then low and depressed when the relationship broke up. (By now you probably have noted that one's "highs" are often followed by "lows" because the highs are based on unreal expectations.) In Rachel's case, the "dream" was of the strong man who would sweep her off her feet and make her life happy forever after.

Now, however, Rachel is beginning to enjoy her independence. She has lost weight and is beginning to take part in activities on her own. Her growth will be gradual, however, and she will have many setbacks. Things do not move smoothly "forever after." The resolution of one conflict only provides room for a new one, and then another and then another. It is the *dealing* with these, rather than being irrevocably trapped by any one of them, that is integral to the life process.

Alison is a thirty-seven-year-old woman. "My mother was a household worker and my father worked for the city," she says. "My parents were very good to me and stressed the importance of a good education.

"But when I got out of school I went through a terrible depression. My mother had always told me how 'special' I was, and she had really protected me from the world. When I couldn't find work I liked— and that had everything to do with the fact that I was black—I was really depressed. I did clerical work, but I was dragging through every day.

"Luckily for me I met a nice guy and we fell in love and got married. I had two babies and I was home, you know. I thought the hell with the outside world, I'm just going to do the best job I can raising my kids.

"When the black liberation movement came, though, I realized, 'Hey, it's not your fault you were rejected.' And I joined the struggle. I'm like a different person now. I really have a lot of energy but I wasn't using it. I wasn't using myself. I do work for several black organizations now and I feel good. When I find myself becoming depressed, it's usually because I want to change everything overnight and I can't. But I try to tell myself, don't get mad at yourself, honey. Get mad at the world! *That* usually works."

Alison began to withdraw when she felt her pain was too heavy a burden to carry. She immersed herself in her husband and children, but was quietly depressed. She had become resigned to her fate; her dreams and hopes were banished.

However, when the black liberation movement came along, she realized how "dead" she felt. The movement helped give meaning to her life. She became *involved* in fighting for what she believed in. And out of that sprang a new strength which fed her feelings of aliveness.

Letty is a soft-spoken forty-seven-year-old art therapist. In the middle of a divorce and a custody battle over her two children, she is fighting hard, she says, to keep from succumbing to an incapacitating depression.

"My mother was strong, head of the household. My father was very sweet and loving, although our mother let us know she thought he was weak. I looked at him the way my mother did for a long time.

"My mother married to get away from her sisters. She and my father bought and ran a grocery store together. My mother was always a hard worker. She worked from early in the morning until early the next morning! She complained constantly. I have a vision of her lying on the couch in the back of the store, exhausted and bitter.

"We were a very closed family. We were kind of imprisoned. My parents had no friends and we didn't either. My mother was very critical of the way I looked. But she didn't help me look any better. She was such a negative person. She never praised anyone for anything.

"Both my younger sister and I did quite well in school. And now that I think of it, our parents did encourage us to continue our educations. After school I went to work in a hospital as an art therapist. *But I had the feeling that I was back in the family grocery store!* I had no power then to assert myself. I would get the lowest salary and the worst hours in the hospital. But I never complained. I was probably depressed at the time.

"I think women often feel guilty after they have been assertive. But we play right into people's hands by being easy victims.

"I finally moved into my own apartment. It wasn't nice. I could have afforded a nicer place, but I didn't get one. I had not come to the point where I thought

I had the right to nice things. *Part of depression, I think, is not saying 'I want this.'* And, you know, it is important to live in nice surroundings.

"I then went to a nicer job. I had a friend who encouraged me to spend on myself, who pushed me toward living better. I got a nicer apartment and started collecting art. And I began to feel I wanted to get married.

"I was married for fifteen years. But I couldn't survive with my husband. He is a very controlling man. He has to be the boss. Everything he wanted I went along with. I realized after a while that he didn't hear me or really see me. But we had a nice home and three kids by then. But eventually I realized I was deluding myself with material things. This was not a life for me. I might as well have been dead.

"For example, I was in an automobile accident and we were supposed to go on a trip. He was leaving a day before me. Well, I was hoping he would delay it one day, because I didn't feel up to traveling myself; but he wouldn't do it. I realized that he didn't really care. He had a superficial charm, but he wasn't a feeling person. He was a very ambitious man. I helped him with many projects, but he got all the credit. There was an emphasis on the way things looked. As long as I played the hostess, everything was fine. Finally, I asked him to move out. When he did, I felt so relieved.

"But I became terribly depressed. A small thing like registering the car—something my husband had always done—practically immobilized me. I just couldn't do it for several days.

"I finally left the house, which is now up for sale, and moved into an apartment. My husband moved a block from me. I think he wanted to drive me crazy!

"I also went to a psychiatrist after our break-up and my husband started going to the same one too. I didn't think that was right, but then I began to question that. I think I entered into my own destruction.

When you're depressed you question what you feel. You worry about what you *should* feel rather than what you do feel. So I didn't protest that I didn't like my psychiatrist seeing my husband. But then I finally decided to go to a new psychiatrist!

"I think our break-up has been good for my twelve-year-old daughter. She was withdrawn, but now is more independent. I think part of her independence comes from having seen her mother refusing to remain in a situation in which she was so unhappy. She learned that you can change your life.

"I am having a lot of problems with my children now. I'm depressed and tired and anxious and so I yell occasionally. My husband has the money and he uses it to get them to his side. He says that if they come live with him, they can have everything they want, do what they want. I know he doesn't really want the kids. He just wants to win. He also doesn't want to pay me alimony. But I deserve it. I think women who don't ask for alimony are masochistic.

"I have to keep up my energy to fight all his destructive maneuvers. My depression, I know, will play into his hands. I have to learn not to be frightened."

When Letty went to work as an art therapist, she felt she was "still back in the family grocery store." That was because she didn't feel that she belonged where she was. She could not speak up and ask for a fair wage. She could not "own" her education, nor the belief that she could do a good job. Having developed little emotional autonomy, she continued to do what was expected of her in marrying an ambitious man, helping him with his career, raising children. This is all well and good *if* it is satisfying and productive for the woman involved. We are all different and have different needs and different satisfactions. In Letty's case, it seems that she suffered from chronic depression the whole time she was married. She, too, was resigned, and even her daughter follows in her footsteps and becomes a "withdrawn" child. Here again we see the contagiousness of the "virus" of depression.

Finally, Letty decides she hasn't lived. She decides on divorce. But she feels guilty and in conflict. On the one hand, she feels she *should* make the marriage work. She *should* be a good wife. On the other hand, she *should* suddenly become independent and perform efficiently in every way, even when she is doing things such as getting the car fixed, something that she has never done before. Her feelings almost immobilize her. Hopelessness and helplessness take over. But she keeps telling herself she has to fight her depression and she does.

Both Letty and Stephanie found it necessary to divorce. They had become involved with men who were excessively destructive. Elsewhere we have mentioned how the man who wants to be on top, the one who wins, has to find women like Letty and Stephanie. Once there is a marriage between this kind of domineering man and submissive woman, you have the setting for the playing out of the sado-masochistic relationship. Because of her needs, the woman clings to the myth of "all for love" and permits her partner to do as he will. Finally, hating herself, as well as him, she either resigns herself to a crushed and bloodless existence, or she has to get out.

The man, too, because of his needs, clings to the myth that all means justify the end of mastery, of the dominance he feels he must have or he will collapse. In having his way with his partner, he too finally comes to hate himself (for being such a mean person) and her (for being such a patsy). He, too, either resigns himself to an endlessly hostile stance, or has to get out. There are no winners here. It is only to be hoped that the next time, each one will select a partner (if that happens) who will not be compelled to bring out the worst in the other, but who can be warm and responsive to the other's reaching out.

Letty does not have an easy struggle on her hands. Her husband has spent his whole life "winning." He will probably resort to any means to get what he wants. Letty's hope lies in fighting him for what she believes in—her rights to alimony, to her children, to a decent life for herself. She has to rely on her strength. She knows what she has to do. And she is determined to do it.

18

Anti-depression Exercises

IN THIS CHAPTER we are going to ask you to use your
notebook, the one you are using as a journal or diary.
We think you will find the following exercises useful
and fun.

A. List three or more of your mother's strengths.
B. List three or more of your father's strengths.
C. List three or more of a sibling's strengths. If
you have no siblings, list the strengths of a relative.

After you have made these lists, write as many
things that you know about each item on your list.
For example, if one of your father's strengths was
being able to raise fine home-grown tomatoes, list
things you know about raising tomatoes. These might
include the best time for planting, most suitable
soil conditions, best fertilizer, best plowing arrangement for watering, best plants to use, how to prop
plants up, how to rid soil of damaging insects, etc.

You may have never planted yourself, but you will
find you know something about these items just from
living with people who did.

Why will these items be of use to you? Because, as
we've seen, tapping and exploring your roots is one
way to pull out hidden strengths. Charlotte, for example, was the daughter of a wealthy and powerful
businessman. When he died she was the only person
alive to run his business. Up to that time she had been

a depressed, self-effacing woman who had had one tragic love affair after another. But when she *had* to run her father's business she realized she knew quite a bit about it. After all, she had spent years listening to her father talk about it. She threw herself into learning all she could. In a short period of time she felt more confident about her abilities. She knew she still had much to learn, but she had explored a strength that had been there all the time. She had, however, negated it, rejected it, been unconscious of it.

D. Make a list of fifteen or more things that you have done recently, or as a younger person, or as a child.

These do not have to be career achievements, or achievements of any particular significance to anyone except yourself. They might be activities you have participated in, or skills you have acquired as a worker, mother, volunteer, wife. It might be easier if you start with your early childhood. For example, you may remember making something with your father when you were five. Or embroidering samplers with your mother when you were six. Then work your way up with each year or period of your life.

After you have made your list go over it again and write a short paragraph on each item. This will be time-consuming and take a good deal of effort, but it will be worth it.

Tolly's list included the following: at twelve, I was in a school play; at sixteen, I contributed to the year-book; at eighteen, I helped to decorate the school gym; at thirty-one, I organized a car pool in my neighborhood. Of course, Tolly has done many other things; this is only a sampling.

Tolly began to see that she had acquired strengths through ordinary life experiences. Under her experience in the school play, she wrote that her strengths included: being able to memorize her lines; being able to appear on stage without being overwhelmed by shyness. She helped the teacher to design the costumes with colored paper and pin them together. She learned something of stage mechanics. She remembered how much she had learned and contributed during this experience many years ago. When she was asked to help with the annual presentation the brownies were preparing, she almost refused to help, sincerely feeling she could contribute nothing. But her recollections of her childhood led her to change her mind. The reviewing of her theater experience helped her retain her confidence to accept this new challenge.

E. Let's move now to the present. Check those items below that you can do, enjoy, or might enjoy. Then write a short paragraph about each one. For example, if you check cooking, write what you like to cook, in what new ways you could use your cooking ability, if any, and if there is anything more you would like to learn about cooking.

Jean had been an excellent home economics student and had been thinking of a career in that field. But then she married and forgot about a career. Eight years later she was "looking for something to do." By working with this list, she was able to see that one of her real loves was cooking. But she had not thought of it as a marketable ability. She and a friend began a small catering service to the businesses in her area. "I've never had so much fun," she says today.

Look at the list and check off things you enjoy. *Depressed women often don't have enough pleasure in their lives.* They are too busy doing what they think they *should* be doing. That's why a list like this one can be a good take-off.

listening to music	exploring
making music	traveling

sewing	meeting new people
cooking	writing down thoughts
decorating	working with children
selling	working with old people
working on projects alone	cleaning house
working on projects with someone	discussing books
organizing groups	seeing movies
attending classes	seeing plays
making money	visiting museums
reading	learning about art
working with hand crafts	learning about history
reading the newspaper	sports
gardening	birdwatching
babysitting	hiking
political action	dancing
community work	religious work
acting	charity work
singing	other

This list is limited. Add as many of your own items as you like. If you are an outdoors person, add those interests. If you have a special skill, you will have other items to include. Don't rush this part. You might spend much more than one sitting at this. Let your list get as long and as detailed as you wish. You may find that your work on this section will take on a life of its own. One thought will lead to another. If this happens, enjoy it! You will find yourself immersed in the *creative process*. Try it. You can do it too.

F. Now that you've tried writing up your feelings and experiences concerning the past and present, you are ready for the next step. Ask yourself the question: What would I like to have done by the end of next year? The end of three years? The end of five years?

If this question is anxiety-provoking, take the unit of time that you feel most comfortable with. Let's say you want to have your basement painted by next year. Make your own list which you can pattern, if you like, on this one.

1. Goal: Paint basement.
2. Purpose: To make me feel more comfortable when I entertain there.
3. Time: By the end of next year.
4. Preliminary steps:
   a. Discuss color scheme.
   b. Look up painters.
   c. Interview painters for estimates.
   d. Check budget.
   e. Clean out junk in room.
   f. Plan for donating unused items to charity.
5. Major procedures:
   a. Arrange convenient time schedule for self, family, and painter.
   b. Plan to have windows washed after painting, but before window dressing goes back up.
   c. Decide on any new decorating such as new rug, curtains, lamps, pictures, and other items. These can be worked on after the painting is done and can be acquired slowly piece by piece.
   d. Try to get household help for cleaning out closets, moving or packing things. If none available, discuss with family how they can help.
   e. After painting is done, take some time off before continuing the work.
   f. Take plenty of time to put major items back in place.
   g. Enjoy room!

You may have to work with several areas of interest at first. But eventually you may have to eliminate some, for the time being, at any rate. It is easier to work with one idea at a time. If one doesn't seem feasible, move on to the next. If you have several areas of interest, you might list them in order of priority and start at the top.

Once you have decided on one, make your outline again: goal; purpose; time limit; preliminary steps; major procedures. Ask for information, advice, and specific help from anyone you know who might help. Get information that is available in library publications. Subscribe to publications that deal in your area of interest. Talk with your family about plans as long as they are not the type to "wet blanket" you. If they are, don't try to share too much with them, because they'll unwittingly make it more difficult for you.

You can alter the outline form at any time. This one is only to get you started. It is very useful, however, to see your own words, thoughts, and plans on paper. Action seems easier then.

It is important to *find your own goals*. These can be anything you want to experience—taking a trip or a course, planting a garden, getting a job.

Your goal for a five-year period will be of a different nature. A common concern today for many women is a return to the work market. This can arouse almost all of your fears, inhibitions, and any of the problems we have previously mentioned: shyness, low self-esteem, fear of assertiveness, decision-making, etc. However, start with optimism!

Perhaps you can begin your work with these three steps.

1. Define your areas of interest.
2. List the people and places you can contact for information relative to this interest.
3. Write down steps needed to initiate action.

You might try to find a friend or acquaintance who is interested in working on this with you. You can support and encourage each other.

Here are examples of what two women did when they found themselves wanting to change the course of their days. Elsie had been home raising children for twelve years. When she was ready to go to work outside of her home she looked through the newspapers to see what kind of jobs would interest her. She made a list which included working in a travel agency, in an airline office, in a hotel. She then saw that she really wanted to work in a service area that catered to a wide variety of people. She searched through her background and came up with various skills that she could contribute to each area. After all, she had organized many fundraising events for her community, and her friends depended on her to help them with their anniversary parties. She felt those were useful skills, and she was right.

She began calling everyone she knew to see if they knew of any openings. Eventually, she took a job as an administrative assistant to the manager of a hotel. She felt she could learn a great deal about the business from him; and she was right again. Eventually she was able to convince him to let her help order food and arrange decorations for the hotel's many functions. She was so good at this that she went on to do the entire job.

Flora had done some work with runaway teenagers in her home town. She also had counseled rape victims. She conveyed great understanding and rapport, and people responded to her. When she went to look for a job, she listed these skills as being among her most valuable assets. Then she asked herself: In what fields would these assets be most valuable? She decided on personnel work.

Both Elsie and Flora had to overcome their own inertia. They had to look around and see what they could do that they had some preparation for. They found that the process of looking and searching can be creative and fun all by itself.

If you are working and would like to change jobs or advance in your job, you can establish a five-year plan for that eventuality also. List in detail what your goals are. Under that, list any and all steps you can take in order to reach those goals. For example, if you don't know what your next step is in advancing, look to see where people who've had your job have gone. What can you do to learn new skills? How can you become noticed? Are there any courses you can take to advance yourself? What contacts can you make? Can you work for someone whose job you can eventually move into? Can you practice becoming more assertive? Can you set up a time schedule or long-range career plan? Is there someone you can collaborate with if you want to work a little more independently but not completely alone? Can you read to learn more about the job area you're interested in? Can you join a professional association? What successful people do you know in business who can give you some advice?

Asking such questions usually leads to other questions, other ideas. In this you can see how the process of growth is a self-perpetuating one, once you have initiated a new beginning. It is this beginning that we want to encourage you to attempt. We have given you a few suggestions you can use. And we can almost promise you that if you try some of them, you'll soon come up with your very own. That is when the fun really starts, when you feel new strength, when you feel that maybe, after all, it's been worth the effort.

Remember, in order to overcome feeling depressed, you have to set your own goals—goals that will give *you* satisfaction and pleasure.

19

Recovery

DEPRESSION is your way of coping with feelings that are too painful and too frightening. Yet while this numbing process serves to *protect* you from those feelings, it also incapacitates and immobilizes you, saps your energy, and makes you feel hopeless about ever feeling better, about ever changing those elements that you think contribute to your depression in the first place.

Depression is the result of living by a "should" system. And depression, as a way of coping, can become addicting—a habit. This is why we call the depression we've been talking about *chronic, low-grade depression.* This is also why some women will be unwittingly reluctant to relinquish their depression, keeping it as a kind of handy security blanket (for familiarity and comfort) to fall back on when things become too anxiety-provoking. Generally speaking, it might be said that all addictions have that same quality of familiarity and comfort, in spite of their obvious and devastating self-destructive character.

To begin to dissipate the inertia of depression, physical activity is almost mandatory. Try to move yourself in any way that you can. Move your arms and legs. Massage your face. Try to take a walk. If you can, sing, play a game, run around the block. Listen to what the women who talked about getting in touch with their bodies had to say. Physical activity is crucial in overcoming depression. Let your body help you.

In every depression you feel: loss of your dream, lost pride, anger, guilt, self-hatred, hopelessness, and helplessness. These feelings compose the substance of conflict which makes itself felt through anxiety. In an attempt to suppress anxiety, which can be the most agonizing of all human feelings, one may become depressed. The function of depression, then, is to cover, to subdue, to mask, to depress not only anxiety itself, but all of those malignant feelings which invariably give rise to the anxiety. The following diagram illustrates how all these feelings flow toward each other in an unending confluence.

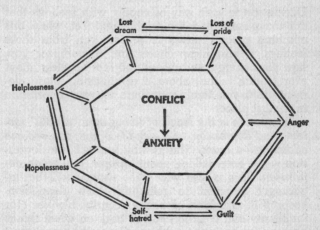

Come back to this diagram when you have time and compile a list of questions in your notebook. Use the following as a guide.

1. Do I feel I've *lost* something? If so, what? How? Was it a person, position, prestige, pride?

2. Am I *angry?* What am I angry at? Parent, friends, husband, lover, child, employer, sibling, myself? Why am I angry with so-and-so? Am I disappointed about something I expected?

3. Do I feel *hopeless?* About what? About whom?

Is the hopelessness based on fact? Can I bring evidence from the past to show it was not always hopeless?

4. Am I feeling *helpless?* Is it true? Is there any small and real way I can be less helpless? Have I explored all possibilities?

5. Do I feel *guilty?* If so, at what? What do I expect of myself? Is someone else inducing my guilt? Am I inducing it myself?

6. Do I *hate* myself for something? What have I done to arouse that hatred? What haven't I done? Do I feel that I'm a terrible person? If so, what evidence can I find to refute that feeling?

7. Am I in *conflict?* Do I want two opposing things at the same time? Am I unwilling to relinquish one of them? Do I want time for myself and yet won't stop giving all my time to my family? Do I want to remain uninvolved and yet want to be close and committed to someone at the same time?

8. What can I do to confront these feelings? To tackle them? To reduce them?

These questions, altogether, may seem quite overwhelming to you, but they can be taken gradually, slowly, one at a time. Or you can make up your own. That's one reason we suggest that you use a notebook. Just write down one question, and then write your responses to it. You can ask the same question many times and answer it in many different ways.

Remember, this is your very own work. There are no rules, no "shoulds," no expectations. Take it and leave it as you choose. Make your responses your own creations. There is no pattern; you create their design as you go. This is a way you can get to know yourself. If you find yourself becoming anxious, just stop. Take it up another day.

Your defenses, or compulsive "shoulds," are the means you have used to defend yourself against your anxiety. The three main defense systems, as we have seen, have been the compulsive search for love, for mastery, for uninvolvement. However, when you violate a "should," or when you have two simultaneous but opposing "shoulds"—a common example being the need to win and the simultaneous need to always please—your defensive system breaks down and your anxiety surfaces once again.

One of the most important and helpful things you can do for yourself is to begin to see how your expectations, or "shoulds" influence the quality of your life, your dissatisfactions with yourself and with others. Recognition does not occur suddenly or miraculously. You don't wake up in the middle of the night and say, "This is my problem! Now I'm going to change completely and live happily ever after for the rest of my life." Change is a gradual process. You may, of course, have a quick insight into certain situations. You may have a dream which you feel is important. A friend may say something which provides food for thought. These are all opportunities to examine yourself and to work with yourself.

If you have any expectations that you are going to solve your problems immediately, however, you are going to be in trouble. Be kind and gentle with yourself. Pace yourself realistically. Change is a process; health is a process. Day by day, throughout your life, you will be striving and growing.

Anger is a large component of all depressions. This anger can be anger at yourself, anger at your family, anger at your friends, anger at your oppression, marriage anger. What can you do about your anger? To feel better, you are going to have to get it out. If you are the kind of person who has dealt with your anger by depressing and thus masking it, you will continue to be depressed if you cannot dissipate it in some way. For you, as long as anger remains in such tremendous quantities, you will probably remain depressed.

If it helps, picture your anger as a tornado, a force inside you. Wishing it away will not work; your anger must come out. This doesn't mean that you have to be tactless and self-destructive and tell off the entire world. But it will help to express your anger and dissatisfaction to someone or some people whom you can trust. This doesn't have to be a family member. Find someone who can "take it."

We also suggest pounding a pillow and loud crying, or shouting. One woman reports that she remembers feeling relieved when she dared to have a loud shouting argument with her sister-in-law. At the time she didn't understand the basis for her relief. But she did feel better.

Depression results from pressing down, from masking your feelings. In order to begin to recover from depression, then, you are going to have to unmask and express these feelings. That means your anger too. Release of your anger will release other feelings you are trying to keep from yourself. These include feelings that contribute to your well-being—enthusiasm, interest, optimism.

Your anger must be analyzed as well as expressed. Are you angry with yourself for not meeting impossible standards, standards usually set up by someone else? Are you angry because your "shoulds" are so perfectionistic that they are causing you to feel constant dissatisfaction? What can you do about that? Can you begin to work with your anger by altering your expectations? Can you feel compassion for yourself by recognizing your limitations? Can you try to root out the "shoulds" that oppress you?

What about anger toward parents whom you may feel have "ruined" you? What can you do about it? You have to decide if it might be better to pound a pillow in your room rather than scream at your mother and father. Can you try to talk with them? Can you tell them how hard you've tried to do what they want, and how you feel that it's killing you inside to keep trying?

New ways of dealing with them have to be found, so that your own needs and wishes are acknowledged and respected. Self-respect includes exercising your abilities to achieve satisfaction. It includes asserting yourself.

And what about your marriage anger? What can you do about that? Can you work with it? Deal with it? Analyze your expectations in the relationship? See areas for change and growth in your marriage? Help your partner to grow also?

What about your children? Are you angry with them because they aren't the children you fantasized? The children you expected and must have? What can you do about this?

Can you begin to discover what your lost dream is? Is there a way you can cast out some of your unreasonable and unrealistic expectations and fantasies and begin to replace them with expectations that can be realized? Are there any fantasies that you can begin to build on to live a more satisfying life? Which lost dreams can develop you to live a productive life?

What roots of strength can you tap? Energy? Will power? Skills? A wish for change? Let the women with whom we've talked help you. Read over what they've said. Remember the woman who said, "I can't begin to expect change overnight." Remember another who said, "I have to begin to take my own needs seriously. I can't feel guilty about asserting myself." Remember a third who said, "I'm using myself now." And a fourth said, "If you can pull out a new aspect of creativity in yourself, you'll be all right." Take from each woman what you think will be helpful to you.

Perhaps you will have to exorcise some of your destructive ideas about femininity. To be feminine does not mean to be self-effacing. As we have said, and it is worth repeating many times, if dependency is seen to be a natural state for women, then depression will always be a natural state, too. We are not talking about healthy interdependency and relationships which are loving and encourage growth. We are referring to destructive relationships, morbidly dependent ones, which keep you from authentic living.

Women do not get nearly enough support from their

society—from doctors, the media, the business world. This is a fact. But if you are dissatisfied with your place, you must begin to change it yourself. No one can or will do that for you. Women are beginning to try to change some features of the society, to support each other, to do many things they feel they want to do. Women are as capable, honest, good, and able as men are. And don't let anyone tell you otherwise! But how is a woman to change her society unless she can first change herself? How is she to protest discrimination if she is overcome with inertia, or if she persists in self-effacing behavior and thereby discriminates against herself and contributes to her own oppression? How is she to help other women if she cannot first help herself?

The first most positive way you can help yourself is to recognize that you are suffering from an illness, depression. There is a reason for your feeling of tiredness, listlessness, inertia, restlessness, boredom, or deadness. That alone should help you take heart; for once you can define and diagnose a problem, you can begin to deal with it. As we have so far suggested, the main ways you can help yourself now are:

Step 1. Experience yourself through physical means. Let your body help you.

Step 2. Express your anger and your dissatisfaction.

Both forms of expression will help you to fight depression. Another thing we have asked you to do is to keep a notebook in which you can write down your feelings. This is something only you can do for yourself. You must make the time for this.

Step 3. Take stock of yourself and your problems. Set aside at least a half hour each day, if you possibly can. Keep a diary of your dreams, for example, and begin to work with them.

This is an important alternative to wallowing in your depression. People often let themselves sink deeper and deeper into despair and may derive some kind of morbid satisfaction from their suffering, or they may impress others with their overriding needs. Sometimes depression is the only way a person allows herself to express vindictiveness, since her suffering can cause anguish and guilt in those around her.

As we've said again and again, talking to other people is crucial. To let yourself remain isolated when you are depressed is to ask for trouble.

Step 4. Decide what *you* want.

Often, as we've seen, the woman who is depressed has been doing what she thinks she *should* do. She has not looked to her own needs as the originator of many of her actions. Others have to "start her engine." She is not a self-starter, but she can be if she learns to plan and take step by step.

When you are feeling particularly blue, pamper yourself. Get a manicure or have your hair done. Even simple things like buying a new lipstick or going to a movie can help. This is especially true if you're the type of woman who has trouble deciding to do nice things for herself.

Step 5. If you have no job, it's an excellent idea to have something to look forward to each day, whether it's shopping, reading a book, working on a project, meeting a friend for lunch. If you have a job, planning your time when you aren't working is equally crucial.

Step 6. Do things with your hands. Build something, sew a dress, needlepoint a pillow, garden, knit a scarf. These are all forms of expression which are interesting, fun, and very helpful.

Step 7. Try to face and deal with your conflicts.

One of the reasons you are depressed is that you are in conflict. Remember, conflict (as well as anger and guilt) is one of the cornerstones of depression. In order to regain health and vitality, you are going to have to explore these conflicts.

Conflicting "shoulds," or the constant back and forth between Perfect and Despised Self, can also keep you depressed. Your lost dream of perfection (i.e., your child isn't brilliant or your project didn't turn out as well as you thought it *should*) can lead to intense anxiety and self-hatred, which is then blanketed by the novocaine reaction, depression. The loss of pride in perfection is felt as a humiliation.

Step 8. Suspect excessive fantasizing as a sign of depression. But, your fantasies may be a way to make you feel alive, to compensate for inertia. When you begin to fantasize, ask yourself what you can do about your fantasy (assuming it's a constructive one) to give it birth, to make it a reality. On the other hand, if it is a destructive or morbidly dependent fantasy (a masochistic fantasy or a fantasy of a man who will come to sweep you off your feet), it would be in your best interest to try to do something else. Try calling a friend. This will take tremendous discipline at first, but will ultimately benefit you greatly.

Step 9. As you plan your goals, remember not to take on too much at one time. Do not expect too much right away. And as you make decisions about your goals and plans, do not worry whether you have made the "right" choice. After due thought, choose your best bet. There are bound to be some doubts ("Can I really do this?" "Did I make a good choice?") but try to avoid putting yourself down or agonizing unduly. How will you ever know that you've made the perfect choice? It is still better to make an "educated" choice than no choice at all.

Step 10. If you suffer from inertia, remember that inertia is composed of impossible expectations, anxiety, anger, and conflicts. The conflict can come from your resistance to doing what you feel you *should* be doing rather than what you want to do. Must you do what you feel is expected of you? Totally? Can you set your own goals?

If your inertia is related to perfectionism, you're going to have to try to both relax your "shoulds" as well as learn to tolerate greater amounts of anxiety for longer periods of time. Most anxiety won't kill you. Consider also that inertia may be an unconscious demand that you *should* get what you want without too much pain, struggle, or effort.

Step 11. Recall that boredom is so often associated with depression. Depression can serve to subdue your anxiety at not living up to standards others have set for you—and which you have internalized and set up for yourself. If you can recognize and understand this, you'll be better able to cope. Boredom or restlessness, which are sometimes a need for excitement and drama, are often an indication of a painful, inner emptiness.

This can be the result of what we talked about earlier, that in nurturing others, women have often deprived themselves of essential self-nurturing. This is especially true of the love-addicted woman who has a compulsive need for love and approval, and who feels great anxiety when she is not receiving the love, attention, and devotion she feels she needs. Much of the anxiety of the morbidly dependent woman is generated by not having a man who will meet her needs; she blames herself for her inability to find such a man and is constantly trying to fight off, or deny, her feelings of self-blame.

Self-nurturing begins with doing things for yourself—strengthening yourself through work, through pleasure, through positive relationships.

Step 12. When you become depressed, ask yourself this question: What options do I have? If you can't think of any, talk to someone. Once you see some options, some possible changes or solutions, your hopelessness will greatly diminish. And hopelessness, as we've seen, is another of the cornerstones of depression.

Step 13. If you are depressed, you are going to have to accept your need to grow. You are presently using despair to feed self-hatred. If you are depressed, you have lost not only your self-esteem, but yourself. You are repressing your needs, wishes, and desires, as well as your conflicts, your anxiety, your anger. This repression results in the loss of your ability to reach out for what you want. *But you have a right to be yourself.* Increasing your pleasure, your involvement, your effort—*that* is what will feed your feelings of aliveness.

We are not necessarily talking about earth-shaking changes. A temporary separation, for example, may be a necessity in one case, a change of jobs in another. But it is more than likely that any *small change*— not going to the country every weekend if you want to remain in the city, not visiting your mother-in-law as often as she demands, finding an interest that is all your own, making a new friend, joining a singing group—can make an enormous amount of difference in the quality of your life.

You have to establish *your own goals.* Not somebody else's. Not your mother's. Not your society's. Not your best friend's. But yours.

Investigate what you want and set it within realistic bounds. Know your limits as well as your strengths. You want to take up skydiving? Great. You want to work with orphans? Marvelous. You want to start your own business? Fantastic. You want to learn Russian? Do judo? Write an article? Become more active? Write poetry? Study philosophy? Raise cows? Go to church every day? Try transcendental meditation? Lead a Girl Scout troop? Sell hats? Play tennis? Own a cat? Sail a boat? Run for office? Talk to your child more? Learn to drive a car? Make more money? Fight for clean air? Meet some new people? No matter what, we're on your side. Your family members aren't too much help? Perhaps you can find other help.

This is a time of great stress for women. We are in a period of transition. For some women, there is dissatisfaction with the housewife role, and still there is not yet an equal place for women in the world at large. Other women may like staying at home, but feel needlessly guilty about their preference. Men and women are going through tremendous changes in relating to one another, and this has caused added tension. Right now the best that women can do for themselves is to learn to express their aspirations, to become assertive, to work at eradicating uninvolved or love-addicted behavior, to take their own needs seriously. As Karen Horney once said, "The prime privilege is to work at oneself." In other words, *to find yourself is to create yourself.*

You will have to keep trying to find your lost self through your own efforts, your own strengths. These are the wellsprings of your own hopefulness. To recover, to be well, is a *possible dream.* Be persistent; be tenacious; be courageous. And most of all, be hopeful.

ABOUT THE AUTHORS

HELEN A. DE ROSIS is a distinguished psychiatrist, living in New York City, who has a special interest in women's problems. She is editor of the *American Journal of Psychoanalysis;* training and supervising analyst at the American Institute for Psychoanalysis of the Karen Horney Psychoanalytic Clinic and Center; attending psychiatrist at the Roosevelt Hospital; associate clinical professor in psychiatry, New York University School of Medicine. She is also the author of *Parent Power/Child Power* (1974) and *Working With Patients: Guidelines for Beginning Psychotherapists* (1976).

VICTORIA Y. PELLEGRINO is the former editor-in-chief of *Pageant* magazine, and a coauthor of *The New York Woman's Directory*. She has been a columnist for *WomenSports* and *Viva* and has written for *New York, Ms., Glamour, Redbook, Cosmopolitan, The Sunday Daily News, Parade, The Village Voice,* and *The Working Woman*. She is also the director of Victoria Associates, a counseling firm, and runs a series of career workshops for women.

READ THE WOMEN
WHO TAKE STANDS
AND ACT ON THEM

Bantam
On Psychology

Bantam Book Catalog

Here's your up-to-the-minute listing of over 1,400 titles by your favorite authors.

This illustrated, large format catalog gives a description of each title. For your convenience, it is divided into categories in fiction and non-fiction—gothics, science fiction, westerns, mysteries, cookbooks, mysticism and occult, biographies, history, family living, health, psychology, art.

So don't delay—take advantage of this special opportunity to increase your reading pleasure.

Just send us your name and address and 50¢ (to help defray postage and handling costs).